INTERPERSONAL SKILLS

Goal-directed behaviour at work

John Hayes

London and New York

First published 1991
by HarperCollins Academic,
London and New York

Reprinted 1994
by Routledge
11 New Fetter Lane, London EC4P 4EE

Simultaneously published in the USA and Canada
by Routledge
29 West 35th Street, New York, NY 10001

Typeset in 10 on 12 point Sabon
Printed in Great Britain by
Biddles Ltd, Guildford and King's Lynn

British Library Cataloguing in Publication Data

A catalogue record for this book is available
from the British Library

Library of Congress Cataloging in Publication Data

A catalog record for this book is available on request

ISBN 0–415–10943–4

Contents

To Mercia, Sarah and Jonathan
All of whom strongly recommend that I read
Chapter 2 at least once a week

List of Figures

Preface and acknowledgements

The decision to write this book was prompted by my experience of working as a consultant on the management of change with a number of large, sometimes multinational, organizations. Most of the people I work with are technically and professionally very competent. If they were not they would not have been promoted to the senior positions they now occupy. There are, however, some of these technically and professionally competent managers who are less successful than others when it comes to achieving goals and getting things done without too much unnecessary disruption. A distinguishing factor between these and the more successful managers appears to be their level of interpersonal competence. Those who pay attention to interpersonal relationships and who, when necessary, are able to consciously manage the way they relate with others seem to be much more successful in terms of achieving their goals.

This book is about interpersonal skills, those goal-directed behaviours that can be used in face-to-face interactions in order to bring about a desired state of affairs.

Although it was originally intended for managers and students of management, this book deals with skills that are equally applicable in many other work (and non-work) situations. A quick glance down the contents page will show that a wide range of people (including teachers, doctors, social workers and police officers) working at different levels in organizations will find that the skills included in this book are skills which can be applied in many of their day-to-day relations with others.

Throughout the book gender is used to help identify the parties to a relationship, for example, in Chapter Four the interviewer is female and the interviewee male. Whenever reference is made to a single person, she or her is used to avoid the he/she syndrome.

I would like to thank all of those people who have read and commented on early drafts of the manuscript and Joan Camm who, because of her remarkable talent for deciphering my handwriting, has typed this final manuscript in record time.

CHAPTER ONE

The conscious application of interpersonal skills

People spend a considerable part of their working day relating with others. One of the findings of the early work activity studies (Burns, 1954, 1957; Horn and Lupton, 1965), echoed more recently by Oshagbemi (1988), is that managers and others consistently underestimate the amount of time they spend in face-to-face contact. There are also indications that they underestimate seriously the effect that their behaviour has on the way others behave and, therefore, on the achievement of personal and organizational goals.

Simple examples may serve to illustrate this point. The selection interviewer needs to obtain from applicants as much relevant information as possible, so that she can determine which of them will be most suitable for the job. To achieve this end she needs to manage the interaction in a way that encourages each applicant to provide the maximum amount of relevant and the minimum amount of irrelevant information. This objective is likely to be frustrated if the interviewer does most of the talking, if she prevents applicants from giving full answers by over-using the kind of questions that limits their responses to yes or no, and if she asks questions in a way that prompts them into giving the answer that they think she wants to hear.

In negotiations, there is evidence that a negotiator's opening bid has an important influence on the expectations of her opponent and that this can affect the outcome. There is also evidence that, in competitive negotiations, concessions are more likely to be reciprocated when the person offering the concession is perceived, by her opponent, to be in a relatively strong position. And it is possible for a negotiator to create this impression by behaving in certain ways.

In decision-making groups, one of the factors that can influence the quality of a decision is the extent to which the knowledge and skill of group members is applied to the task. Some of this task-relevant knowledge may not be available to the group because a knowledgeable but non-assertive member of the group lacks the confidence to make his views known, or because some members fail to pay attention or give appropriate weight to the views of others. The person who is able to recognize what is happening, and who can use this awareness to intervene, to act consciously in ways that make it more likely that relevant knowledge will be applied to the task, can make an important contribution to improving group performance.

Diagnostic and action skills

In his book *Power and Performance in Organisations*, Mangham (1986) argues that:

> one's success as an executive is dependent upon one's ability to consider oneself in the complexity of the organisation as a subtle, insightful, incisive performer. Successful executives appear to have a natural and/or a highly developed ability to read the actual or potential behaviour of others around them and to construct their own conduct in accordance with that reading. Not that this ability is peculiar to them – we all read behaviour and react – just that the more successful amongst us appear to do social life with a higher degree of skill than the rest of us manage.

This book offers a series of conceptual frameworks that can be used for 'reading behaviour': that is, for diagnosing what is going on, and for constructing conduct to ensure that desired objectives are achieved. It also focuses attention on how these conceptual frameworks can be used to develop diagnostic and action skills. A football analogy illustrates the importance of these two complementary sets of skills: that is, diagnostic skills and action skills.

At half time, it is normal practice for the members of a football team to engage in a detailed review of how the game is progressing. Players use their diagnostic skills to understand what has happened, what they might have done differently to secure a better outcome and what, in the second half, they need to attend to if they are to achieve the result they desire. Good players also do this for themselves on a continuing basis throughout the match, so they are always aware of what kind of contributions they should be making. Action skills are concerned with intervening and making these contributions. Players invest a lot of effort in developing action skills such as marking, running with the ball, passing and shooting which enable them to deliver an appropriate contribution when required.

Although football players give a high priority to skill development in their work situation, training in other work situations tends to emphasize technical and professional skills, and relatively little attention is given to the development of interpersonal skills. Most people learn how to relate with others on the basis of experience, through trial and error. Sometimes this approach is successful, but often it is an unreliable and ineffective process of skill development. It is not unusual for people to develop habitual modes of relating with others that consistently yield unsatisfactory results. For example, when managers and supervisors interview job applicants they may find it difficult to get them to talk about themselves and, even though they may have come across this problem many times before, they may not be aware of how their own behaviour contributes to the problem. Furthermore, they may have little awareness of alternative ways of behaving that could improve matters. Sidney, Brown and Argyle (1973) report that untrained and unskilled interviewers only do marginally better than chance when it comes to predicting satisfactory performance: a sobering thought when we remember that the interview is the most widely used selection tool. Trained interviewers, on the other hand, do very much better at predicting performance: evidence that the intentional development of interpersonal skills can produce tangible results.

Does the conscious application of interpersonal skills entail manipulation?

Honey (1988) argues that what he labels 'interactive skills' can and should be learned consciously and that the objective of this learning is to increase the possibility of achieving a desired objective. He goes on to argue that on many occasions people need to organize their behaviour *consciously* in order to achieve this end. This raises the issue of whether the conscious management of one's own behaviour with the intention of increasing the probability that others will respond in particular ways entails manipulation. In this context, manipulation is taken to mean controlling others by unfair or insidious means.

The author's view is that, while manipulation does involve the conscious management of one's own behaviour to control others, the conscious management of one's own behaviour per se does not necessarily constitute manipulation. This book is full of examples where certain behaviours are advocated as a means of bringing about a desired state of affairs, but these desired states of affairs usually involve promoting the welfare of the other party and always involve respecting their rights. For example, in Chapter 6 an underlying theme is that effective helping involves helping clients to learn to manage their problems for themselves. A step towards this desired goal involves building a trusting relationship between helper and client, so that the client will be more prepared to share sensitive information with the helper. This trust could be abused by the helper and she could use it to achieve her own ends at the expense of the client. That would be manipulation. But building a trusting relationship in order to offer more effective help is not manipulation. Similarly, a theme in Chapter 7 is assertiveness. This involves standing up for one's rights and can involve expressing unpopular opinions, refusing requests and requesting that others change their behaviour. But again, the importance of behaving in ways that respects the rights of others is stressed.

People will be motivated in ways that will bring about a desired state of affairs irrespective of whether they have acquired their repertoire of interpersonal skills and behavioural responses unconsciously, through experience, or via a deliberate and conscious process of self-development. The person who has learned through experience that she can satisfy her needs by behaving aggressively towards others might achieve her goals by using others for her own ends and by denying them their rights. On the other hand, somebody who attempts to satisfy her needs by consciously applying assertion skills that she has learned intentionally may also achieve her goals, but do so in a way that respects the right of others.

Interpersonal skills

Interpersonal skills are goal-directed behaviours used in face-to-face interactions, which are effective in bringing about a desired state of affairs. The approach adopted in this book is to focus attention on micro skills, or small units of behaviour, which can be combined into larger elements. An example will illustrate this hierarchical organization of goal-directed behaviours. The *accent*, a one or two word restatement that focuses attention on what somebody has just said, is one of seven behaviours that can be grouped together under the broader heading of following skills. *Following skills* are behaviours that help a person to encourage somebody else to talk and help the listener to concentrate on what the speaker has to say. Following skills are one of four sets of behaviours which, at another level, are referred to collectively as listening skills. *Listening skills*, which involve an active search for a full and accurate understanding of the meaning of another's message, are, in their turn, just one of the sets of behaviour that comprise *helping skills*.

Chapters 2 to 4 are concerned with skills that are important in their own right (listening, listening to non-verbal messages, information getting, and explaining and presenting skills) but which also form an important element of more complex skills. Some of these more complex skills (helping, influencing, negotiating and working in groups) are considered in Chapters 6 to 9.

Chapter 2 examines listening skills. The various micro skills (including accents) are considered under four headings: preparing, attending, following and reflecting.

Chapter 3 considers listening to non-verbal messages and opens with the proposition that there is more to listening than meets the ear. Attention is given to behaviours associated with the determination of meaning and the deciphering of contradictory signals, and many of the non-verbal signals that can convey important information are reviewed.

Chapter 4 examines the skills involved in presenting information and offering explanations to others. These skills are organized under a number of headings, including preparing, attention getting and presenting.

Chapter 5 looks at information-getting skills. The way the interviewer and respondent interpret each other's behaviour is examined and the implications this has for the quantity and quality of information offered by the respondent is explored. Consideration is also given to a range of micro skills, especially those concerned with the formulation of questions.

Chapter 6 is concerned with helping, and under this broad heading the skills of empathy, probing, giving feedback and challenging are examined. The deployment of these skills is discussed within the context of a problem management approach to helping.

Chapter 7 looks at influencing from two perspectives. The first focuses on assertiveness and examines those behaviours that help a person to stand up for her rights and communicate important messages to others. The second takes a more macro perspective and considers influencing as a political process.

Chapter 8 looks at negotiating, which is defined as a process of joint decision-making in which people with different preferred outcomes interact in order to resolve their differences. Climate setting, bidding and bargaining skills are some of the behaviours that are considered within the context of competitive and collaborative negotiating strategies.

Chapter 9 is concerned with working in groups and examines those behaviours that can influence key variables that affect group performance. These variables are the level of effort that group members expend collectively on carrying out the task, the amount of knowledge and skill members bring to bear on the group task, and the appropriateness to the task of the performance strategies used by the group.

The final chapter presents a range of conceptual models that provide a more macro view of social interaction and offers a range of diagnostic questions and action strategies which offer a basis for managing relationships more effectively.

References: Chapter 1

Burns, T. 1954. The directions of activity and communication in a departmental executive group. *Human Relations*, 7: 73–97.

Burns, T. 1957. Management in action. *Operational Research Quarterly* 8: 45–60.

Honey, P. 1988. *Face to Face: Practical Guide to Interactive Skills*, 2nd edn. Aldershot: Gower.

Horn, J. H. and Lupton, T. 1965. The work activities of middle managers: an exploratory study. *The Journal of Management Studies* 2, 1: 14–33.

Mangham, I. L. 1986. *Power and Performance in Organisations: an Exploration of Executive Process*. Oxford: Blackwell.

Oshagbemi, T. 1988. *Leadership and Management in Universities*. New York: Walter de Gruyter.

Sidney, E., Brown, M. and Argyle, M. 1973. *Skills with People*. London: Hutchinson.

CHAPTER TWO
Listening

Listening is a core competence. People who cannot listen cannot relate. Nichols and Stevens (1957) estimate that 45 per cent of all communication time is spent listening compared with 30 per cent speaking, 16 per cent reading and 9 per cent writing. Despite the fact that people spend so much time listening, few ever receive any formal training on how to listen effectively. Poor listening undermines the ability to communicate with others. Anyone who wants to be an effective negotiator, interviewer, coach, consultant, leader or group member needs to be a good listener.

Listening involves more than just hearing what somebody has said. Drakeford (1967) defines the 'physiological sensory process by which auditory sensations are received by the ears and transmitted to the brain' as *hearing* and differentiates this from *listening*, which he regards as a much more 'complex psychological procedure involving interpreting and understanding the significance of the sensory experience'. Listening involves the search for a full and accurate understanding of the meaning of another's message. Lundsteen (1971) talks about listening as the process by which messages are converted into meaning in the mind. Listening involves more than merely attending to verbal messages. To be a good listener a person has to be able to 'read' both verbal and non-verbal messages. A more detailed treatment of non-verbal communication is reserved until the next chapter.

Hargie *et al.* (1987), after reviewing the work of others, identified four main types of listening.

Comprehension listening is the kind of listening people engage in when conducting fact-finding interviews or attending lectures.

It involves listening for facts, ideas and themes that may be of future use.

Evaluative listening is the kind of listening people engage in when trying to make judgements concerning the persuasive messages others, such as sales persons and negotiators, are using to influence their attitudes, beliefs or actions. It involves listening for the main propositions being made by the speaker and being able to determine the strengths and weaknesses of each.

Empathic listening is the kind of listening people engage in in counselling sessions, appraisal interviews and more generally when faced with someone who has a need to talk and be understood by another person. It involves the listener demonstrating a willingness to attend to and understand the thoughts, beliefs and feelings of the speaker.

Appreciative listening is the kind of listening people engage in for pleasure. It might occur when listening to poetry or children playing. It involves the listener seeking out signals or messages that she wants to hear.

The content of this chapter is not concerned with appreciative listening. Many of the concepts and techniques discussed here will apply equally to comprehension, evaluative and empathic listening; however, most attention will be focused on empathic listening, because experience suggests that this is the kind of listening that managers find most difficult.

The first part of this chapter considers those factors that influence the ability to listen. The reasons why some kinds of information are attended to and others are ignored will be examined, and also some of the variables that determine how information is interpreted and messages given meaning. This will be followed by a more detailed look at the process of communication and some of the common listening problems associated with the listener, the speaker, the message and the environment.

The second part of this chapter considers the steps people can take and the skills they will need to develop if they are to improve their capacity to listen effectively.

FACTORS INFLUENCING THE ABILITY TO LISTEN EFFECTIVELY

There are many competing demands for a listener's attention. In an interview, the total attention of a member of the appointing committee might not be focused on what the candidate is saying. The interviewer might be more interested in how the candidate is dressed, the mark on his collar and the smell of tobacco smoke that surrounds his person.

The effect of selectivity Various factors can influence where the interviewer's attention will be directed. There are external factors such as *intensity*: for example, a colleague's loud voice or the candidate's bright shirt; *contrast*: the interviewer might only notice the typewriter next door when it stops or the draught on her neck when the fan is first switched on; or *movement*: her attention might be drawn back to the candidate if he suddenly changes from a relaxed posture and sits bolt upright.

A number of internal factors will also influence where the interviewer will direct her attention. She might have a greater *interest* in the replies to her own questions or, because of her marketing background, in any answer that demonstrates a concern for the customer. *Expectations* can also be important. If the job involves a liaison role between product engineering and manufacturing, a pre-interview briefing might alert the interviewer to look for evidence of the candidate's appreciation of ways in which design and product engineering can affect manufacturing cost and product quality. Without the pre-briefing the importance of such information might not be recognized and therefore relevant answers might be ignored. The *personal needs* of the interviewer might also influence what she attends to. Because she is a non-smoker and believes that working in a smoke-filled atmosphere affects her asthmatic condition, she might notice and attribute greater importance to the smell of smoke surrounding the candidate than a fellow interviewer who happens to be an occasional smoker.

Interpretation and personal bias Not only do different people attend to different things, they also interpret the information they receive in different ways.

Past experience might mean that what is easily understood jargon to one person is jibberish to another.

Background and culture might influence the meaning attributed to certain behaviours. For example, a tendency for the interviewee to look away and not engage in eye contact may be interpreted as evidence of a serious lack of confidence by one interviewer and as an appropriate reflection of relative status differences between candidate and interviewers by another.

An interviewer's values will also determine what she is likely to interpret as 'good' or 'bad', and her personal needs will influence how the candidate's answers will be understood.

Being aware of one's own personal filters can help a person listen more effectively. In the interview example the interviewer could prepare a check list to help make sure that she pays attention to all the relevant messages and that the effects of selectivity are minimized. An awareness of personal bias can also help with the interpretation of information. The empathic listener might deliberately work to suppress her own biases, she might think about the speaker's background, experience, attitudes, etc., and try to understand what he is saying from his point of view.

A more detailed look at the process of listening will highlight some other potential barriers to effective communication. Following Hargie *et al.* (1987) these problems can be grouped under four headings: the listener, the speaker, the message and the environment.

The listener

Listening is not a simple process in which A talks and B listens. While A is talking B listens, evaluates what she hears and even begins to think about what she will say in reply. These activities interfere with pure listening. The effect of working out a reply before the other party has finished speaking can be illustrated by thinking about what you picture when you hear the words:

WOMAN, TABLE, KNIFE, CLOTH

For most people if these words were followed by 'emergency, surgeon, blood, intestines' the message or picture in their mind would change dramatically. The person who had stopped listening after the first four words (in order to prepare a reply) would be unable to offer an appropriate response to the speaker. Effective listening requires the listener to give her full attention to the task of listening to everything the speaker has to say.

The motivation of the listener can influence how well she attends. If the listener feels that the speaker has something useful to say or if she is committed to helping him work out a problem, then she is likely to work harder at listening than if she expected the message to be boring or irrelevant, or if she had no interest in helping the speaker.

Another fact that can influence how well the listener attends is her physical condition. A listener who is ill or tired might find it more difficult to concentrate than someone who is well rested and alert. It is not unusual, for example, for trainees to find it easier to listen to a lecture in the morning than immediately after a heavy lunch, when they are feeling sleepy, or late in the evening after a busy day.

People who can make sense of a message are more likely to listen attentively than those who cannot understand what is being said. One factor that can influence this is the ability to organize incoming information, to identify key elements of the message and to store these in appropriate conceptual compartments. Hargie *et al.* (1987) suggest that linguistic aptitude might be correlated positively with the ability to comprehend what is being said because those with a wider vocabulary can more readily understand and assimilate a wider range of concepts.

The speaker

Who the speaker is can affect how the message is interpreted. Sometimes people hear who the other person is rather than what he is saying. Messages from high status people may receive more attention than messages from low status people. A common problem, which detracts from the effectiveness of work groups, is the inappropriate way in which members often weigh the contributions of others (see Chapter 9). A speaker's task-relevant expertise might be discounted in favour of his gender, age or lack of seniority.

Speech rate can also affect listening. The normal speech rate is about 140 words per minute. Wolff *et al.* (1983) report that listeners:

> prefer to listen, can comprehend better, and are more likely to believe a message that is presented at the rate of 190 words or more per minute.

They go on to suggest that listening can improve up to 280 words per minute, but there is evidence that with higher rates it begins to deteriorate. Although people can think at a rate considerably faster than this, they require a reasonable differential between speaking and thinking rates to process what they have heard. Slower rates of speech, especially when they drop much below 125 words per minute, can impair effective listening just as much as excessively fast rates. The listener's capacity to process information is under-utilized, so her attention begins to drift. Day-dreaming, thinking about a difficult situation at home or a challenging new assignment at work are the kinds of interference that can affect listening when the speaker is talking too slowly. Of course, the optimum speech rate in any situation will always be influenced by the complexity of the message being communicated.

Hargie *et al.* draw attention to 'emotionality' as an important barrier to effective listening. When a speaker expresses high levels of emotion (for example, anger or despair) the listener may be overwhelmed by the emotional content of the message and find it very difficult to listen to the words. They suggest that one way of managing this kind of problem is to allow the speaker time to ventilate his emotions, to have his say. If the listener is to understand the speaker's message she cannot ignore the emotional content, it is important. However if she allows herself to be overpowered by it she may fail to pay proper attention to the factual content of the message and, therefore, may fail to fully and accurately understand what the speaker has to say. By sustaining the interaction and allowing the speaker to ventilate his emotions the listener can help him reach a point where, on the one hand he is able to communicate a more balanced message and, on the other, is more ready to listen to a reasoned response.

The message

The structure of the message can influence how easy or difficult it will be to comprehend. It is not unusual to hear critical comments about people who seem unable to 'stick to the point' or whose messages are 'as clear as mud'.

Difficulties can arise if the speaker incorrectly assumes that the listener is in possession of important background information and/or knows what it is that the speaker is attempting to achieve. If the speaker makes these kind of assumptions he might only bother to communicate part of the message, thus leaving the listener with the problem of making sense of a message that is incomplete or ambiguous.

The amount of detail, either too much or too little, and the order in which information and arguments are presented can influence comprehension (see Chapter 5).

The significance that different parts of the message might have for the listener can also be linked to order of presentation in a way that can either help or hinder listening. If one bit of the message is highly significant for the listener she might continue to think about its implications after the speaker moves on to talk about his next point. In this way the listener might miss important parts of the message. Elements of the message that the listener might want to think about need to be taken into account when the speaker is formulating the structure of a communication, and the listener needs to be ready either to store significant information for later processing or signal to the speaker if subsequent parts of the message go unheard.

The environment

The environment is a variable that intervenes between the speaker and the listener in a way that can influence the quality of the message that the listener receives. For example, the level of noise in a machine shop might make it very difficult to hear what the speaker is saying. If the message is important, those involved might decide to move to a quiet office, to change the nature of the environment.

Auditory noise is only one of many environmental problems. The quality of ventilation can influence the ability to listen as can the presence of anything which competes with the message for the listener's attention: for example, a letter left where it can be read or an interesting view from a window.

Effective listening involves more than simply hearing what the speaker has said, it involves the search for a full and accurate understanding of the meaning of another's verbal and non-verbal messages. Active listening offers an approach to understanding other people's messages in a way that deals with many of the problems identified so far.

ACTIVE LISTENING

The aim of this second part of the chapter is to identify and elaborate the skills needed by the listener in order to improve her ability to listen effectively. This involves developing the skills which:

(a) help the speaker 'tell his story' to the best of his ability
(b) keep the listener's attention focused on the speaker's message
(c) help the listener give appropriate weight to what the speaker says
(d) assist the listener to organize the information she receives so that she can make sense of even complex or badly structured messages; and
(e) minimize the problems of personal bias.

The skilled listener needs to be skilled at attending to both the factual and affective content of a message. She should neither ignore nor be overwhelmed by the speaker's emotional state, and she needs to be able to interpret what is said in a way that reflects accurately what the speaker is thinking and feeling about the content of the message.

There is considerable agreement about the kinds of behaviour that promote good listening. Egan (1986) identifies four basic communication skills: *attending*, which refers to the way the listener orients herself to the speaker, both physically and psychologically; *listening*, which involves receiving and understanding the verbal and non-verbal messages transmitted by the speaker; *empathy*, which involves the listener understanding the speaker's message from within his frame of reference and communicating this to him; and *probing*, which involves encouraging and prompting the speaker to talk about himself and define his problem more concretely and more specifically. Deetz and Stevenson (1986) discuss the importance of *attending to others* and *taking the perspective of others*, Hargie *et al.* (1987) mention a range of responses required in active listening such as *verbal following, reflecting* and *probing* and Bolton (1986) identifies twelve separate listening skills which he groups into three skill clusters: *Attending Skills, Following Skills* and *Reflecting Skills*.

Listening skills will be discussed in this chapter under four headings: preparation, attending, following and reflecting.

PREPARATION

There are a number of things which the listener can do to prepare for listening. Preparation is possible because many of the occasions when you need to listen, such as an appraisal interview, project review or daily debrief with the kids after school, can be anticipated. Deetz and Stevenson (1986) note that all too often the opportunity for preparation is lost because potential preparation time, if used at all, is spent worrying about what to say rather than how to listen. The kind of preparation that the listener can engage in involves:

(a) arranging important listening tasks for a time when she is least likely to be stressed or fatigued, or eating a light meal and avoiding alcohol immediately prior to an important meeting;
(b) increasing her receptivity by making a conscious effort to put aside temporarily preoccupying concerns, such as a recent row with her boss or the need to book a holiday flight as quickly as possible;
(c) arranging an environment that contains as few distractions as possible, thereby encouraging all parties to concentrate on communicating;
(d) reviewing background material, such as notes and reports, or issues to be discussed. This kind of preparation can stimulate interest and help create the right mental set, which in turn can facilitate understanding by assisting the listener to identify key messages and organize incoming information into appropriate conceptual compartments.

ATTENDING

The second set of listening skills involve the listener letting others know that she is with them.

Everybody, at some time or other, has been told by a friend or colleague that they have not been listening and they have leapt to their own defence by repeating most of what had been said. They had heard, they could repeat the message like a tape recorder, but if the truth were known they had not been listening and this fact had been apparent to the speaker.

People want to feel that the listener is genuinely interested in what they have to say and that she will work hard to understand their message. It will be more difficult to develop rapport, and the speaker will be much less likely to give a full account of himself, if he feels that the listener is preoccupied and disinterested.

The listener, all of the time, is giving out cues and messages with her body. Egan (1986) argues that, by being mindful of the cues and messages she is sending, the listener can deliberately develop and project an image that tells the speaker that she is 'with him'. Egan offers the mnemonic SOLER as an aid to remembering ways in which the listener can project a sense of presence.

S: Face the speaker Squarely This is a basic posture of involvement, which tells the speaker that the listener is with him. Sitting 'squarely' need not be taken too literally. In some situations an anxious listener might be overpowered by too much attention, so a slight angling of the position might be called for, but if the listener turns too far away the message she communicates might be one of indifference or rejection. We have all heard the expression 'he gave me the cold shoulder'.

O: Adopt an Open posture Tightly crossed arms or legs can communicate to the speaker that the listener is in a defensive mood and/or not open to influence. Uncrossed or loosely crossed limbs communicate a sense of openness and approachability.

L: Lean the upper part of your body towards the speaker A slight inclination of the listener's body towards the speaker communicates interest and attention. An enthralled audience can sometimes be described as 'sitting on the edge of their seats'. Leaning backwards or slouching can be taken to mean that the listener is not in tune with the speaker or is bored by the message she is hearing. As with facing the speaker squarely, leaning too far forward can be overpowering in some circumstances. The good listener is alert to feedback, which tells her whether to lean more towards the speaker or to back off slightly at different points in the interaction.

E: Maintain good Eye contact Maintaining good eye contact with the speaker is one of the most powerful ways of communicating that the listener is with him and wants to hear what he has to say. Good eye contact does not mean maintaining a hard, fixed stare. This can project an image of hostile confrontation. To communicate involvement the eyes should be focused softly on the speaker's face and, rather than maintaining uninterrupted contact, the gaze should shift occasionally, to a gesturing hand or to the notes the speaker has in front of him, and then return to his face. Looking away, especially if this happens too frequently, signals that the listener is not involved. Consider how you feel when talking to somebody who keeps glancing over your shoulder to look at other people in the room or who keeps glancing at her watch or the clock on the wall! Taken to an extreme, the almost total absence of eye contact usually signals indifference or boredom. Many people are passive listeners. They pay close attention to what is being said but they doodle on their pad or look out of the window while the speaker is talking. Although they are listening, the message which the speaker receives is that they 'don't want to know'. This can be very inhibiting for the speaker and is one of the reasons why this part of the chapter is headed 'Active listening'. The communication process can be considerably more effective if the listener engages actively in the process of listening.

R: Try to be relatively Relaxed, while engaging in these behaviours If the listener is too tense or nervous the speaker will not feel at ease. The aim is neither to be so relaxed and laid back that the speaker feels the listener is not prepared to work at understanding what he has to say, or so tense that he is frightened off and disinclined to talk. What is required is the projection of a relaxed but alert posture, which suggests both a comfortable relationship and a genuine interest in what the speaker has to say. The listener who is too tense is likely to hold her body too still and create an impression of being very controlled and aloof. Smooth movement, especially if it responds to and reflects what the speaker is saying suggests listening with empathic understanding.

The SOLER mnemonic offers a set of pointers to the kinds of behaviour that communicate a sense of presence to the speaker. These need not always be adhered to strictly. They are not rules, rather they are reminders of the importance of non-verbal behaviour. The listener's body is a vehicle for communication and she should constantly be aware of all the cues and messages she is sending.

FOLLOWING SKILLS

Bolton (1986) argues that while one of the primary tasks of the listener is to stay out of the other's way so that the listener can discover how the speaker views his situation, this aim is often frustrated because the 'listener' interrupts and diverts the speaker by asking too many questions or making too many statements. All too often listeners do too much of the talking.

The listener can encourage the speaker to talk, can better concentrate on the task of listening and can gently seek out more information to help promote a better understanding of the speaker's message by using door openers, minimal prompts, accents, statements, questions, attentive silences and a number of special concentration techniques.

Door openers Careful attention to non-verbal clues can often signal when somebody is pre-occupied or worried and may want to talk. In these circumstances the listener might be able to help the other by offering what Bolton (1986) describes as a non-coercive invitation to talk; this might be either an invitation to begin a conversation or an encouragement to continue if the speaker shows signs that he is unsure about saying more. Bolton suggests that door openers typically have four elements:

(a) A description of the other person's body language, for example:

'You are not looking yourself today'
'You sound a bit low'

(b) An invitation to talk or continue talking:

'Feel like talking?'
'Do you want to tell me about it?'

(c) Silence – not rushing the other person but giving him time to decide.
(d) Attending – engaging in the attending behaviours already discussed, especially eye contact and a positive involvement that demonstrates the listener's interest in and concern for the other person.

Door openers will not always receive a positive response. The other person may be reluctant to talk. However, it can sometimes be helpful to encourage a reluctant speaker with more than one *non-coercive* invitation to talk, but remember that door openers should be perceived as non-coercive and the reluctant speaker must not be pushed too hard. There is a marked distinction between gentle seduction and rape. A relationship can be seriously damaged if the over-eager listener attempts to coerce a reluctant speaker.

Minimal prompts Hackney and Cormier (1979) suggest that the counsellor often uses 'minimal verbal activity' as a reinforcer or prompt to further exploration. In conversation, prompts such as:

'uh – huh'	'right'
'mmm'	'really'
'yes'	'and . . .'
'tell me more'	'wow'

can signal to the speaker that you are listening and may encourage him to continue. Sometimes, on the telephone, if the listener has remained silent too long, the speaker feels the need to ask 'are you still there?' In face-to-face conversation, a minimal prompt can take the form of a gesture, a nod of the head or a slight inclination of the body.

Bolton (1986) makes the point that minimal prompts do not imply agreement or disagreement. 'Yes' means 'yes, I hear what you are saying, go on' rather than 'yes, I agree with what you are saying'. The purpose of the minimal prompt is to let the speaker know that he has been heard and that the listener would be interested to hear more. It is not used to offer a judgement on what the speaker is saying.

The 'accent' Another response that can help uncover relevant information is the accent. Hackney and Cormier (1979) define it as 'a one or two word restatement that focuses or brings attention to a preceding client response'. For example:

Manager: 'Most of the customer reports seemed OK'
Colleague: '*Seemed OK?*'
Manager: 'Well, I suppose I'd hoped for better. What I had expected was . . .'

The 'accent' can be used to encourage others to say more fully what they have only half said or hinted at.

Statements Egan (1986) suggests that if the listener asks too many questions the speaker might end up feeling that he is being grilled. An alternative to some questions might be the kind of statement that makes a demand on the speaker to say more, to elaborate or clarify. For example, the statement:

'What you have been saying seems to have made you very angry'

might encourage the speaker to talk about his feelings of anger without feeling that he is being quizzed.

Infrequent questions Bolton (1986) believes that many listeners make an excessive and inappropriate use of questions. The main reason for this is that often questions are designed to yield information related to the concerns of the listener rather than those of the speaker. This kind of self-centred questioning might be useful when the aim of the listener is to better comprehend information that will be of use to her later or to evaluate the worth of another's persuasive argument, but it will be less appropriate when the listener is using questions in an attempt to understand accurately the thoughts and feelings of the speaker. It is even possible to undermine the effectiveness of comprehension and evaluative listening by asking too many or the wrong kind of question. The different kinds of question the listener can ask are dealt with elsewhere (Chapter 3).

With empathic listening, questions can be used to good effect when the listener has not followed what the speaker has been saying or when she feels a need for more information in order to develop a better understanding of the speaker's point of view. They can also be used to provide a useful prompt to encourage the speaker to think a little more deeply about what he has been saying. For example:

> 'Could you say a little more about why you felt the negotiations broke down?'

Egan (1986) even suggests that the speaker can be helped to sort out his own thoughts by being encouraged to ask relevant questions of himself. For example:

> 'What are some of the important questions you need to ask yourself regarding the breakdown in negotiations?'

Some of the dangers associated with the overuse of questions are well stated by Benjamin (1981, p. 71), cited by Egan (1986):

> I feel certain that we ask too many questions, often meaningless ones. We ask questions that confuse the interviewee, that interrupt him. We ask questions the interviewee cannot possibly answer. We even ask questions we don't want the answers to and, consequently, we do not hear the answer when forthcoming.

Attentive silences People sometimes ask too many questions because they cannot cope with even a short silence. They need to fill the gap.

Learning the art of silent responsiveness has been described as the key to good listening. Bolton (1986) suggests that a silence can give the speaker time to consider what to say. It enables him to go deeper into himself and examine his thoughts. Whether or not the speaker is using the silence for this purpose can often be detected by the direction of his gaze. If, when he stops talking, the speaker fails to make any eye contact with the listener, this is likely to be a sign that he is thinking and that in time he will continue talking. If, on the other hand, he stops talking and looks towards the listener, he is probably signalling that he has finished and now it is her turn. The listener might respond to this cue with a statement or a question or she might allow the silence to continue in order to gently nudge the speaker into saying more. A silence used in this way can be a powerful prompt, especially if it is accompanied with any of the non-verbal behaviours which indicate that the speaker has the listener's full attention and she is waiting to hear more.

Aids to concentration The listener can improve her ability to follow what the speaker is saying by using one of a number of techniques that aid concentration. Hargie *et al.* (1987) discuss the use of intrapersonal dialogue. The listener concentrates on what the speaker is saying and heightens her receptivity by asking herself questions such as 'why is she telling me this now?' or engaging in covert coaching and telling herself whenever she is not paying enough attention. Memory devices (see Smith 1986), such as using rhymes to remember names, or visualization, whereby the listener creates a mental picture of what the speaker is saying, can help the listener to concentrate on the message and remember it later. The listener might also find the kind of listening framework proposed by Egan (1986), which focuses attention on experiences, behaviours and feelings, a helpful aid to concentration as well as providing a useful structure within which to organize incoming information. This kind of framework can also suggest areas that might be explored beneficially with the speaker. Egan (p. 82) suggests people talk about:

Experiences – that is, what happens to them. If a client tells you he was fired from his job, he is talking about his problem situation in terms of an experience.

Behaviours – that is, what do they do or fail to do. If a client tells you he has sex with underage boys, he is talking about his problem situation in terms of his behaviour.

Affect – that is, the feelings and emotions that arise from or are associated with either experiences or behaviour. If a client tells you how depressed he gets after drinking bouts, he is talking about the affect associated with his problem situation.

Egan advocates the use of this framework to help clients clarify their problem situation or explore their unused opportunities. If the listening task involves a personal problem Egan believes that it will be clear to both speaker and listener when it is seen and understood in terms of specific experiences, specific behaviours and specific feelings and emotions.

Note-taking can also aid concentration but, because it interrupts eye contact, it can inhibit free communication. In some circumstances the speaker might also feel less free to talk if notes are being taken that might be shown to others later.

REFLECTING

A reflective response, according to Bolton (1986), is when the listener restates the feeling and/or content of what the speaker has communicated and does so in a way that demonstrates understanding and acceptance. This kind of restatement not only provides an opportunity to check that the speaker has been understood, but it can also help the speaker clarify his own thoughts.

Understanding is not easily achieved, especially if it is to include an awareness of what the message means to the speaker. Defined in this way, understanding involves the listener taking the speaker's perspective into account. Deetz and Stevenson (1986) suggest that this calls for an imaginative reconstruction of what he thinks, feels and sees in a situation. They go on to argue that this is not accomplished by magic, luck, or feeling good about the speaker. It is based on knowledge. This knowledge is gained by listening to the messages he sends, but at the same time being constantly aware of the things that influence how he sees the world: his values, culture, attitudes, etc. Information gained in this way can be used to formulate hypotheses about what the message means to the speaker. These hypotheses can then be tested against new information or they can be checked out by reflecting them back to the speaker.

Acceptance must not be confused with sympathy or agreement. Egan (1986) makes the point that sympathy, when aroused in the listener, can distort the stories she hears by blinding her to important nuances. Acceptance means withholding judgement, especially in the early part of a conversation, neither agreeing nor disagreeing with what the speaker has said. It involves a readiness to understand the message from the other's point of view and to communicate this readiness to the speaker by letting him know that what he has said has been both received and understood.

There are basically two types of reflective response: content responses and affect responses (Danish and Hauer 1973).

Paraphrasing deals with facts and ideas rather than with emotions. Bolton (1986) defines a paraphrase as a concise response to the speaker which states the essence of his content in the listener's own words. The paraphrase can be distinguished from a detailed word-for-word summary (sometimes referred to as parroting), because it is brief, focused and is presented in the listener's own words, reflecting her understanding of the speaker's message.

Reflecting back feelings Many listeners ignore the emotional dimension of a conversation and focus attention on the factual content of the message. Consider what this might mean in the context of an appraisal interview. By listening to the 'facts' a manager might build up an accurate picture about the quality of the work that her subordinate had been doing but, by filtering out the affective component of the message, might fail to appreciate that he finds his work very enjoyable and would would be very unhappy with any change.

Bolton (1986) suggests a number of techniques the listener can use to become more aware of the affective component of a message. She can listen for feeling words such as happy, sad, afraid, angry, surprised, disgusted; she can pay attention to the general content of the message and ask herself what she would be feeling; and she can observe body language. People often express their feelings without talking about them. A newly promoted employee who talks listlessly about his work and stares at the floor might not actually say that he is unhappy, but his non-verbal behaviour suggests that this might be the case. The skilled listener checks out her understanding (her hypothesis that he is unhappy), by reflecting back to the speaker the emotions he appears to be communicating.

Feeling and content can be reflected back together. The reflective responses offered by a listener who has used a listening framework similar to that proposed by Egan (see p. 23) might involve the expression of core messages in terms of feelings, and the experiences and behaviours that underlie these feelings. After listening to the newly promoted employee the manager might reflect that:

> 'You feel unhappy about your promotion because you used to enjoy what you were doing and because you miss your friends'

Carkhuff (1973) suggests that using a 'You feel . . . because . . .' format for reflective responses offers an easy and useful way of combining both feelings and fact.

Summative reflections Bolton (1986) defines a summative reflection as a brief statement of the main themes and feelings that have been expressed by the speaker over a longer period of conversation than would be covered by the other two reflecting skills. In addition to providing the listener with an opportunity to check out her understanding of the overall message, summative reflections can help both the listener and the speaker develop a greater awareness of themes by tying together a number of separate comments. They can offer an especially useful way of helping the speaker to appreciate the bigger picture. If, after listening for some time to what the speaker has to say, the listener summarizes, and reflects back to him her understanding of his predicament by making a statement along the lines of:

> The problem doesn't just seem to be that you are unhappy about giving up the old job and losing contact with the people you used to work with. You also appear to be anxious and insecure in the new job because you think that you don't have what it takes to successfully supervise other 'professionals'.

the speaker might begin to appreciate that there may be links which he had not previously considered and, as a result, may begin to think about his problem differently.

Summative reflections are also useful because they can reinforce positively the speaker's effort to communicate by providing direction to the conversation, creating a sense of movement and confirming that the listener is working hard to understand the speaker's message. Summative reflections also offer a very useful way of restarting interrupted conversations.

SUMMARY

Listening has been defined as the active search for a full and accurate understanding of the meaning of another's message.

The first part of this chapter considered those factors that influence the ability to listen. The reasons why some kinds of information are attended to and others are ignored were examined, as were some of the variables that determine how information is interpreted and messages given meaning. This was followed by a more detailed look at the process of communication, and some of the barriers to effective communication associated with the listener, the speaker, the message and the environment were examined.

The second part of the chapter identified and elaborated some of the key skills that can be deployed to improve listening. These skills were grouped under four headings: *preparation skills*, which include what the listener needs to do to prepare herself to listen; *attending skills*, which include the behaviours she needs to engage in to let the speaker know that she is paying careful attention to what he is saying; *following skills*, which include keeping the focus of attention on what the speaker has to say and encouraging him to tell his story; *reflecting skills*, which provide the listener with the opportunity to check out her understanding and communicate this to the speaker and to help the speaker to clarify his own thoughts.

The listening skills record sheet presented in Figure 2.1 can be used as an aid to skill development. Observe several people as they listen. Identify people whom you have experienced as good listeners and others whom you regard as poor listeners. Record the frequency with which they use the skills listed on the listening skills record sheet. Some of the preparatory behaviours are difficult to observe in others, as are the concentration techniques they might use (other than note taking). Nonetheless

SKILL

PREPARATION

arranged an appropriate time to listen	Yes ☐	☐ No
put aside other concerns	Yes ☐	☐ No
arranged environment free of distractions	Yes ☐	☐ No
reviewed background material	Yes ☐	☐ No

ATTENDING

facing speaker squarely	most of time ☐	☐ little of time
adopting open posture	☐	☐
leaning towards speaker	☐	☐
maintaining eye contact	☐	☐
appearing relaxed	☐	☐

FOLLOWING	No. of times used
non-coersive invitations to talk	☐
minimal prompts	☐
accents (one or two words re-statements)	☐
statements	☐
questions	☐
attentive silences	☐
note taking and other concentration techniques	☐

REFLECTING	No. of times used
paraphrasing	☐
reflecting back feelings	☐
summaries	☐

Figure 2.1 Listening skills record sheet

try and identify differences in the skills used by good and poor listeners.

Before you attempt to change the way you listen, construct a profile of the listening skills you use. Behave as you normally behave when listening and, as soon as possible after the listening episode, review and record the skills you think you used. Do this a few times in order to identify your typical listening style. Consider how your profile compares with those you have constructed for good and poor listeners. Which are you most like?

Finally, note the skills you either do not use, or use least frequently. Think through some recent listening episodes and consider how you might have made greater use of these skills. Then find opportunities to practise them. If there are a lot of skills that you do not normally use pick two or three to practise first. Commit yourself to find at least three occasions each day to put these skills into practice. Gradually widen your repertoire until you are regularly using a wide range of preparation, attending, following and reflecting skills every time you listen.

The next chapter is concerned with listening to non-verbal messages; a rich source of information about people's feelings.

References: Chapter 2

Benjamin, A. 1981. *The Helping Interview*, 3rd edn. Boston: Houghton Mifflin.

Bolton, R. 1986. *People Skills*. Sydney, Prentice-Hall of Australia.

Carkhuff, R. R. 1973. *The Art of Helping: an Introduction to Life Skills*. Amherst, Mass.: Human Resource Development Press.

Danish, S. J. and Hauer A. L. 1973. *Helping Skills: a Basic Training Programme*, New York: Behavioral Publications.

Deetz, S. A. and Stevenson, S. L. 1986. *Managing Interpersonal Communication*. New York: Harper and Row.

Drakeford, J. 1967. *The Awesome Power of the Listening Ear*. Waco, Tex: World Books.

Egan, G. 1986. *The Skilled Helper*, 3rd edn. Belmont, Calif.: Brooks/Cole.

Hackney, H. and Cormier, L. S. 1979. *Counselling Strategies and Objectives*, 2nd edn. Englewood Cliffs, NJ: Prentice-Hall.

Hargie, O., Saunders, C. and Dickson, D. 1987. *Social Skills in Interpersonal Communication*, 2nd edn. London: Croom Helm.

Lundsteen, S. 1971. *Listening: Its Impact on Reading and Other Language Acts*. New York: National Council of Teachers of English.
Nichols, R. G. and Stevens, L. A. 1957. *Are You Listening?* New York: McGraw-Hill.
Smith, V. 1986. Listening. In O. Hargie (ed.) *A Handbook of Communication Skills*. London: Croom Helm.
Wolff, F., Marnik, N., Tracey, W. and Nichols, R. 1983. *Perceptive Listening*. New York: Holt, Rinehart and Winston.

CHAPTER THREE

Listening to non-verbal messages

There is more to listening than meets the ear. The spoken word is not the only way people present information. The rate at which words are spoken, the tone of voice used, and its pitch and volume can all convey meaning, as can the way the speaker is dressed, his gestures, eye contact and body movement. If the words are heard in isolation and the accompanying non-verbal signals, audio-vocal and visual-gestural, are ignored, then the listener will miss important information and her understanding of the message will be incomplete.

The relationship between verbal and non-verbal signals

Argyle and Kendon (1967) make the point that verbal utterances are closely dependent on non-verbal signals, which keep the speaker and listener attending properly to each other, sustain the smooth alternation of speaker and listener and add further information to the literal messages transmitted. The link between verbal and non-verbal signals is further elaborated by Knapp (1978). He identifies six different ways in which non-verbal behaviour can be related to verbal behaviour. These are:

1 Repeating The non-verbal signal simply repeats what was said verbally: for example, while telling somebody the way to the railway station, the speaker points in the proper direction.

2 Contradicting The non-verbal behaviour contradicts the verbal behaviour: for example, banging the table and shouting

'I'm not angry'. (We will return later to take a closer look at which of the contradictory signals should be believed.)

3 *Substituting* The non-verbal behaviour substitutes for the verbal message. In response to the question, 'how did the interview go?' the other offers a thumbs down gesture. Sometimes, when the substitute non-verbal behaviour fails, the communicator might resort to the verbal level. For example, the woman who wants her date to stop making sexual advances may stiffen, stare straight ahead, act unresponsive and cool. If this does not deter him she might say something like 'Look Fred, please don't ruin a nice friendship'.

4 *Complementing* Non-verbal behaviour can elaborate or modify a verbal message: for example, a slight forward inclination of the body and a smile might signal that you are satisfied with the verbal report you are giving and that you expect it to be received with enthusiasm by your boss. If his reaction is cold and critical, your annoyance at his response might be signalled, as you continue with the report, by a change of posture and facial expression. A verbatim transcript of the interaction might totally fail to capture and record these affective elements of the message.

5 *Accenting* Non-verbal behaviours such as a nod of the head or a gesture of the hand may be used to emphasize or accent part of the spoken message.

6 *Regulating* Non-verbal behaviours can also be used to regulate the communicative flow between people. The importance of a person's regulatory skills is reflected by the evaluative statements we often make about others, such as, 'talking to him is like talking to a brick wall', 'you can't get a word in edgeways' or, 'she keeps butting in'. A number of non-verbal signals can be used to synchronize the sequence of utterances. Argyle (1975), summarizing the experimental work of others, lists many of the behaviours that signal when: (a) the listener wants to take the floor (such as interrupting or making impatient non-verbal signals like triple head nods); (b) the speaker wants to keep the floor (for example, by raising the volume of his

voice when interrupted or keeping a hand in mid-gesture at the end of a sentence); (c) the speaker wants to yield the floor (such as gazing at the other when he stops speaking or by ending a sentence by trailing off, saying 'you know', etc.); (d) the listener wants to decline an offer of the floor (such as merely offering a nod or a grunt when the other pauses).

The expression of feelings

Although Bolton (1986) acknowledges that there is considerable overlap between the type of information that is transmitted verbally and non-verbally, he maintains that words tend to be best for communicating factual information and non-verbal signals are best for communicating emotions.

Sometimes we deliberately signal our emotions in order to influence others (for example, anger or suffering), but often people work hard to camouflage what they are feeling, especially when they fear that open expression will involve some sanction: for example, that the quick-tempered candidate will be passed over for promotion.

The majority of people find it easier to control the words they utter than to control the way they behave and the non-verbal signals they transmit. Non-verbal signals offer a rich source of data about emotional states (such as anger) and interpersonal attitudes (such as being angry with a particular person). The most difficult non-verbal signals to control are autonomic displays such as perspiration and skin colour, but leakages can occur in many areas.

The observation of body language is an important element in effective listening, because it can provide you with many useful clues to what the speaker is really feeling. However, great care needs to be exercised when interpreting non-verbal signals, otherwise their true meaning may not be understood.

DETERMINING MEANING

Verbal and non-verbal signals need to be 'listened to' together if you are to properly understand the messages being presented by the speaker. Taken in isolation it is difficult to be sure what any one signal means. Knapp (1978) maintains that non-verbal signals can have multiple meanings and multiple uses. For example, a smile can be part of an emotional expression (I am happy), an attitudinal message (I like you), part of a self-presentation (I'm the kind of person your customer will like), or a listener response to manage the interaction (I'm interested in what you are saying).

Non-verbal signals have little or no meaning in themselves: they acquire meaning in particular contexts. Argyle (1975) illustrates this well. He argues that the significance of touching another person will vary depending upon whether the other person is '(a) one's spouse, (b) someone else's spouse, (c) a complete stranger, (d) a patient, (e) another person in a crowded lift'. The meaning of a non-verbal signal can depend on its position in time and its relation to other signals. For example, two men kissing on the football field immediately after one has scored a winning goal may have a completely different meaning from the same kiss in the privacy of a hotel bedroom.

Eisenberg and Smith (1971) have identified two factors that have important implications for the way we determine the meaning of non-verbal messages. The first is *discrimination*, the recognition of a non-verbal element that has potential message value, and the second is regrouping or *pattern recognition*, the process whereby discriminated elements are sorted into meaningful patterns. For example, somebody might fail to reply when you speak to them. You recognize this as unusual (you discriminate), because normally you spend a lot of time in conversation with this person and you both get on well together. This might prompt you to search for other signals that will help you determine whether he just did not hear you or there was some other reason for his failure to reply. If you notice that he goes on to break the lead of his pencil, slams a drawer shut and marches out of the room without saying goodbye, you might begin to build up a more complete picture, which helps you determine what his failure to reply means (pattern recognition). You might conclude that it was more likely that he was upset about something (possibly something he attributed to you), rather than that he didn't hear what you said.

The next section of this chapter offers a brief review of some of the non-verbal signals that can convey important information, signals that can be helpful when attempting to develop a full and accurate understanding of the meaning of another's message.

THE FACE

Most people pay a lot of attention to other people's faces because they are a rich source of both emotional expressions and interaction signals.

Several studies have attempted to identify those emotions that can be most readily distinguished from facial expression. In practice it would appear that this can sometimes be more difficult than many people imagine. A major problem is that the subject might be expressing more than one emotion at the same time (for example disappointment and anger), thus presenting a confusing expression. Nonetheless, there is evidence that people are able to identify six primary emotional states without too much difficulty. These are surprise, fear, anger, disgust, happiness and sadness (see Figures 3.1 to 3.6).

In an attempt to determine how accurately emotions can be recognized from facial expressions, Ekman *et al.* (1971) developed a scoring system, which involved dividing the face into three areas: (a) the brows and forehead, (b) the eyes, lids and bridge of the nose, and (c) the lower face, including the cheek, nose, mouth, chin and jaw. They presented coders with photographs of each facial area, giving examples of the six emotions. The coders were then asked to score a range of photographs by matching them against the examples provided. It was found that after being given six hours training the coders were able to identify emotional expressions with high levels of accuracy. On the basis of the evidence from this and other studies, Ekman *et al.* (1972) concluded:

> Contrary to the impression conveyed by previous reviews of the literature that the evidence in the field is contradictory and confusing, our analysis showed consistent evidence of accurate judgement of emotions from facial behaviour.

This conclusion is based on evidence derived from studies that used posed rather than spontaneous expressions. There is the

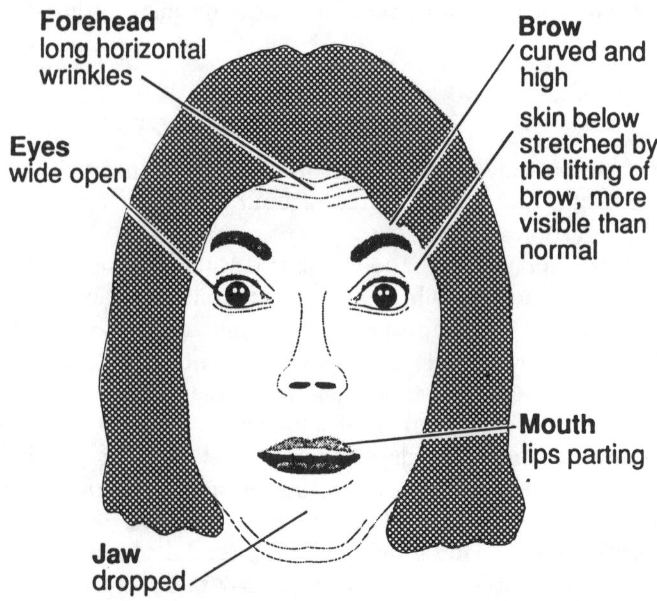

Figure 3.1 **Surprise** tends to be signalled by curved and raised brows, a wrinkled forehead, clearly visible whites of the eye (the sclera often being visible below as well as above the iris), dropped jaw and loosely opened mouth.

danger that these may be caricatures of natural expression, which both simplify and exaggerate what occurs spontaneously. Some researchers have tried to base their studies on actual emotions. One of the earliest such attempts was by Dunlap (1927). The way he tried to elicit emotions is illustrated by the following quotations. It makes entertaining reading:

2 **Amusement.** This was readily evoked by the use of a carefully selected stock of jokes, casually introduced as if suggested by the details of the work. . .
4 **Startle.** A pistol was fired, unexpectedly, behind the sitter. . .
5 **Expectation.** After the pistol had been fired, it was brought into the sitter's view and, after time had been given for the sitter to become composed, he was told that the next pistol would be deliberately fired to the slow count of one–two–three. . .

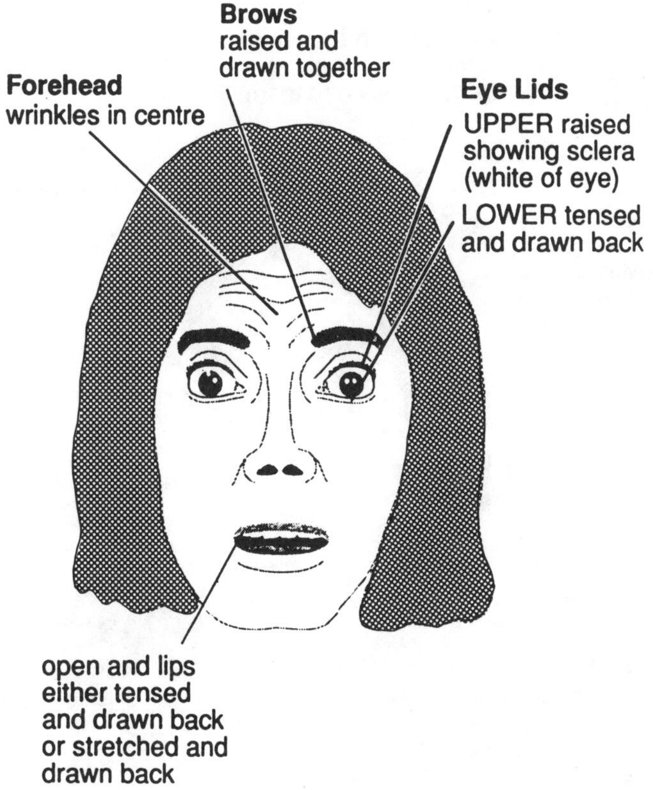

Figure 3.2 Fear is expressed through raised brows that are drawn together, a wrinkled forehead (but, unlike surprise where the wrinkles tend to go across the entire forehead, with fear the wrinkles are concentrated in the centre), tensed lower eyelids but with the whites of the eye showing above the iris, and the mouth open with lips that are tensed and drawn back.

6 **Pain.** . . . The stimulation consisted in bending a finger joint backwards forcibly.
7 **Disgust.** (The sitter was asked to smell). . . a test tube in which tissues dissected from a rat had reposed, corked, for several months.

More recent experiments have been less contrived and have, for example, made use of newspaper photographs to capture

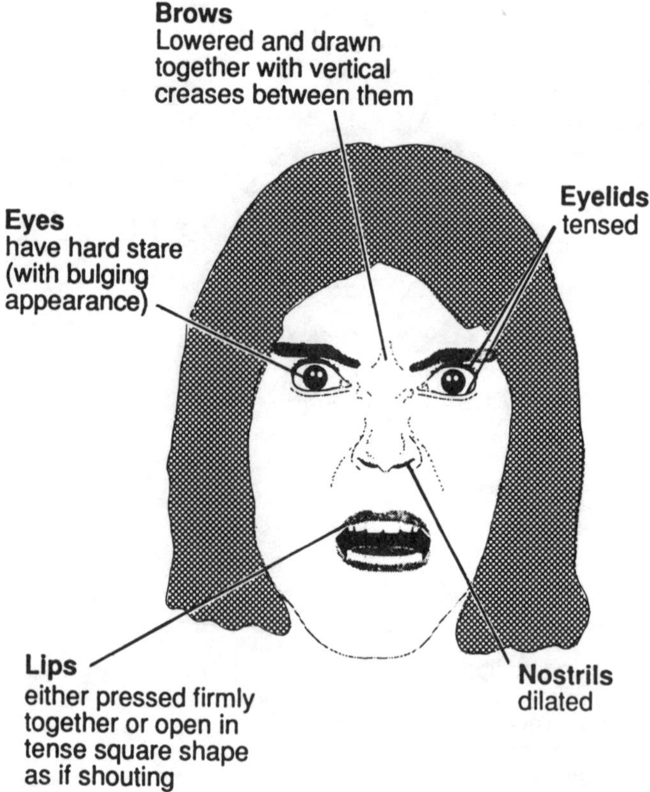

Figure 3.3 **Anger** is portrayed by brows that are lowered and drawn together, with vertical creases visible between the brows. The upper and lower lids are tensed and the eyes have a hard stare. The lips can either be pressed firmly together or open in a tense square shape, as if shouting.

spontaneous behaviour. Argyle (1975) reports that such studies achieved levels of accuracy of identification comparable with those derived from studies using posed photographs, approximately 70 per cent in both cases.

It would appear, therefore, that it is possible to identify some emotional states from facial expressions. Accuracy is likely to be greater when a simple or 'pure' emotional state is being experienced. When the face conveys multiple emotions it might be considerably more difficult to interpret these 'affect blends'. In

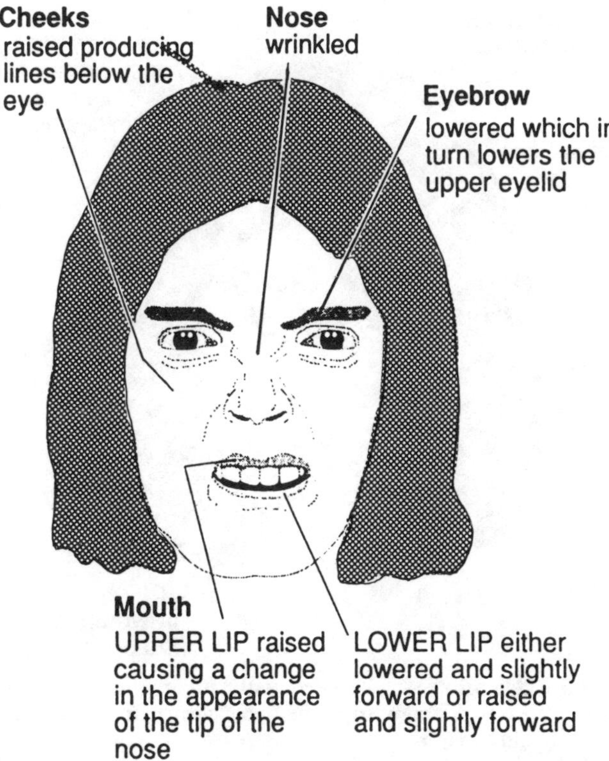

Figure 3.4 **Disgust** is signalled by a lowering of the brow which in turn pushes down the upper lid. The cheeks are raised and, most important, the nose is wrinkled. The upper lip is raised, but the lower lip can be either pushed up to meet the raised upper lip or lowered and pushed out.

such circumstances, it is especially important to pay attention to pattern recognition. Knapp (1978) refers to several studies which show that additional knowledge concerning the context within which a particular facial expression occurred can positively affect the accuracy of judgement.

Facial expressions can also be used to regulate an interaction. A greeting signal, which has been observed across a wide range of cultures, is the eyebrow flash (Morris 1972). At the moment of recognition the head tilts back, the eyebrows arch up and the face breaks into a smile. Head nods and smiles, as mentioned

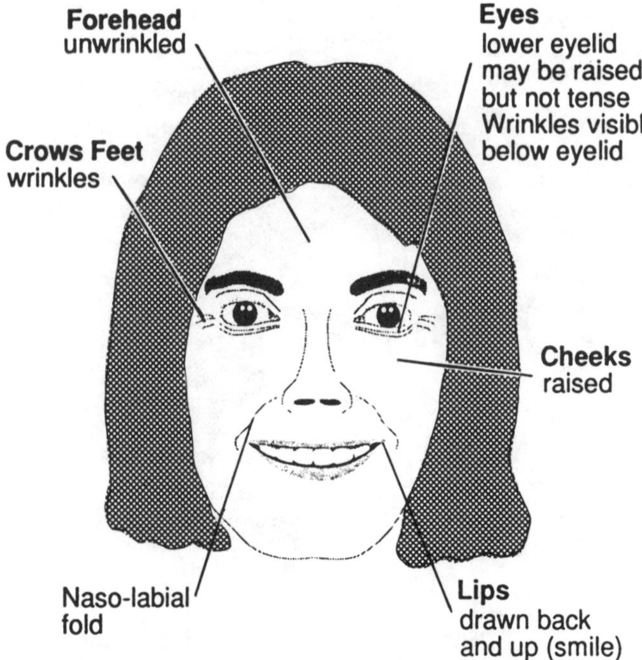

Figure 3.5 **Happiness** is associated with an unwrinkled forehead, crow's feet creases radiating from the outer corner of the eyes, raised cheeks and folds that run from the nose to just beyond the outer edges of the lip corners, which are drawn back and up to produce a smile.

in the previous chapter, can also play an important role in the synchronizing of conversations and in listening behaviour. A person's looking-behaviour can also be important in this respect.

GAZE

Looking-behaviour can signal a desire to communicate. A glance across the room at a manager engaged in conversation with others can tell her that you would like a word when she has finished. At a party, a similar glance might signal to a member of the opposite sex that you would like to initiate some contact, and a glance towards a waiter or a barman might be used to signal that you desire some attention.

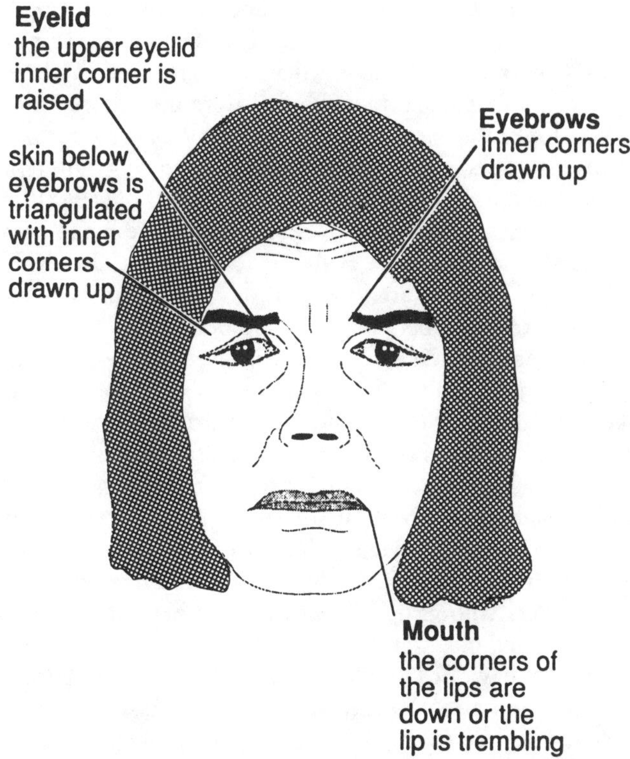

Figure 3.6 **Sadness** is expressed through eyebrows, which are drawn up at the inner corner, revealing a triangle of skin (with the apex pointing inwards and slightly upwards below the brows and above the upper eyelids, whose inner corners are raised). The corners of the lips are turned down and the lip may be trembling.

In Chapter 9 it is suggested that by paying attention to the direction of gaze you can identify important relationships during meetings. Speakers often look to leaders for permission to speak or for feedback on what was said. They may also look towards possible opponents for their reactions. Observing the pattern of such glances over a period might reveal alliances, because people are likely to glance most at the person who is championing their cause.

Looking-behaviour can provide a lot of information about the nature of relationships. Argyle (1975) reports that people look most at those they like. This conclusion is well supported by experimental evidence. It has also been found that gaze is perceived by others as a signal that they are liked. Mehrabian (1972) found that when two subjects were interviewed the one who was looked at most inferred that she was preferred.

Status also affects gaze. In a small group, people will tend to look most at the person with highest status. Efran (1968) found in triads where a freshman addressed a senior–freshman pair, he or she tended to look most at the senior. There is also evidence that those people who are looked at most see themselves as the most influential members of the group.

Hostility and aggression can be conveyed via looking behaviour. It has been found that a gaze of longer than ten seconds is likely to induce irritation and discomfort in many situations. The long hard stare is often used to threaten others.

Looking-behaviour can signal a desire to influence. Another study by Mehrabian (Mehrabian and Williams 1969) showed that when a person is trying to be more persuasive he will tend to look more. Knapp (1978) also reports that listeners seem to judge speakers who gaze most as the most persuasive, truthful, sincere and credible.

Looking-behaviour can also signal a desire to co-operate, to be included and an interest in what the other is saying.

A change in the pattern of eye contact can provide the 'listener' with useful information. Cutting off gaze is a powerful signal that, for example, a flirtatious glance has been recognized and the implied invitation rejected or, in response to a threatening stare, that the person cutting off the gaze is willing to submit or seek appeasement.

Less eye contact can also signal that a person is ashamed or embarrassed about something, or that she is too sad or preoccupied to engage the other in conversation. The wish to avoid involvement also tends to result in limited eye contact. When the chairman of a meeting is seeking a volunteer for some undesirable task it is not unusual to observe a marked reduction in eye contact – people look away. The same thing happens when a teacher asks a question to which no one knows the answer. Lack of confidence also tends to result in limited eye contact as does lack of interest, a point that received attention in the previous chapter on listening.

GESTURES

It is possible to distinguish between gestures that are intended to communicate and those that signal private reactions to what is going on. Ekman and Friesen (1969) offer three categories of gestures intended to communicate: emblems, illustrators and regulators.

Emblems are gestures that have a specific verbal translation and are used as a substitute for words. They are often employed when the verbal channel is blocked, for example by divers working under water or by the floor staff in a television studio who need to inform the participants of a chat show that they must draw their conversation to a close. They can also be used in everyday interactions: for example, rubbing hands for coldness, thumbs up for approval or the nose-thumb for mockery. There are, however, many emblems that are specific to one group of communicators (for example, ticktack men on a racecourse) or the members of one culture. Outsiders may not be able to translate the meaning of such emblems or may interpret them in a way that was not intended by the communicator. 'The ring' is an example of a gesture that means different things in different cultures. It is formed by holding the hand up, palm facing away, with the thumb and forefinger touching to form a circle. In Britain this is the A-OK gesture signifying that something is good. In some parts of France it can mean that something is worthless and in Sardinia it is a sexual insult. Most emblem gestures are formed by the hands, but this need not always be the case: the nose can be wrinkled as a sign that something smells or is in some other way undesirable.

Illustrators are non-verbal acts that are directly tied to speech. They are used to repeat, compliment or accent the verbal content of the message. Illustrative gestures may be used in many ways, for example to point to objects or people, sketch a train of thought, to demonstrate a rhythm or to depict spatial relationships. Bull (1983) summarizes a number of studies that provide evidence that some illustrators do assist the process of communication. One of the studies he cites tested the hypothesis that visual information is communicated more easily through hand gestures (Graham and Argyle, 1975). English students were asked to communicate information about some two dimensional shapes to others without the use of hand gestures. The decoders were asked to draw what they thought the shapes were and the results were rated in terms of their similarity to the original. The experiment was repeated with a group of Italian students. It was found that when gestures were permitted the results were significantly more accurate. It was also found that this effect was more pronounced for the Italian students: a result which suggests that gestures make a more important contribution to accurate communication in some cultures.

Illustrative gestures can also facilitate the comprehension of speech by enabling the speaker to stress certain words or phrases. Desmond Morris, in his popular book *Manwatching* (1977), provides a wealth of examples of such signals including the 'hand chop', a straight hand slashed downwards through the air, possibly indicating that the speaker wants her ideas to cut through the confusion that may exist, and the 'vacuum precision grip' where the tips of thumb and forefinger are brought together as though holding some small delicate object, suggesting that the speaker wants to express herself with great exactness.

Illustrators can also communicate the speaker's enthusiasm for her subject and can help to increase the listener's level of attention by providing greater stimulation. It is important to note, however, that inappropriate gestures, such as picking one's nose or rubbing one's crutch, can be very distracting for the listener, but these are not illustrative gestures and will be considered later.

Regulators have been defined as those non-verbal acts that maintain and regulate an interaction. They tend to be associated with greetings, turn-taking and partings, and include gestures such as the eyebrow flash, waving and nodding, which have already been discussed.

Unintentional gestures are those gestures which signal private reactions to what is going on. They can take several forms but they usually involve some form of self or object touching. Morris

(1977) suggests that the most common form of self-touching is self-intimacy: movements which provide self comfort because they are unconsciously mimed acts of being touched by somebody else. People stroke their own face, clasp their hands, gently press their knuckles against their lips, caress their own hair, cross their legs so that one limb feels the comforting pressure of the other, rock their bodies, etc. In order of frequency, the most common self-intimacies appear to be the jaw support, the chin support, the hair clasp, the cheek support, the mouth touch and the temple support.

In addition to indicating a need for comfort and reassurance, self touching can signal that a person is experiencing negative attitudes towards the self. Ekman and Friesen (1969, 1972) found that when people experienced shame they tended to cover their eyes. Others have suggested that hand over mouth can also be associated with shame or self blame and that picking fingers, nose, ears and teeth can also be linked to feelings of self blame.

Attitudes towards others can be signalled through self touching. Experimental results suggest that the hand to nose gesture is associated with fear or anxiety, and that anxiety is also signalled by tightly clenched hands. The fist gesture implies aggression. The exposure of parts of the body can be a sexual invitation, whereas covering up the body can signal a wish not to get involved, as can the gesture of folding ones arms across the chest. Flight behaviour, reflecting a wish to get away from others, can be signalled by restless movements of hands and legs.

Unintentional gestures, which serve the function of relieving tension can also involve the touching of objects rather than self. Morris (1977) describes these gestures as displacement activities, agitated fill-in actions performed during periods of acute tension. He offers the example of a girl waiting for an interview. She wants very much to attend the interview, but at the same time is very scared and would like to flee the waiting room. This inner conflict makes it extremely difficult for her to wait calmly to be called. She reacts by filling the behaviour void with displacement activities. These can take many forms: fiddling with the clasp on her bracelet, polishing her glasses, smoking.

TOUCHING OTHERS

Bodily contact and touching behaviour is the most basic way in which people can express such interpersonal attitudes as aggression and affiliation.

Children pat, slap, punch, pinch, stroke, lick, suck, kiss, hold, kick and tickle others much more than adults do. Maturity tends to bring with it a considerable reduction in touching behaviour, many of the functions normally served by such behaviours being fulfilled by facial and gestural expressions. Nonetheless, adults touch others to offer encouragement, express tenderness and show emotional support. They also touch others, but in different ways (slapping, punching, kicking), to express aggressive interpersonal relationships. Sexual intimacy is another area of social interaction that inevitably involves bodily contact.

Many factors influence the meaning of touching behaviour. Context can be important, as is illustrated by the kissing example cited by Argyle (see p. 34). Intensity and duration can also be important. Handshakes can be formal and polite or they can express real warmth. Warm handshakes tend to involve a firm grip and are sustained for a longer period than the merely formal greeting. Knapp (1978) suggests the possibility of plotting touch behaviour along an intimacy continuum, ranging from touch and release (least intimate), through touch and hold, to touch and stroke (most intimate). The meaning can also be influenced by the kind of touch. A pat is usually interpreted in terms of encouragement or play, whereas a stroke suggests comfort and/or intimacy.

The importance of touch is well illustrated in several studies. Agulera (1967) found that the touch behaviour of nurses increased the verbal output of patients and improved patients' attitudes towards nurses. Fisher *et al.* (1976) found that in those situations where library clerks touched some students when returning their library cards, those who were touched evaluated the clerk and the library more favourably than those who were not touched.

It is possible to gain some clues about differences in status by observing touching behaviour. Usually it is the high status person who touches first. Often this occurs within the context of managing an interaction. People touch others when guiding them. They may also hold or squeeze the other when accenting part of the message. Touch can also be used as a means of attracting attention.

POSTURE

Several factors influence the posture a person will adopt. They include context, culture and attitudes towards others. Mehrabian (1968) found that subjects adopted different postures towards those whom they liked and disliked: for example, with people they disliked there was an increased tendency to adopt an arms-akimbo posture. In a later study (Mehrabian 1972), it was found that people adopted a more relaxed posture (consisting of asymmetrical arm positions, sideways lean, asymmetrical leg positions, hand relaxation and backwards lean) with others of lower status. Argyle (1975) cites a report by Goffman (1961), which supports this finding. Goffman noticed that the most important people at meetings in mental hospitals sat in the most relaxed postures.

It has been found that when people are presented with sketches of stick figures they tend to attribute similar meanings to different postures. Some of these interpretations are presented in Figure 3.7.

Observe the different postures people adopt in different situations. The manager conducting a disciplinary interview is much more likely to sit upright and appear more tense than when she is reading her young daughter a bedtime story later the same day. The affection she has for her daughter is likely to manifest itself in a much more relaxed and open posture. The mother is also much less likely to position herself so that there is a piece of furniture between herself and her daughter, whereas at work she may well have conducted the disciplinary interview across her desk.

THE USE OF FURNITURE

It has long been recognized that the shape of a table in a meeting room, the layout of chairs in a lecture room and the arrangement of furniture in a sitting room can have an

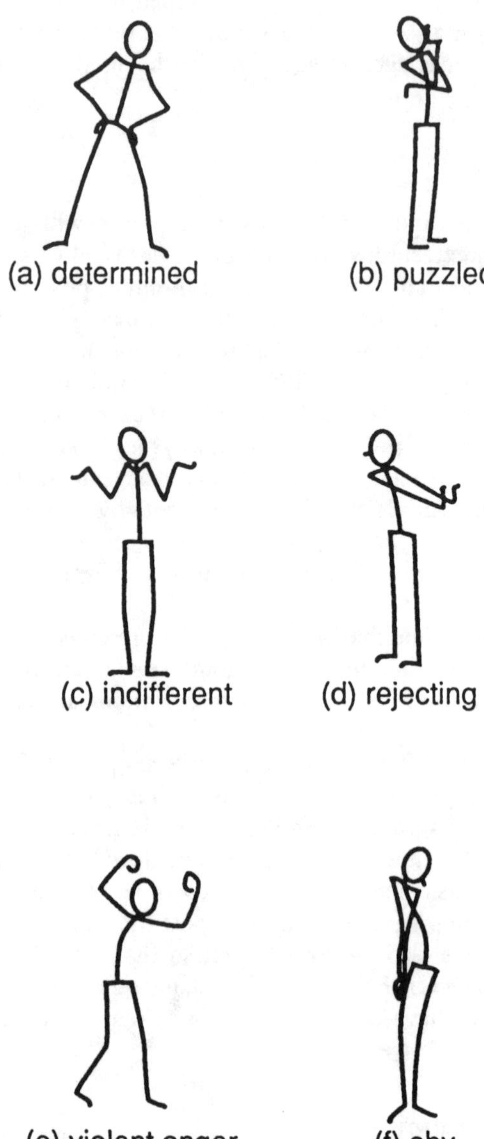

Figure 3.7 Posture: interpretations of stick-figure diagrams (based on an experiment by Sarbin and Hardyck 1953)

important effect on the flow of communication. For example, people sitting along the same side of a long boardroom table may experience problems in communicating with each other because eye contact, apart from that with immediate neighbours, is difficult.

The way people arrange or use the furniture in their office or home can provide valuable clues to how they are feeling. The manager who feels insecure in a meeting may prefer to keep a desk between herself and the person or persons she is interacting with. The manager might also prefer to stay behind her desk as a way of signalling that the meeting is formal; for example, in a disciplinary interview. However, on those occasions when she wants to encourage a more informal relationship, for example, when counselling a colleague, she may decide to come from behind her desk and move to a more informal seating arrangement. She may also prefer this kind of setting when meeting people she likes or when she is less pressed for time. An interesting study of doctor-patient relationships suggested that the presence or absence of a desk can alter the patient's 'at ease' state (White 1953). It was found that when the doctor sat behind a desk only 10 per cent of the patients were perceived to be at ease, whereas when the desk was removed the proportion was 55 per cent.

Furniture can be used to key the climate for an interaction. Sitting behind a desk with your back to a window so that a visitor can only see a silhouette of your face deprives the other person of the opportunity to observe your facial expression. Experiments suggest that the silhouetted person is likely to be perceived as being more dominant, especially if the visitor is seated in a lower chair.

SPATIAL BEHAVIOUR

The distance between people signals something about the nature of their relationship. Four proximity zones have been suggested for different kinds of relationship (Hall 1959).

Intimate: Up to 18 inches. At this distance bodily contact is easy. Each person can smell the other and feel their body heat. They can see, but

	not very well, and they can talk in a low whisper.
Personal:	18 inches – 4 feet. At this distance people can touch each other but they are sufficiently far apart to see better and not smell the other's breath.
Social-consultative:	9 – 12 feet. This is the distance at which important relationships are conducted, for example, talking to somebody across a desk. A louder voice is needed.
Public:	12 feet and above. This is the distance associated with public figures and public occasions. Public figures addressing an audience are often on a stage. Even where there is no stage the public figure usually stands apart when speaking to a large group.

In the UK, friends or colleagues talking about agreeable matters tend to stand about 24 inches apart. Problems sometimes arise when people from different cultures, with different concepts of personal space, engage each other in conversation. One may feel comfortable standing close to the other, whereas the other may experience discomfort because he feels that his personal space has been invaded. It is not unusual in such circumstances to see the latter turning away or taking a step backwards to restore a comfortable distance.

There is evidence that in an interaction between people of different status the more junior person may require more personal space and the senior person may inadvertently make the junior feel uncomfortable because she approaches too close. The author has observed inexperienced drilling teams on oil rigs lose their rhythm of working together when a senior manager visiting the rig has approached too close in order to observe their work. During certain operations this loss of rhythm has been known to be the cause of accidents.

Experiments have shown that when a person's personal space is invaded, measures of emotional arousal, such as skin resistance, go up.

APPEARANCE

Appearance is included here as an important element of non-verbal communication because it is something that can be manipulated. People can choose what clothes to wear and how they will wear them; they can choose the kind of jewellery, badges and accessories to adorn themselves with; they can choose how to dress their hair or care for their skin. They can even choose how they will smell and, to a lesser extent, what kind of physique they will have.

When people deliberately exercise this kind of choice they will usually be making decisions that reflect the impact they want to have on others, decisions concerned with impression management. Power-dressing is a modern term which has come to mean choosing what to wear in order to create an influential/dominant image.

This chapter has not adopted the perspective of the actor and her attempts to create some impact. The theme has been interpretation and the focus has been those clues that might help the listener better understand the messages she is receiving. A person's appearance can provide the listener or observer with messages about personality, status and interpersonal attitudes.

Argyle (1975) suggests that people with certain kinds of personality prefer certain colours and other features. For example, people who are sociable and extroverted prefer brighter and more saturated colours and conformists also conform in the clothes they wear.

Uniforms signal rank, as in the army, or disguise rank as in some (e.g. Japanese) work organizations. Status differences and social class are often communicated by the cost and 'cut' of the clothes people wear and by the condition of their body, especially their hands and finger nails.

Appearance can also convey messages about one person's attitude towards others. Certain kinds of clothes worn within a certain context might signal a person's sexual availability. Respect for another might also be communicated through appearance. Arriving at a business meeting in worn, dirty, casual clothes might give others, especially customers, the impression that they are not highly regarded. Skinheads and rockers might also be seen as aggressive and threatening by some people because of the clothes they wear and their general appearance.

VOCAL CUES

This chapter opened with a statement that the rate at which words are spoken, the tone of voice used and its pitch and volume can convey meaning. Research in this area has been fraught with difficulties, largely because of the problem of separating the meaning of the words spoken from the vocal expression. Various approaches have been tried to eliminate verbal information. Some researchers have experimented with meaningless content, speakers being asked to express emotions by reciting numbers or nonsense syllables; others have used a standard passage, which has been spoken in different ways, and others have filtered the statement electronically to eliminate verbal information. The results of all these experiments have been encouraging and seem to provide clear evidence that people are able to make reasonably accurate judgements from audio-vocal messages about another's emotions and feelings as well as about many personal characteristics such as age, sex and status.

Davitz (1964) has summarized many of the research findings in the area of emotional sensitivity in an attempt to produce an Emotion–Vocal Cue Dictionary. The key variables identified by Davitz are loudness, pitch, timbre, rate, inflection, rhythm and enunciation. Figure 3.8 presents the different patterns of vocal expression for two emotional states: affection and anger.

Mention has already been made of the way in which vocal cues can help to regulate the interaction between people. Changes in pitch – for example, raising the pitch at the end of an utterance – is just one vocal cue that can influence how the other will behave. The change in pitch signals a question that demands an answer. The audible inspiration of breath, changes in volume, changes in the frequency and duration of silences and interrupting are just some of the many vocal cues which can be used to regulate turn-taking in conversations.

Vocal cues are also used by people to make judgement about another's personality. However, research evidence suggests that

FEELING	LOUDNESS	PITCH	TIMBRE	RATE	INFLECTION	RHYTHM	ENUNCIATION
AFFECTION	soft	low	resonant	slow	steady & slight upward	regular	slurred
ANGER	loud	high	blaring	fast	irregular up & down	irregular	clipped

Figure 3.8 Characteristics of vocal expression

while 'listeners' do tend to agree on the judgements they make – for example, breathiness suggests females who are more feminine, prettier, more petite, more effervescent, more highly strung and shallower than others, and nasality in both males and females suggests a wide array of socially undesirable characteristics (see Addington 1968) – many of these stereotypes do not correlate with the scores achieved by speakers on personality tests. Nonetheless, these stereotypes, even though often inaccurate, may well have an important influence on the way we interpret what others say and how they behave.

DECIPHERING CONTRADICTORY SIGNALS

This chapter has looked at the ways in which attending to another's non-verbal behaviour can contribute to effective listening. It has been argued that it is important to 'listen' to both verbal and non-verbal signals because, while there is overlap, words tend to emphasize the factual content of messages, whereas non-verbal signals emphasize the affective content. However, problems can arise when the words and the non-verbal signals appear to be sending contradictory messages.

Returning to the exchanges cited earlier in this chapter: what is the true meaning of the message if a red-faced man bangs the table with a clenched fist and declares that he is not angry? Research evidence suggests that non-verbal behaviours generally offer the most reliable clues to what a person is really feeling, in spite of his denial that he is angry.

It appears that people are less likely to inhibit or manipulate certain signals. These tend to be those which they are least aware of, believe others pay little attention to or are beyond their control. Morris (1977) has proposed a 'Believability Scale' for different kinds of action. He suggests that autonomic signals are the most believable and verbalizations are the least believable. The seven elements in his scale are:

1 **Autonomic signals.** These include sweating, skin colour, respiratory patterns, etc. They are almost impossible to control because they result from physiological changes within the body. However, although they offer a very reliable indication of a person's emotional state, their occurrence tends

to be limited to a relatively few dramatic situations. The body actions listed below tend to occur more frequently and therefore deserve attention.

2 **Leg and foot signals.** People tend to focus most attention on the face, possibly because it is a highly expressive area. Even when it is possible to observe the whole body it is the face which receives most attention. It would appear that we normally pay least attention to those parts of the body which are furthest away from the face and, probably for the same reasons, we exert least deliberate control over these same parts of our own body. Since the feet are as far away from the face as you can get, it is not unreasonable to assume that they will provide valuable clues to a person's true mood. Foot actions that you might observe include aggressive toe jabs that may be at variance with friendly words and a smiling face, or restless and repetitive foot movements, which suggest that the person is anxious to discontinue the interaction and get away. If we consider the leg as a whole, it may be possible to observe the soothing leg squeezing, mentioned above, which suggests that a seemingly confident person is seeking some self assurance, or flirtatious leg displays that conflict with upper body primness.

3 **Trunk signals.** Posture can reflect the general muscular tonus of the whole body and, therefore, can be a useful guide to mood states. Somebody who is keyed up and excited will find it much more difficult to adopt a slumped posture than someone who is bored, unhappy or depressed.

4 **Unidentified gesticulations.** People tend to be more aware of hands, their own and others, than they are of feet. However, their awareness still tends to be relatively low, especially when the hands are used to make the vague and indefinite actions that accompany speech. Assertive finger wagging, imploring palm-up hand gestures or hand chops are some of the signals that can indicate what a person is really feeling. These 'illustrative gestures' are a better guide to the truth than the 'emblems' that are included in the next category.

5 **Identified hand gestures.** We tend to be more aware of those hand gestures that are precise units of communication and are deliberately performed. For this reason, emblems such

as the A-OK or the victory V signs cannot be trusted if they appear as part of a contradictory signal. A person might deliberately signal A-OK or thumbs up when she is feeling less than satisfied with her state of affairs. Consequently, such signals merit less weight than those discussed above.

6 **Facial expressions.** It is relatively easy to lie with the face. Most of us can fake anger or surprise with relative ease and, therefore, when contradictory signals are observed it might be best to ignore facial expressions. However, the careful observer might be able to see through many faked facial expressions and observe frozen smiles or other minute facial movements that provide clues to what the other is really feeling.

7 **Verbalizations.** As already mentioned, people are able to exercise most control over the verbal messages they give out. For this reason, they are the least reliable guide to true feelings when contradictory signals are observed.

IMPROVING YOUR ABILITY TO LISTEN TO NON-VERBAL SIGNALS

Observe other people in conversation and ask yourself what they really feel about each other, about the issues being discussed and about themselves. Ask yourself who has the highest status and who is taking the lead in managing the interaction.

Think about the non-verbal behaviours you attended to when making your assessment. Figure 3.9 offers examples of some non-verbal signals which have been organized under the headings discussed in this chapter. Using this as a framework, keep a record of the signals you attend to. After you have observed and recorded a number of interactions between people you will have a profile of the signals you attend to most and least.

Note whether you attend to a wide or a narrow range of non-verbal behaviours. Bearing in mind Morris's 'Believability Scale', ask yourself whether you are paying sufficient attention to the most reliable signals.

You might find it useful to start observing those signals that you tend to neglect, and to monitor how those observations improve your ability to better understand the meaning of the messages you receive from other people.

Which non-verbal behaviours do you attend to?

FACE
- brows and forehead ☐
- eyes, lids, bridge of nose ☐
- cheek, nose, mouth, jaw ☐
- other, specify ______

GAZE
- direction ☐
- frequency ☐
- length ☐
- soft/hard ☐
- cut off ☐
- lack of ☐
- other, specify ______

GESTURES
- **Emblems:** eg: A-OK thumbs down. ☐
- **Illustrators:** eg: hand clap, finger wagging, vacuum precision grip. ☐
- **Regulators:** eg: nodding, eyebrow flash. ☐
- **Self touching:** eg: self intimacies, picking and scratching, hand over eyes. ☐
- **Object touching** ☐
- other, specify ______

TOUCHING OTHERS
- kind of touch. ☐
- target of touch. ☐
- duration of touch, ☐
- frequency. ☐

POSTURE
- upright ☐
- slumped ☐
- tense ☐
- relaxed ☐
- other, specify ______

FURNITURE
- as barrier, ☐
- as status symbol, ☐
- other, specify ______

PROXIMITY ZONES
- intimate 18in. ☐
- personal 18in. - 4ft. ☐
- consultative 9ft.- 12ft. ☐
- public 12ft. + ☐

APPEARANCE
- clothes. ☐
- hair. ☐
- skin. ☐
- smell. ☐
- other, specify ______

VOCAL CUES
- loudness ☐
- pitch ☐
- timbre ☐
- rate ☐
- infliction ☐
- rhythm ☐
- enunciation ☐
- other, specify ______

Figure 3.9 Non-verbal signals.

One final point. Remember that it can be dangerous to over-interpret the meaning of an isolated behaviour. The art of effective listening to non-verbal messages is to recognize behaviours that may have potential message value and then to search for other behaviours that suggest a pattern. It is these patterns of behaviours, interpreted within context, which will enable you to determine the meaning of what you have seen and heard with a greater degree of confidence.

References: Chapter 3

Addington, D.W. 1969. The relationship of selected vocal characteristics to personality perception. *Speech Monographs* 35: 492–503.

Agulera, D. C. 1967. Relationships between physical contact and verbal interaction between nurses and patients. *Journal of Psychiatric Nursing* 5: 5–21.

Argyle, M. 1975. *Bodily Communication*. New York: International Universities Press.

Argyle, M. and Kendon, A. 1967. The experimental analysis of social performance. *Advances in Experimental Social Psychology* 3: 55–98.

Bolton, R. 1986. *People Skills*. Sydney: Prentice-Hall of Australia.

Bull, P. 1983. *Body Movement and Interpersonal Communication*. New York: Wiley.

Davitz, J.R. 1964. *The Communication of Emotional Meaning*. New York: McGraw-Hill.

Dunlap, K. 1927. The role of eye-muscles and mouth muscles in the expression of emotions. *Genetic Psychology Monographs* 2: 199–233.

Efran, J. S. 1968. Looking for approval: effect on visual behavior of approbation from persons differing in importance. *Journal of Personality and Social Psychology*. 10: 21–5.

Eisenberg, A. and Smith, R. 1971. *Nonverbal Communications*. Indianapolis: Bobbs–Merrill.

Ekman, P. and Friesen, W. V. 1969. The repertoire of non-verbal behaviour: categories, origins, usage and coding. *Semiotica* 1: 49–98.

Ekman, P. and Friesen, W. V. 1972. Hand Movements. *Journal of Communication* 22: 353–74.

Ekman, P., Friesen, W. V. and Ellsworth, P. 1972. *Emotion in the Human Face: Guidelines for Research and Integration of Findings*. Elmsford, NY: Pergamon.

Ekman, P., Friesen, W. V. and Tomkins, S. S. 1971. Facial affect scoring technique: a first validity study. *Semiotica* 3: 37–58.

Fisher, J. D., Rytting, M. and Heslin, R. 1976. Hands touching hands: affective and evaluative effects of an interpersonal touch. *Sociometry* 39: 416–21.

Goffman, E. 1961. *Asylums*. New York: Anchor Books.

Graham, J.A. and Argyle, M. A cross cultural study of the communication of extra-verbal meaning by gestures. *International Journal of Psychology* 10: 57–69.

Hall, E. T. 1959. *The Silent Language*. Garden City, NY: Doubleday.
Knapp, M. L. 1978. *Non-verbal Communication in Human Interaction*. New York: Holt, Rinehart and Winston.
Mehrabian, A. 1968. The inference of attitude from the posture, orientation and distance of a communication. *Journal of Consulting Psychology* 32: 296–308.
Mehrabian, A. 1972. *Non-verbal Communication*. Chicago: Aldine–Atherton.
Mehrabian, A. and Williams, M. 1969. Non-verbal concomitants of perceived and intended persuasiveness. *Journal of Personality and Social Psychology* 13: 37–58.
Morris, D. 1977. *Manwatching: a Field Guide to Human Behaviour*. London: Cape.
Sabin, T. R. and Hardyk, C. D. 1953. Contributions to role taking theory: role-perception on the basis of postural cues. Unpublished, cited by T. S. Sarbin 1954, Role Theory, in G. Lindzey (ed.) *Handbook of Social Psychology*. Cambridge, Mass.: Addison–Wesley.
White, A. G. 1953. The patient sits down: a clinical note. *Psychiatric Medicine* 15: 256–7, cited in Argyle, M. 1975

CHAPTER FOUR

Information-getting

One of the most common definitions of the interview is 'a conversation with a purpose' (Bingham, Moore and Bruce 1942). This is a wide ranging, umbrella-like definition, which encompasses many kinds of purposeful conversations ranging from disciplinary interviews to counselling sessions, and possibly even including negotiations. In this chapter, a much narrower definition has been adopted and the interview is defined as a face-to-face interaction in which one (or more) person(s) seeks information from another. For example, the interviewer may want information that will help assess a person's suitability for a job, determine why customers are unhappy with a product, anticipate people's reactions to the introduction of flexi-time or decide whether an insurance claim is justified. Such interviews are more focused than most conversations because the interviewer has a clear purpose: to obtain certain kinds of information. She may have little interest in much of the information that the interviewee may be prepared to talk about, nor may she have the time to listen to it.

The effective interviewer is someone who is able to structure and manage the encounter in such a way that information irrelevant to the purpose of the interaction is largely eliminated and relevant information is fully and accurately communicated in a relatively brief period of time. Many interviewers engage in interactions that are very different from this. They fail to manage the interaction and allow, maybe even encourage, the respondent to spend much of the time talking about things which are irrelevant to the purpose of the interview. The aim of this chapter is to identify and discuss many of the skills that can help an individual conduct an effective information-getting interview.

The information-getting interview is not restricted to objective fact-finding. Nadler (1977) argues that the interview is an effective instrument for obtaining several kinds of information. These include: (a) descriptive accounts (a systems analyst, for example, might interview members of a department in order to discover how some system or procedure works); (b) diagnostic evaluations (the analyst may not only want to know how the system or procedure operates but also how effective it is, so she may ask respondents for their assessment of whether or not it is fulfilling its purpose); (c) affective reactions (even if the system is working effectively people may or may not like it. Affective reactions are the positive or negative feelings that people have, they may feel satisfied or dissatisfied, challenged or frustrated). In other words, information-getting can involve gathering many different kinds of information, including other people's attitudes, values, hopes and fears. It is not restricted to obtaining 'objective facts' and often involves asking people to talk about private thoughts that they may not normally share with others, or about partially formed attitudes or personal feelings that they may never have articulated before.

THE INTERVIEW AS A SOCIAL ENCOUNTER

Obtaining full and frank answers from another person is not an easy task. The interview is a complex social encounter in which the behaviour of each party is influenced by the other. An often used but over-simplified model of the interview presents the process solely in terms of the interviewer getting information from the respondent (see Figure 4.1) and fails to take full account of the interactive nature of the encounter. Respondents are aware that interviewers are observing what they say and do and, on the basis of these observations, are making inferences about them. Consequently, respondents may not openly and honestly answer all the questions they are asked; they may attempt to manage the way they respond in order to maximize their personal benefit from the interaction rather than help the interviewer achieve her purpose.

Goffman (1959), Mangham (1978) and others have used drama as a metaphor for describing and explaining a wide range of interactions, and this metaphor can usefully be applied

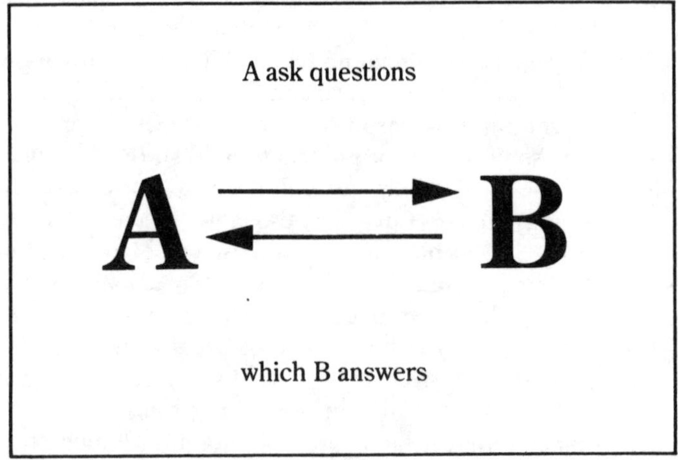

Figure 4.1 Over-simplified model of the interview

to the interview. Goffman talks about putting on a performance for an audience and argues that a person's portrayal of action will be determined by his or her assessment of the audience. He also notes that actors use mirrors so that they can practise and become an object to themselves, backstage, before going 'on-stage' and becoming an object to others. Similarly, interviewees may anticipate the nature of their audience, the interviewer(s), and rehearse the way they want to present themselves. Problems can arise, especially in selection interviews, if interviewers (the audience) interpret what they observe as being a true reflection of stable personal dispositions of the interviewees, when in reality the interviewees' behaviour may well be a performance, a reaction to the situation as they perceive it, and consequently may not be a good predictor of how they will behave in different situations.

The problem can be further complicated because in the interview situation the respondent's ability to manage their behaviour, 'to put on a performance', might be impaired. Farr (1984) argues that, if respondents are too sensitive to the fact that others are evaluating them, they may become apprehensive and this may cause them to perform poorly. This could be an important problem for the chronically shy and may help to explain why those who lack confidence may fail to do well in selection interviews.

The nature of the social encounter involved in an interview is illustrated in Figure 4.2. Let us assume that we are looking at an appraisal interview and that the interviewer is A and the respondent is B. The interviewer is likely to structure the situation and behave in a way that she feels will best project her definition of the purpose of the interview and the role she wants to assume in the interaction. Mangham (1978) suggests that this behaviour not only says a lot about whom A wishes to be taken for, but also about whom A takes B to be and the role B is expected to play. A attempts to influence B's interpretation of the situation and to focus his attention on those issues that she regards as important. Much of what takes place at this stage involves what Wicks (1984) refers to

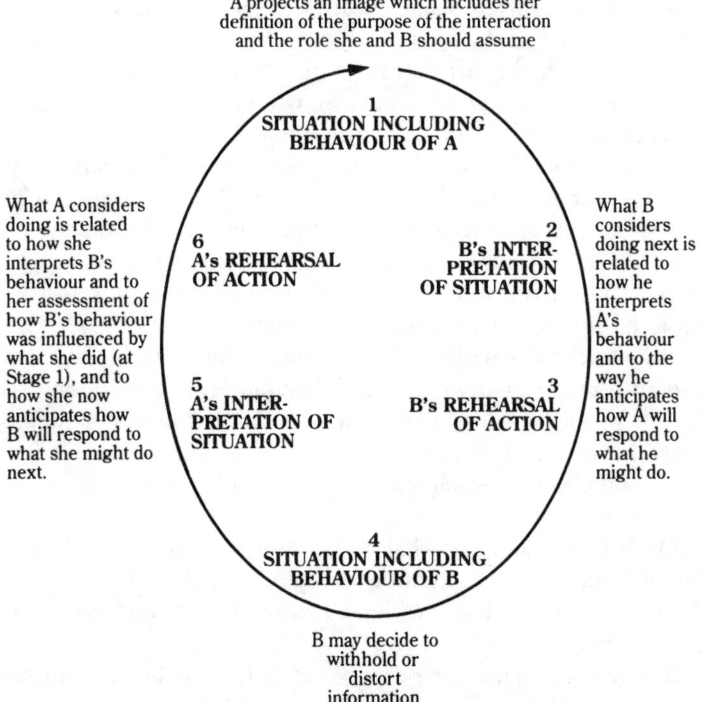

Figure 4.2 The interview as a social encounter

as cognitive scene setting, which will be discussed in more detail later.

At stage 2, in Figure 4.2, B seeks to understand what it is that A is projecting and what implications this has for him. Does A, for example, see the appraisal interview as an evaluation exercise, during which she will collect information from B in order for her to make decisions about his work, rewards and career progress, or does she see it as a developmental exercise, which involves joint appraisal and shared decision-making?

B might detect a difference between the performance A consciously and deliberately gives and what Mangham refers to as the information she 'gives off'. A may attempt to perform in a way that gives the impression to B that she is committed to a shared approach to appraisal; however, she may actually 'give off' signals, verbal and non-verbal, that contradict this intended impression. (The interpretation of non-verbal behaviour is considered thoroughly in Chapter 2.) Thus, as the interview progresses through stages 3 and 4, B may decide to cooperate with A and give her the answers she wants or may decide not to be completely open and to distort or withhold information until he is more confident about her intentions.

Reference has already been made to rehearsal of action. At stage 3, B has to decide, on the basis of his interpretation of the situation, how to respond to A. Farr (1984), discussing the work of Mead, notes that man not only acts but re-acts to his own actions. He reacts to his own behaviour on the basis of the actual or *anticipated* reaction of others. He can anticipate their reactions through simulation or rehearsal. He can try out, in his own mind, a few pieces of behaviour and test them for fit. Mangham even suggests that he can simulate several stages into alternative futures for an interaction, a form of mental chess in which various moves and their consequences are tested.

Once B has decided what to do and has responded to A's initial behaviour, the situation changes. Both A and B, at stage 4 on the circle, are faced with a situation that includes the most recent behaviour of B.

If A did not make her purpose explicit, B might have misinterpreted her behaviour and acted in ways that A either did not anticipate or feels are inappropriate to the situation.

A has to assess this situation (stage 5) and attempt to understand the meaning of B's behaviour. Her interpretation of B's response offers a basis for assessing the relevance and validity of any information communicated by B. Good interviewers have the ability to empathize with the other party. They can assume the other's role in the interview situation. They can put themselves in the other's shoes and replay in their mind the situation that the respondent faces. And they can interpret their behaviour, including their answers to questions, from this perspective.

On the basis of her interpretation of the situation, including B's behaviour, A can rehearse her next move (stage 6) before deciding what to do and/or say. This then forms part of the unfolding scene to which B will have to respond, and so the process continues.

Many of the problems associated with interpreting behaviour are considered in Chapter 2 (on listening) and in the next section of this chapter, and therefore will not be discussed here, other than to note that people cannot attend to all that is happening in the interview and therefore attend selectively. A number of factors also determine how meaning is attributed to the selected information. For example, the McGill studies on decision-making in interviews (Webster 1964) found that, in selection interviews, the decision to accept or reject the candidate was made in under four minutes and that, for the rest of the interview, the interviewer sought confirmatory evidence, her decision predisposing her to perceive and accept information that was congruent and to neglect information that was incongruent with that decision.

An underlying theme of this section of the chapter is that the interview can be viewed as a social encounter. The nature of the encounter will influence how both the interviewer and respondent interpret what they hear. It will also influence the quantity and quality of the information that the respondent is prepared to offer.

BIAS IN INTERVIEWS

Interviews can be used to acquire information for a number of purposes: to determine whether things are going according to plan and, if not, why not; to ascertain people's attitudes and feelings regarding something or somebody; to predict future performance, as in the selection interview, etc. The extent to which the interview can be an effective instrument in helping to achieve such purposes will be determined, at least in part, by the accuracy of the information acquired.

Kahn and Cannell (1957) in their seminal book, *The Dynamics of Interviewing*, reviewed some of the early evidence that pointed to the prevalence of error and bias in the interview. They found:

1 *Persistent and important differences between interview data and data obtained from other sources.* For example, it was found, in one study, that one out of every nine families receiving city relief failed to report this when asked a specific question in the course of an interview. People might not have wanted to admit to the interviewer that they were receiving relief payments, because this was incongruent with the image they wished to project. We might have expected more accurate answers if the question had enquired about something less sensitive, such as the respondent's gender.

2 *Differences between two sets of interview data when respondents were re-interviewed.* Kinsey, in his study of sexual behaviour (Kinsey *et al.* 1948), re-interviewed 150 respondents and found that, although the answers to some questions showed close agreement, the answers to others evidenced considerable variability. Many factors could have accounted for these differences, including the possibility that the answers to some of the questions in the first interview were less accurate than others (maybe for the kind of reasons already discussed). Where answers in the first interview represented deliberate distortions of the truth the respondents might have experienced more difficulty recalling the answers they gave, whereas they may have experienced less difficulty recalling and repeating accurate (truthful) answers.

3 *Differences between the results obtained when two interviewers interviewed the same individuals.* Two selection interviewers questioned independently twenty-three job applicants regarding their work experience, family history and social and

personal characteristics. A comparison of the two sets of interviews showed a considerable lack of agreement, with an average reliability of 0.71 for all items. An explanation of this might be that the respondents were motivated to respond differently to the different interviewers; however, Kahn and Cannell (1957) also found research evidence to suggest that the source of this kind of inaccuracy was not always the respondent. In a study into the causes of destitution, it was noticed that the results reported by one interviewer were very similar for all his interviews, but were very different from the results obtained by another interviewer. The first cited alcohol abuse as the chief cause of destitution, whereas the other tended to emphasize social and industrial conditions. This suggests that the interviewer's own preconceptions might have influenced her interpretation of what respondents said.

Bias can arise for many reasons.

Background characteristics, such as the age, sex, race or status of both interviewer and respondent, might influence the quality of information exchanged in the interview. There is, for example, a wealth of evidence suggesting that respondents avoid telling interviewers things which they may find hurtful or things of which they might disapprove. Hyman *et al.* (1954) report that in a study in which negroes were interviewed by either whites or negroes, significantly more information on resentment over discrimination was given to the negro interviewers. Khan and Cannell (1957) also report a study by Robinson and Rohde (1946) in which three groups of interviewers questioned New Yorkers on their attitudes towards Jews. The first group of interviewers were people who were non-Semitic in appearance and name, the second group included people who were Semitic in appearance but non-Semitic in name and the third group comprised people who appeared to be Semitic both in appearance and name. It was found that the more likely the respondents were to identify the interviewers as Jewish, the less likely they were to make anti-Semitic statements.

In terms of the model outlined in Figure 4.2, no matter how hard the interviewer (A) tries to perform a role and project an image that will encourage the respondent (B) to provide full and frank answers, A's background characteristics might 'give off' signals to B that will have an important influence on the way he will behave in the interview. Similarly, A might find it equally difficult not to respond to the background characteristics of B.

Psychological factors, such as attitudes, motives and expectations, can also be important sources of bias. The motivation of the interviewer and respondent to engage in the interview might be different. For example, in an appraisal interview the interviewer might be motivated to help the appraisee develop and realize his full potential, and, therefore, might regard seeking accurate information about the appraisee's strengths and weaknesses as an important objective of the interview. The appraisee, on the other hand, might be motivated to obtain more pay or rapid promotion and, therefore, his objective might be to hide his weaknesses and emphasize his strengths so that he can convince the appraiser that he deserves such rewards. The appraisee will want to create a good impression and will be alert to cues that provide him with feedback on how he is regarded by the appraiser. If she appears to approve of certain of the attitudes he has expressed or activities he has engaged in, he is likely to be motivated to repeat or emphasize them. He is also likely to avoid expressing feelings or describing activities that are in conflict with those that seem to be approved of. If, on the other hand, the appraisee interprets the appraiser's behaviour as disapproving of an attitude or activity, he may attempt to avoid the risk of further disapproval by modifying his view and/or withholding certain kinds of information. Thus the appraisee's behaviour may frustrate the appraiser's objective of collecting accurate information about his strengths and weaknesses. If the appraiser is unaware of the appraisee's motives, she might accept the appraisee's answers at face value and not realize that he is trying to mislead her.

Even in interviews where the respondent attempts to give full and frank answers to the interviewer's questions, the interviewer's own attitudes, expectations and motives might influence the way she interprets what she hears. For example, a journalist who is a committed pacifist might find it hard not to let her own attitudes influence the way she interprets the answers she receives from the chief executive of a company that manufactures battle tanks. Similarly, a manager who believes that most workers have an inherent dislike for work, will avoid it if they can and must be coerced and closely controlled if they are to perform effectively, might find that these beliefs influence the way she interprets what she is told in an appraisal interview.

The interviewer's behaviour can also be an important source of bias. Kahn and Cannell (1957) illustrate this point well with a report of a study that showed that four interviewers obtained different responses to certain questions, and that these differences arose because of the different interviewing methods used rather than from the interviewer's own attitudes towards the topic covered by the questions. It was found that some interviewers were more likely to rely on the initial answers they received without any additional probing. It was also found that responses were recorded incompletely, and that some interviewers decided not to ask certain questions if the question appeared to have been answered partially in another context.

INTERVIEWER BEHAVIOUR

The effective interviewer has been described as somebody who is able to behave in ways that will eliminate or reduce as much as possible those forces that cause relevant information to be distorted or withheld in the interview. These behaviours will be discussed under eight headings.

1 Definition of purpose and preparation

Gratis (1988) argues that clarity of purpose aids preparation and the formulation and ordering of questions; it enables the interviewer to adopt a more flexible approach to managing problems without losing control of the interview; it facilitates a more effective evaluation of the interview once it has been completed.

If the purpose of a selection interview, for example, was defined as 'getting as much relevant information from the candidate as might be necessary to allow the interviewer to make an accurate assessment of his suitability for the job as defined by the job specification', this definition would alert the interviewer to the need to prepare for the interview by ensuring that she had (a) an appropriate and sufficiently detailed job specification,

(b) given some thought to the kind of information she would require about each candidate in order to be able to assess whether they would be capable of performing the job to the required specification, and (c) considered how she might go about obtaining the necessary information. It is not sufficient to simply have a vague notion about what you hope to achieve from the interview. The interviewer needs to be clear about purpose and clear about how she needs to behave in order to achieve that purpose.

When the conceptual model of the interview was introduced earlier in this chapter it was argued that early encounters will often be concerned largely with scene setting, with what Wicks (1984) describes as cognitive scene setting and what Hargie *et al.* (1981) refer to as set induction.

2 Set induction

The interviewer needs to communicate her purpose and establish terms of reference for the interview. This involves inducing a state of readiness appropriate to the task that will follow. If a manager calls one of her subordinates into her office he might be unsure why he has been summoned and will probably spend the first part of the 'interview' searching for clues that will indicate what his boss's purpose is. Could it be to enquire into why deliveries have been delayed, could it be to appraise his performance over the preceding twelve months, could it be to assess his suitability for promotion, or what? If the interviewee 'misreads' the situation he may respond inappropriately to the manager's questioning. For example, if her opening statement was 'has there been any improvement in deliveries?' the subordinate might not realize that she was enquiring about whether suppliers have made any more progress towards meeting their commitments under the new 'just in time' contractual arrangements. He may go on the defensive and prepare himself to justify why his department twice failed to get work out on time during the previous month.

Before embarking on the main business of the interview it is important to ensure that the interviewer's purpose is understood clearly by the respondent and that the interviewer is aware of the respondent's goals and how these might interfere with the achievement of her purpose. Usually the former is easier to accomplish than the latter, because the respondent, as in the appraisal example cited earlier, may deliberately conceal his own goals and may feel that his purpose would be best served by behaving as though he accepted the interviewer's goal. Nonetheless, even though it may be difficult, the interviewer should seek to ascertain the respondent's purpose and expectations and, where these are inconsistent with her own, take special care when interpreting what the respondent tells her.

Inducing an appropriate cognitive set involves preparing others for the main business or purpose of the interview. This can be achieved by providing briefing documents or prior instructions, as often happens before an appraisal interview when the appraisee may be asked to bring with him to the interview a list of his main objectives and to prepare his own assessment of the extent to which these have been achieved. It can also be achieved through the interviewer's opening remarks and by some of the non-verbal cues she gives off.

The environmental setting in which the interview takes place will also help to key the respondent into a particular frame of reference. He might respond differently to an interview on 'expense claims' depending on whether it were held in the local police station or the boss's office. A less dramatic example of how physical setting can induce cognitive set might be seating arrangements. If a manager who usually conducts interviews around a coffee table interviews one of her subordinates across her desk, this may signal that the subordinate is in trouble or that something serious is to be discussed.

The interviewer's opening behaviour is important, not only in terms of inducing an appropriate cognitive set, but also in terms of establishing rapport. Gratis (1988) points to the importance of 'meeting and greeting' and Hargie *et al.* (1981) emphasize the need for what is described as social set induction, a process that involves helping the respondent feel more at ease, establishing his confidence and trust in the interviewer and breaking the ice so that the interview can get off to a good start.

Rapport can be established in a number of ways. The interviewer might stand up to greet the interviewee, shake his hand, use his name and offer welcoming remarks in a tone of voice that puts him at ease. She might demonstrate that she is interested in the interviewee by exhibiting many of the attending behaviours discussed in Chapter 2 and she might break the ice by talking about non-task issues such as the weather or the journey. She might also start the interview by asking the kind of question that the respondent will find easy to answer and will not cause embarrassment or pose a threat of any kind. Empathic listening throughout the interview will also build rapport. Nadler (1977) reports that where more empathic approaches are adopted respondents seem more willing to open up and disclose sensitive information.

Rapport and motivation can be closely linked. What happens in the early stage of the interview can have important implications for the interviewee's motivation, which in turn will influence the quantity and quality of information that will be available to the interviewer. Where motivation is low, the respondent may disrupt the interview, may refuse to answer any questions or may give false answers deliberately, thus defeating the interviewer's purpose.

3 Content and coverage

With the purpose of the interview in mind, the interviewer needs to give some thought to the kind of information she requires. For example, a selection interviewer might use Rodger's seven point plan (Rodger 1952) to reduce the likelihood that she may overlook important information and to ensure that similar kinds of information are collected about all candidates. Rodger argues that four points need to be considered when deciding what categories of information to include in an interview plan. (1) They should be relevant to the purpose of the interview; for example, in the selection interview they should pinpoint influences connected commonly and demonstrably with success or failure to perform the job. (2) They should be independent; they should be separable from one another sufficiently to enable the interviewer to avoid making overlapping assessments that could be wasteful. (3) They should be assessable in the circumstances in which the assessment is to be made. (4) They should be few enough to keep the risk of hasty and superficial judgements to a minimum, but numerous enough to cover the ground adequately.

Rodger's seven point plan, which has been used extensively in selection and vocational guidance interviews, includes:

(a) *Physical characteristics.* Physical abilities of occupational importance, such as state of health, vision, hearing, speech, appearance, bearing.
(b) *Attainments, training and experience.* Educational background and attainment, training, work experience, personal achievements in other areas such as sports, music, etc.
(c) *General ability,* especially general intelligence and cognitive skills (words, numbers, relationships). These are best assessed by the use of psychometric tests, but the interviewer may be able to make estimates in these areas by seeking information that indicates what the respondent has managed to do, especially in those situations where he has been fully stretched.
(d) *Special aptitudes,* especially occupationally relevant talents, for example scientific, mechanical, mathematical, practical, literary, artistic, social skills.
(e) *Interests.* Type of interests (intellectual, practical, physical, social, artistic) and how they are pursued can be important, because they may indicate the directions in which the respondent's other attributes might best be employed.
(f) *Disposition/Personality.* Rodger argued against the use of abstract nouns such as sociability and leadership and favoured questions that fasten the interviewer's attention on facts. For example, how do other people take to him? Do they take notice of what he says or does? Is his behaviour fairly predictable? Does he work things out for himself?
(g) *Circumstances.* The context of the person's life in relation to how it affects his ability to perform the job to the required specification.

A plan of this kind does not represent an ordering of the questions to be asked in an interview. It provides a framework, a set of pigeonholes into which relevant information can be posted as and when it is obtained. It also provides a check list to ensure that all the necessary points have been covered before the end of the interview.

4 Organization of topics

When deciding the order in which topics are to be addressed in an interview, a useful guiding principle is to put yourself in the shoes of the respondent and select an ordering that is most likely to help him understand the questions and motivate him to respond.

A respondent might easily misunderstand complex or subtle questions if he has not been given cues that will key him into an appropriate frame of reference. Topics can be ordered in such a way that the respondent is encouraged to think about a range of issues before answering a question on a more complex topic. For example, before enquiring whether the company's security budget should be cut, the interviewer might first explore the respondent's views on a wide range of security related issues. These might include data protection, kidnap and hostage policy, whether innovations should be patented or kept secret, pilfering, use of company equipment for personal ends, etc. This approach ensures that the interviewee fully understands the nature of the question on the security budget. However, care must be exercised to ensure that the respondent is not conditioned or led to answer in a particular way by the ordering of topics. An extract from *Yes, Prime Minister* (Lynn and Jay 1986, p.106) offers a classic example. Humphrey Appleby shows Bernard, the PM's Principal Private Secretary, how the way that opinion pollsters organize the questions they ask can influence the response they receive. Sir Humphrey explains that when the Man in the Street is approached by an attractive female researcher he wants to create a good impression. Above all else, he does not want to make a fool of himself. Pollsters are aware of this and may decide to ask a *series* of questions designed to elicit *consistent* answers in order to produce a desired outcome.

Sir Humphrey proceeded to offer Bernard an example. He asked a series of questions that prompted Bernard to respond in favour of the re-introduction of National Service, and then asked another series of questions that persuaded him to oppose its re-introduction.

Q. Bernard, are you worried about the rise in crime among teenagers?'

A. Yes

Q. Do you think there is a lack of discipline and vigorous training in our Comprehensive Schools?

A. Yes
Q. Do you think young people would welcome some structure and leadership in their lives?
A. Yes
Q. Do they respond to a challenge?
A. Yes
Q. Might you be in favour of re-introducing National Service?
A. Yes

Bernard volunteered the information that he could hardly say anything but 'Yes' without looking inconsistent. Sir Humphrey's second series of questions were:

Q. Bernard, are you worried about the danger of war?
A. Yes
Q. Do you think there's a danger in giving young people guns and teaching them how to kill?
A. Yes
Q. Do you think it is wrong to force people to take up arms against their will?
A. Yes
Q. Would you oppose the re-introduction of National Service?
A. Yes

Thus, while on the one hand the organization of topics in an interview schedule can provide the respondent with a frame of reference that will help him to better understand a difficult or complex question, the organization of topics can also lead the respondent to answer in a particular way. This can be dangerous when the aim of the interviewer is to explore how the respondent really feels about an issue.

Other considerations might also influence the organization of topics. It might be that some questions that are seen to be very personal or threatening are best asked in the middle or towards the end of an interview, when maximum rapport and motivation have been established.

For all these reasons, questions that the interviewer may see as being closely related may best be asked at different points in the interview in order to increase the likelihood of the respondent providing full and accurate answers. This reinforces the importance for the interviewer of having some kind of framework or set of pigeonholes (such as the seven point plan) in which information can be stored and cross referenced as the interview progresses.

5 Formulation of questions

The way in which the interviewer formulates her questions can have an enormous impact on the quantity and quality of information the respondent will disclose. Three aspects of question formulation will be considered here: choice of words, the extent to which the question signals an expected or preferred response (leading questions), and the degree of freedom given to the respondent to answer (open versus closed questions).

Choice of words is important at one level because, if the interviewer uses a *vocabulary* that is unfamiliar to the respondent, he may not understand the question he is being asked, and in some circumstances may not be prepared to admit his ignorance for fear of losing face. At another level, questions might be phrased in such a way that they lack *precision*, causing different respondents to reply to what they perceived to be different questions. For example, if members of a church congregation were asked about their attitudes towards tithing and if one of the questions were 'Would you be prepared to give a tenth of your income to the church?', the word income might be interpreted differently by different people. By some it might be taken to mean gross earnings, by others as earnings after tax, and by yet others as disposable income after taxes, mortgage, housekeeping and school fees had been deducted.

Choice of words can also facilitate understanding by providing the respondent with a *frame of reference*, the importance of which has already been emphasized. Thus, there is a greater likelihood that a manager will understand his boss's question and provide relevant information if he is asked:

> 'How are things between you and the storeman since you insisted on better record keeping?'

than if he were simply asked:

> 'How are things?'

If the respondent were grieving the loss of his wife, this second question might be interpreted as an enquiry about how he was coping with his bereavement.

Kahn and Cannell (1957) suggest that if respondents are to be encouraged to answer freely and honestly questions should be worded in such a way that a wide range of responses is perceived to be acceptable. *Acceptability of a wide range of responses* can be achieved by incorporating a brief introductory statement into the question. For example, rather than asking a married coal miner:

> 'Do you ever do the washing and ironing at home?'

a more truthful answer might be elicited if the question were worded

> 'Recent research has shown that many men share household chores with their wives. Do you ever do the washing or ironing?'

Worded in this way the question informs the respondent that it is not unusual for men to do housework and indicates that the interviewer has no preconceived ideas about what kind of answer would be acceptable.

Leading questions When phrasing questions, great care needs to be taken to avoid signalling a preferred response. Where the expected or preferred answer is implied in the question, this is referred to as a leading question. There are several different kinds of leading question: for example, questions that anticipate the answer that the respondent would have given anyway, such as 'Isn't it a lovely day?' are called *conversational leads*. They are often used in the early stages of an interview to convey friendliness and interest and to encourage the respondent to participate.

Hargie *et al.* (1981) have identified three other kinds of leading question: simple leads, implication or complex leads, and subtle leads.

Simple leads are questions that are unambiguously intended to lead a respondent to a given answer. Whereas the conversational lead anticipates the answer the respondent would have given in any case, the simple lead anticipates the answer the interviewer expects, for example:

> 'You are not a member of the Union, are you?'

Many writers suggest that leading questions should aalways be avoided. Gratis (1988) states that the two objectives of questions are to obtain accurate information and to motivate the interviewee to respond freely, and a leading question negates both. There are, however, a number of circumstances where leading questions can contribute to the quantity and quality of information that will be given to the interviewer. It has already been argued that conversational leads can help build rapport, and Hargie *et al.* (1981) suggest that there is evidence that the use of simple leads that are obviously incorrect may induce the respondent to provide information in order to correct the apparent misconceptions inherent in the question. This point is illustrated by Beezer (1956), who conducted interviews with East German refugees. He found that by using simple leading questions that were obviously incorrect, such as:

> 'I understand you don't have to pay very much for food in the East Zone because it is rationed?'

the refugees gave very full replies in an attempt to correct the interviewer's impressions of life in East Germany.

Implication or complex leads exert much more pressure on the respondent to reply in a particular way. An example of such a question might be:

> 'At times like this it is important that we all pull together to maintain the stock market's confidence in the Company.

So don't you feel that all managers should hold on to their bonus shares even though the price is falling?'

The kind of introductory statement that prefaces this question, unlike those discussed above which are designed to signal that a wide range of responses is equally acceptable, clearly indicates that only one answer is acceptable to the interviewer. If the respondent offers the 'wrong' answer he has to accept that the interviewer may well label him as someone who is disloyal.

Prosecution lawyers are tempted to use leading questions because they can often persuade the accused to reveal more than he intended. Hargie *et al.* (1981) suggest that implication leads put the respondent under considerable pressure to justify his position. For example, if asked the question 'did you know that what you were doing was dishonest?' (Loftus 1982), the respondent must either accept the negative implication of dishonest or respond at length.

Subtle leads are questions that may not be immediately recognized as leading questions. Harris (1973) reports studies demonstrating that the way a question is worded can influence the response. For example, asking somebody how tall a basketball player was produced greater estimates than when respondents were asked how short the player was. The average guess of those who were asked 'how tall?' was 79 inches as opposed to 69 inches for those who were asked 'how small?'. Hargie *et al.* describe a study by Loftus (1975) which reported similar findings when 40 people were asked about headaches. Those who were asked 'Do you get headaches frequently and, if so, how often?' reported an average of 2.2 headaches per week, whereas those who were asked 'Do you get headaches occasionally and, if so, how often?' reported only 0.7 per week. Some interviewers may deliberately use subtle leads to obtain the answers they desire but often neither the interviewer or respondent are aware of the extent to which the wording of the question can influence the response.

Open and closed questions The degree of freedom given to a respondent to answer a question can have an important influence on the nature of the information available to the interviewer.

Closed questions are those which require the respondent to reply by selecting a response from a series of predetermined categories offered by the interviewer. There are three main types of closed question. The most common is where the respondent is offered the two categories Yes and No, for example:

> 'Are you over 21?'

There is usually a correct answer to this kind of question, and therefore it can be an effective way of obtaining specific information quickly. In an accident investigation the investigator might need to identify which of the people who were present actually saw the accident occur, and therefore ask the question:

> 'Did you see the collision?'

A similar kind of closed question, sometimes referred to as the identification question, requires the respondent to identify and offer a correct factual response, for example:

> 'How old are you?'

The third kind of closed question offers the respondent a range of alternative answers from which he is required to select the one that best approximates to his own opinion. This form of question is sometimes referred to as a forced choice question, for example:

> 'Which colour do you want your office painting, grey, red or blue?'

The respondent may not be keen on any of these colours and may prefer green, but faced with the choice of grey, red or blue may choose grey on the grounds that it is the least offensive.

Closed questions tend to be easier to answer than open questions and therefore can be useful ice breakers at the start of an interview:

> 'Can I take your coat?'

'Would you like some coffee?'

They also enable the interviewer to exercise control and focus the respondent's attention on relevant issues. A customs officer, for example, may not be interested in whether a returning holidaymaker has enjoyed his holiday or whether his flight was delayed. However, she may want to know whether he is aware of the duty free allowances, how many cigarettes or bottles of wine and spirit he has and whether he is importing goods over a specified value. A series of closed questions, for example:

> 'Are you aware of the duty free allowance?' (a yes–no question) 'How many cigarettes do you have?' (an identification question)

will enable her to elicit this information, and only this information.

Closed questions can also be employed usefully in those situations where it is necessary to collect and compare responses from a large number of respondents. For example, a market researcher might use closed questions when interviewing potential customers, because answers to closed questions tend to be brief and therefore easier to record. Also, since the range of possible responses to closed questions is likely to be more limited than the range of possible responses to open questions, it is often easier to anticipate, categorize and therefore analyse the responses obtained.

This said, closed questions also have a number of limitations. A question that offers the respondent the choice of answering only 'yes' or 'no' might deny the interviewer access to important information. For example, three managers who answered 'yes' to the question 'should the company introduce the appraisal scheme that was discussed at the last executive committee meeting?' might have replied in the affirmative for three very different reasons. The first manager might believe that the scheme could help improve productivity by identifying dead wood and making it easier to weed out and get rid of poor performers. The second might favour the scheme because she believes that it could encourage managers to manage their subordinates more effectively, especially those managers who fail to provide their subordinates with clear objectives and helpful feedback. In other words, she might see appraisal as the key to better staff development. The third manager might have supported the introduction of the scheme even though she is opposed to formal appraisal, because she feels that it is inevitable that some form of appraisal will be introduced sooner or later and that the scheme currently being considered by the executive committee has fewer disadvantages than most. Thus, the interviewer who receives the three positive answers might assume mistakenly that all three managers feel the same way about the scheme and may be unaware that they have very different views; that two are highly committed whereas the other is only lukewarm at best, and that of those who are committed their commitment is based on different and possibly conflicting assumptions and goals.

Open questions do not restrict the respondent to answering within a framework of a predetermined set of categories. Respondents are left free to reply in their own words and to answer the question in any way they like. Compare the closed question:

'Do you like your new job?'

with the open question:

'What do you think of your new job?'

The closed question can only elicit a yes–no reply, whereas the open question is likely to not only provide information about the respondent's affective response to his job, but also some explanation of why he feels the way he does.

Open questions that make use of Kipling's six honest serving men (who taught him all he knew – their names were What and Why and When and How and Where and Who) encourage the respondent to talk. 'Yes' would not be an adequate reply to the question 'what do you think of your new job?'

Open questions can also produce answers that the interviewer may never have expected and therefore provide access to information that would not have been revealed by the replies to a series of closed questions. For example, if a car owner were asked:

> 'Why did you buy a Vauxhall Cavalier?' she might reply 'Because the Vauxhall dealership is the nearest dealership to where I live',

a reply which indicates that the geographical location of dealerships is a key factor in influencing the decision on which make of car to buy. This fact might not have been revealed by a series of closed questions that focused on price or design, such as:

> 'Do you think the Vauxhall Cavalier is value for money compared with competing models such as the Ford Sierra or the Peugeot 405?'

It must be remembered, however, that the interviewer is not simply faced with the stark choice of using either open or closed questions. The degree of openness, and therefore the degree of control that can be exercised over the way the respondent will reply, can be varied by the interviewer. Compare:

> 'How are things?'
> 'How are things at work?'
> 'How are you getting on with your new assistant?'
> 'How are you managing your new assistant's negative attitude towards working for women?'

These are all open questions, but some are more focused than others and impose more restrictions on the way the respondent can answer.

6 Sequence of questions

The sequence of questions within a topic can take a number of forms. The *funnel* is a sequence that begins with a very open question and then continues with a gradual decreasing level of openness (see Figure 4.3). All the questions in the sequence can be open questions but, as in the 'how are things?' example above, each successive question might become more focused.

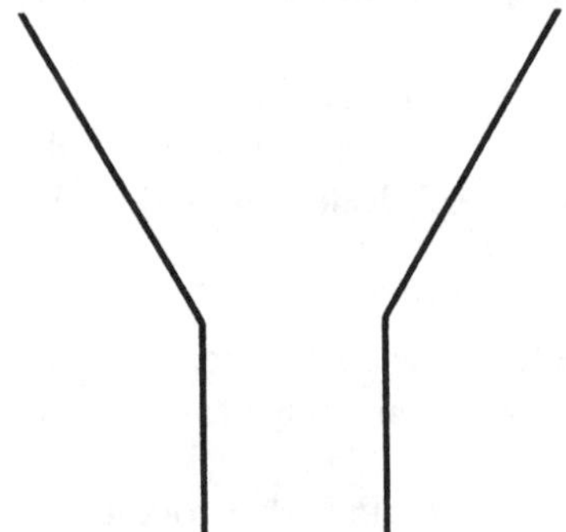

Figure 4.3 The funnel sequence

Alternatively, the sequence might progress from open to closed questions, for example:

Q. 'Why did you buy a Vauxhall Cavalier?' (open)
A. 'Because the Vauxhall dealership is the nearest dealership to where I live.'
Q. 'Why is the proximity of the dealership important?' (open)
A. 'With my last car I was always late for work when I had to take it in to be serviced. The problem was particularly difficult because there wasn't a convenient bus route between the service centre and my work-place.'
Q. 'How many times a year do you expect to have to use the service department?' (closed)

The funnel sequence can be useful in problem-solving interviews where the helper wants to find out whether there is a problem and, if so, what the respondent (colleague/subordinate/patient/customer, etc.) believes it to be. This might be achieved by opening the sequence with the question:

'How are things?' or 'What would you like to discuss?'

The funnel sequence can also help to motivate the respondent by providing him with the opportunity, at an early point in the discussion, to talk about those things that are important to him. Too many closed questions at the beginning of a sequence might force the respondent to suppress his own views and talk about issuees that seem unimportant or irrelevant.

Nonetheless, there are many occasions when it is useful to reverse the process and start with one or more closed questions. For example:

Q. 'Do you own your own car?' (closed)
A. 'Yes'
Q. 'What make and model of car do you own?' (closed)
A. 'Vauxhall Cavalier GL.'
Q. 'Why did you buy a Vauxhall Cavalier?' (open)

The inverted funnel (see Figure 4.4) can be used to help the interviewer gather relevant information: for example, about what happened or why the respondent behaved in a particular way, before seeking to explore the reasons why.

In some interviews, all the questions may exhibit the same degree of openness. For example, if a manager has to interview somebody to assess whether he qualifies for a particular benefit or discount, he may use a predetermined sequence of closed questions that are designed to elicit objective or factual responses as quickly as possible. This is known as the tunnel sequence of questions (see Figure 4.5).

Hargie *et al.* (1981) warn against the dangers of inconsistent or erratic sequences of questions and they point to

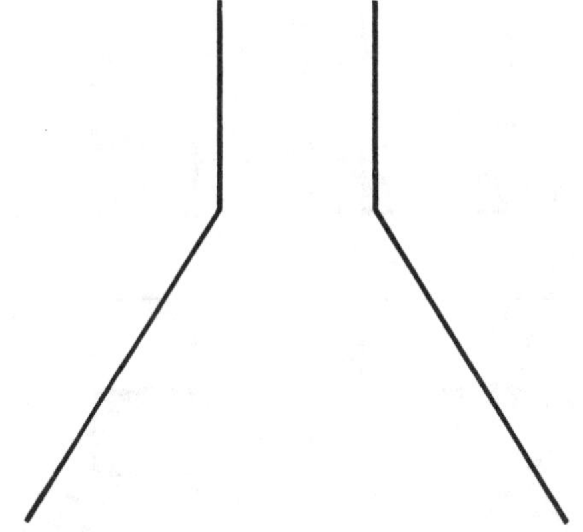

Figure 4.4 The inverted funnel sequence

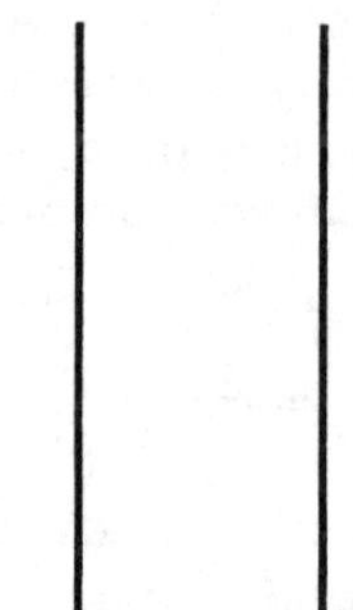

Figure 4.5 The tunnel sequence

research evidence suggesting that a consistent sequence (funnel, inverted funnel, tunnel, etc.) facilitates participation and understanding. However, erratic sequences can be useful in some circumstances. Erratic sequences characterize many of those fact-finding interviews that can be included under the broad heading of interrogation, where the objective is to obtain information that the respondent would prefer not to reveal. Not knowing what kind of question to expect next can confuse the respondent. Kestler (1982) suggests that erratic sequences can be effective in the courtroom because the quick change of focus can catch the witness off-balance, with thoughts out of context. The erratic sequence is illustrated diagramatically in Figure 4.6.

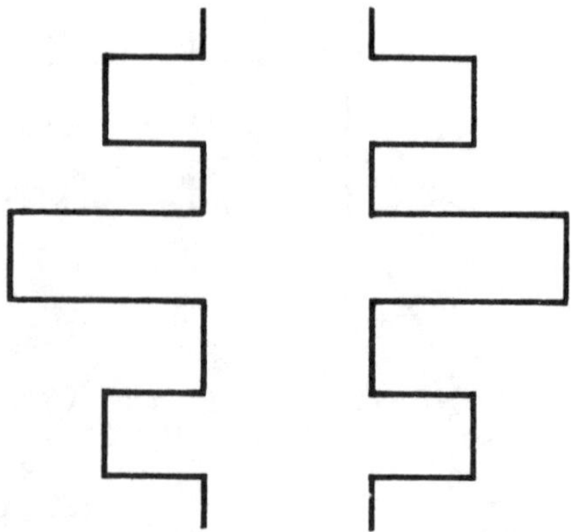

Figure 4.6 The erratic sequence

7 Probing and seeking clarification

No matter how much care the interviewer has exercised in wording and asking a question there will be many occasions when the initial response will be incomplete or inadequate in some way. Probing is the technique that can be employed to encourage the respondent to provide further information. Kahn and Cannell (1957) suggest three criteria for effective probes. They must enable the interviewer to motivate the respondent to engage in additional communication on the required topic. They must enhance, or at least maintain, the interpersonal relationship between the interviewer and respondent. And, most important, they must accomplish this purpose without introducing bias or modifying the meaning of the primary question.

Bias and the modification of meaning are aspects of probing that must be managed carefully. Simplifying, shortening or rewording questions can result in the intended meaning of the primary question being changed significantly. Bias can also be introduced if the interviewer fails to give the respondent sufficient time to answer the primary question before posing a supplementary question, or if the supplementary question suggests an expected or preferred response.

One of the easiest ways to press for further information in a way that avoids these problems is to use minimal prompts such as 'uh-huh', 'and...', 'tell me more'; attentive silences, which suggest to the respondent that the interviewer expects him to say more; or accents which offer a one-word or two-word restatement of what the respondent has just said. These techniques are discussed in Chapter 2 and are referred to by Turney *et al.* (1976) as non-verbal probes and echo probes.

Another type of non-directive probe is the paraphrase or summary (also discussed in Chapter 2), which indicates the extent of the interviewer's understanding and provides an opportunity for the respondent to clarify, restate or elaborate what he has said.

These non-directive techniques, although useful, might not provide sufficient focus, and the interviewer may wish to use a range of probes that enable her to manage, more precisely, the kind of information the respondent will feel encouraged to offer. Turney *et al.* identify seven of these more directive probes:

1 *Clarification probes*, which can be used to elicit a clear, more concisely worded, response:

'What exactly do you mean?'

Clarification probes can also be posed as closed questions:

'Are you saying that you were not responsible?'

2 *Justification probes*, which seek reasons for what the respondent has said:

'Why did you say that?'

3 *Relevance probes*, which require the respondent to explain the relationship between ideas, people, events, etc.:

'How does that relate to what you said earlier...?'

4 *Exemplification probes*, which seek concrete or specific instances of what has been said:

'Does an example spring to mind?'

5 *Extension probes*, which encourage the respondent to elaborate on his initial response:

'What happened next?'

6 *Accuracy probes*, which invite the respondent to reconsider an earlier response and emphasize the importance of accuracy:

'Are you sure it happened before six o'clock?'

7 *Consensus probes*, which enable the interviewer, in a group interview situation, to assess the extent to which a view is shared:

'Do you all agree with that?'

Sometimes, interviewers are tempted to ask supplementary questions following the primary question. The result is a *multiple question* which may leave the respondent confused and provide the interviewer with little useful information. For example:

'Why did you change jobs? Were you unhappy with what you had been doing or was it that the new job offered better pay?

And are you happy with the new job?'

Which question does he answer first. Indeed, can he remember all that he was asked? Maybe his response might be to concentrate on the last question and simply answer "yes".

Hargie *et al.* (1981) suggest that multiple questions may be useful when time is limited and it is important to get some answer from a respondent (for example, in a radio or TV interview), but the information obtained via multiple questions is likely to be inferior to that which might otherwise have been obtained.

8 Closure

When the interviewer is satisfied that the main purpose of the interview has been fulfilled she needs to check this out, ensure that she has understood fully what the respondent has said and signal to him her view that the interview is drawing to a close so that he can manage his own exit from the interaction. The absence of appropriate closure behaviour can leave the respondent unsure about whether he should wait patiently for another question, continue talking or get up and leave, and can waste the time of the interviewer because she fails to stop the respondent talking even though she feels that she has obtained all the relevant information that he can offer.

One of the most useful closure behaviours is the summary. It helps the interviewer check that she has remembered and recorded the main points discussed. It reassures the respondent that the interviewer has listened attentively and provides him with the opportunity to clarify or elaborate. It also provides the respondent with the opportunity to offer new information on additional issues that he feels the interviewer needs to be aware of.

The interviewer might have used summaries at several points during the interview to check understanding, draw points together and identify themes, and provoke the respondent into offering more information. By prefacing the terminal summary with a remark such as:

'*Before we finish* let me review . . .'

the interviewer provides a clear signal that the interview is nearing its end.

Other kinds of closure markers can be used to reward the respondent for participating in the interview:

'That's been very useful and has helped me see things from your perspective.'
'Thanks for your time'.

Such remarks help to persuade the respondent that his participation in the interview has been worth while and can be especially important when the interviewer wants to engage the respondent in a follow-up interview. Closure markers can be non-verbal as well as verbal. The interviewer can gather her papers together, look at the clock, stand up and offer a hand-shake, while thanking the respondent for his time and saying goodbye.

Ideally, the information-getting interview will end when the interviewer is satisfied that she has elicited sufficient information; however, sometimes time runs out and the interview has to be drawn to a close prematurely. This can happen in the best managed interviews, possibly because it is only towards the end of the available time that the respondent gives an unanticipated response to an open-ended question (suggesting a new line of enquiry), or develops sufficient confidence in the interviewer to reveal important information. However, the effective interviewer can normally ensure that it is not a frequent occurrence through careful time management.

Time management is an important interview skill. The interviewer must keep in mind a broad plan of the issues that need to be explored (again emphasizing the usefulness of a framework such as the seven point plan) and a discreet eye on the clock in order to pace the interview appropriately.

Occasionally, it will be possible to extend the interview and time will not be an important constraint, but often other commitments, on the part of both interviewer and respondent, will render this impossible. In such circumstances the interviewer may feel that a follow-up interview would be useful and, therefore, will attempt to draw the first interview to a close in a way that will encourage the respondent to participate in a further encounter. This end might be achieved by:

(1) Leaving the respondent with the feeling that the interview was worth while, that his contribution was useful and that something has been achieved as a result of the interaction:

> 'Thank you that has been very helpful.'

(2) Seeding the idea that a further meeting might be necessary by referring to the purpose of the interview and indicating that more information will be required:

> 'I'd like to check out whether these problems persist by talking to you again once the new system has been operational for at least a week'.

(3) Suggesting a time when the follow-up interview might occur.

> 'Can we meet again at the end of the month?'

DEVELOPING INFORMATION-GETTING SKILLS

The first step in developing information-getting skills is to assess how effective you are at getting information. Probably the best way to test this is to evaluate the outcome of an interview and determine whether you were successful in obtaining the quantity and quality of information necessary to achieve your objective. This may not always be as easy as it might appear. In the selection interview, for example, your objective might be to get as much relevant information as necessary in order to make an accurate assessment of the candidates' suitability for the job. This information will then be used (by you and/or by others) to decide which candidate to appoint. If, later, the appointee proves to be a disappointment, it may be difficult to determine whether this was the result of the quantity and quality of information you obtained during the interview or a result of the way the information was used in the decision-making process.

Nonetheless, even though an accurate attribution of cause and effect may be difficult, this kind of ongoing personal appraisal can be an effective way of monitoring ones own performance.

Another way of assessing information-getting skills is to compare the information you obtain from a respondent with that obtained by somebody else. It is not unusual for a job applicant to be interviewed by more than one person, either in the context of a panel interview or a series of separate interviews. This latter arrangement offers the best opportunity to compare your information-getting skills with others, because each interviewer is responsible for the overall management of his or her own interview. You might ask yourself whether others found out things you missed, whether they obtained a better understanding of issues and whether they interpreted what was said in the same way as you.

Sometimes, but unfortunately not often enough, it is possible to compare the information you have collected with some more objective record of the facts. For example, a community physiotherapist may be given an urgent referral and may have to interview a patient at home before his medical records are available, or after a bank raid a security officer may have to interview counter staff before the tape from a video camera is available. Information obtained in this way can be compared with the medical records or the evidence on the tape later.

Where the results of these kinds of assessment suggest room for improvement you need to determine more precisely which skills require development. One way you can do this is to compare your information-getting behaviour with some standard of good practice. This way forward requires that you have some notion of what comprises good practice and also that you have a method of obtaining feedback on your own behaviour, so that deviations from good practice can be identified.

Definitions of good practice might vary, depending on the purpose of the interview. In an interrogation, for example, erratic interviewing sequences might be more effective than more consistent sequences such as the tunnel. In a screening interview, on the other hand, tunnel sequences that comprise a series of closed questions might be much more effective than a mixture of open and closed questions presented within a funnel or inverted funnel sequence. The content of this chapter provides the interviewer with a basis for determining which behaviours will be most appropriate for different purposes.

On training courses, other people can observe and record how the interviewer interacts with the respondent and can offer the trainee feedback on her performance. In the real world, this opportunity for third-party feedback will rarely be available and, even in the training context, the use of audio or video recorders can improve the quality of feedback by providing a more accurate and objective record of the trainee's behaviour. Back at work it may also be possible to record, with the respondent's permission, real interviews as they occur. The tapes can then be analysed for evidence of the kinds of behaviour that help or hinder the getting of information. Some of the behaviours that might be the focus of this analysis are presented in Appendix 4.1 (see pp. 95–6). For some purposes, it might be sufficient to use a framework similar to that presented in Appendix 4.1 to code behaviours as they occur. The resulting frequency count could show, for example, what kinds of question the interviewer makes most use of, whether she uses summaries, silences, etc.

A more elaborate analysis might involve making a transcript of everything the interviewer says and then categorizing each unit of behaviour (question, statement, silence, nod, etc.) in terms of its function. This approach not only provides a frequency count of the kinds of behaviours used, but also furnishes sufficient information for typical questioning sequences to be identified (tunnel, funnel, etc.) as well as showing, for example, the pattern of probing behaviours employed and other structural aspects of the interviewer's behaviour.

Neither of the above ways of recording interviewer behaviour make it easy to assess how appropriate a particular piece or pattern of behaviour was in terms of accomplishing the interviewer's objective. By making a full transcript of what the interviewer said and the respondent's reply, it becomes possible to determine more effectively the consequences of specific interviewer behaviours.

It may be necessary to analyse more than one interview in order to construct a representative profile of your behaviour. However, once you are confident that you have sufficient information about your interviewing style, you can compare it with what you feel is the ideal profile suggested by all the available evidence of good practice. Deviations from this ideal will pinpoint possible areas for improvement and facilitate the formulation of testable hypotheses about how a change in your behaviour will improve the quantity and quality of information obtained. For example, you might decide that you, typically, allow the respondent too much freedom to determine the content of the interview and, therefore, hypothesize that your coverage of relevant issues would be improved if, before the interview, you were to devise a framework or checklist to guide your questioning and to organize and record the information received.

Summary

This chapter has presented the interview as a social encounter, and has argued that the nature of this encounter will influence both the way in which the interviewer and respondent interpret the behaviour of the other and the quantity and quality of the information they will exchange.

The effective interviewer has been described as a person who behaves in ways that eliminate or reduce to a minimum those forces that cause relevant information to be distorted or withheld. Critical interviewer behaviours have been discussed under eight headings: definition of purpose and preparation, set induction, content and coverage, organization of topics, formulation of questions, sequencing of questions, probing, and closure. The final section of the chapter has discussed ways in which the interviewer can modify her behaviour to improve her effectiveness.

Appendix 4.1

INTERVIEWER BEHAVIOURS

COMMUNICATION OF PURPOSE — overall assessment: Adequate … Inadequate

- pre-interview *(briefing document, memo etc.)*
- start of interview *(opening remarks)*

BUILDING RAPPORT

- welcoming remarks
- early questions *(easy, non-threatening)*
- showing respect/concern for respondent

WORDING OF QUESTIONS

- vocabulary
- clarity of questions
- introductory statements which signal acceptability of wide range of answers — No. of times used

TYPES OF QUESTION

- Conversational leads *(which anticipate answers respondent would give anyway: 'Isn't it a nice day?')*
- Simple and complex leads *(which lead respondent to an expected or preferred answer)*
  Closed questions: Yes-No
  identification
  forced choice
- Open questions
- Multiple questions
- Non-directive probes: minimal prompts
  summaries
- Directive probes which seek:
  clarification *('what do you mean by that?')*
  justification *('why do you say that?')*
  relevance *('how does that relate to x?')*
  exemplification *('give me an example')*
  accuracy *('are you sure it was only six?')*

SEQUENCE OF QUESTIONS	No. of times used
• funnel	☐
• inverted funnel	☐
• tunnel	☐
• erratic	☐
ORGANISATION OF TOPICS	overall assessment yes no
• facilitated understanding of meaning and relevance of questions	○○○○
• avoided conditioning respondent to answer in a particular way	○○○○
• maximized respondent's motivation to answer	○○○○
COVERAGE OF QUESTIONS	
• questions obtained all relevant information	○○○○
CLOSURE	good poor
• concluding summary	○○○○
• closure markers *(verbal and non-verbal)*	○○○○
• time management	○○○○

References: Chapter 4

Beezer, R. H. 1956. Research on methods of interviewing foreign informants, George Washington University, HUM RRO, Technical Reports No. 30.

Bingham, N., Moore, J. and Bruce, V. 1941. *How to Interview*, 3rd edn. New York: Harper & Row.

Farr, R. 1984. Interviewing: the social psychology of the interview. In Cary L. Cooper and Peter Makin (eds), *Psychology for Managers*. London: British Psychological Society.

Goffman, E. 1959. *The Presentation of Self in Everyday Life*. New York: Doubleday.

Gratis, J. 1988. *Successful Interviewing*. Harmondsworth: Penguin.

Hargie, O., Saunders, S. and Dickson, D. 1981. *Social Skills in Interpersonal Communication*. London: Croom Helm.

Harris, J. R. 1973. Answering questions containing marked and unmarked adjectives and adverbs, *Journal of Experimental Psychology* 97: 399–401.

Hyman, H. H. *et al.* 1954. *Interviewing for Social Research*. Chicago: University of Chicago Press.

Kahn, R. L. and Cannell, C.F. 1957. *The Dynamics of Interviewing*. New York: Wiley.

Kestler, J. 1982. *Questioning Techniques and Tactics*. Colorado Springs, Col.: McGraw-Hill.

Kinsey, A. C., Pomercy, W. B. and Martin, C. E. 1948. *Sexual Behaviour in the Human Male*. Philadelphia: W. B. Saunders.

Loftus, E. F. 1979. *Eyewitness Testimony*. Cambridge, Mass.: Harvard Universtiy Press.

Loftus, E. F. 1979. Interrogating eyewitnesses – good questions and bad, in R. M. Hogarth (ed.), *Question Framing and Response Consistency*. San Fransico: Jossey Bass.

Lynn, J. and Jay, A. 1986. *Yes, Prime Minister, Vol. 1*. London: BBC Publications.

Mangham, I. L. 1978. *Interactions and Interventions in Organizations*. Chichester: Wiley.

Nadler, D. A. 1977. *Feedback and Organization Development: Using Data Based Methods*. London: Addison-Wesley.

Robinson, D. and Rohde, S. 1946. Two experiments with an anti-Semitism poll. *Journal of Abnormal and Social Psychology* 41: 136–144.

Rodger, A. 1952. *The Seven Point Plan*. London: National Institute of Industrial Psychology.

Turney, C., Owens, L., Hatton, N., Williams, G. and Cairns, L. 1976. *Sydney Micro Skills: Series 2 Handbook*. Sydney: Sydney University Press.

Webster, E. C. 1964. *Decision Making in the Employment Interview*. Montreal: Industrial Relations Centre, McGill University.

Wicks, R. P. 1984. Interviewing: practical aspects. In Cary L. Cooper and Peter Makin (eds), *Psychology for Managers*. London: British Psychological Society.

CHAPTER FIVE
Explaining and presenting

Almost everybody who is employed in a managerial or professional role has to present information or offer explanations to others. From time to time the presentation will be before a large audience, in a formal setting. More frequently it will be to a small, sometimes informal, group of colleagues, subordinates, customers or senior managers.

The presentation often represents an important opportunity for the presenter. A customer might invite a supplier to come and talk to some of his colleagues about the advantages of a new product. If the manager from the supplying company makes a poor presentation the result could be a considerable loss of business. A personnel manager might be invited to address a managers' meeting about the introduction of a new appraisal scheme. If he fails to convince them that the scheme is a good one he might loose the chance of winning their support, and his job of introducing the scheme could be made much more difficult. A project leader might be required to report on progress to a project review committee. If her presentation is disorganized and she fails to provide the committee with the information they require, she might create the impression that the situation is worse than it really is. If, on the other hand, the presentations are successful, the customer may place a new order, the managers may be enthusiastic about the introduction of the new appraisal scheme and the project leader might create the impression that she is very competent and could possibly manage a bigger project next time around.

A presentation is an occasion when, either literally or metaphorically, the spotlight is on the individual. The presenter is very exposed and her performance can leave a lasting impression.

What would you think of somebody who made a presentation that was difficult to hear and even more difficult to understand, if the arguments lacked structure, if you were denied important information while being overwhelmed by irrelevant detail, and if the session overran its allotted time, making you late for a subsequent meeting? The answer, almost certainly, is that you would not be impressed. The danger is that members of the audience might not only acquire a poor impression of the presenter's presentation skills, they might also assume that she lacks other work-related skills as well. In other words, because making presentations is a very public activity, it is an aspect of an individual's performance which can have a very important influence on what other people think about him or her. There are, therefore, many good reasons why you should consider ways in which you can improve your presentation skills.

At an early point in a good presentation the presenter tells the audience what to expect: he alerts them to the main issues that will be covered. This chapter will consider the ingredients of a good presentation and what the presenter needs to do to ensure that the presentation is successful. Attention will be focused on preparation, what the presenter needs to do beforehand; getting and keeping interest: that is, what the presenter needs to do to involve the audience from the start and to keep them involved until the end; getting the message across, those explaining and presenting skills that enhance clarity of expression and ease the burden of listening; aids to understanding, such as the use of examples, visual displays and demonstrations; and closure, the best way to end the presentation.

PREPARATION

The importance of preparation cannot be overemphasized. Pemberton (1982) quotes the old saying that to fail to prepare is to prepare to fail. A sentiment echoed by Jay (1972), who argues that there is a general law applicable to any project: that the earlier a mistake is made the more profoundly it will affect the whole project and the harder it will be to recover from. Presentations are no exception. Thorough preparation is the basis of success. The presenter needs to define the objective of the presentation, research the audience, identify what information needs to be presented, plan how the presentation is to be structured and finally review the environmental arrangements.

Clarifying the objective The objective of the presentation might be to describe or report what did or will happen. For example, a manager might want to brief his team on company results or present a departmental plan for the next operating period. It may also involve more than a descriptive report. It may include an explanation, an account of why something has occurred. When an explanation is offered the presenter's objective is to help the audience understand a cause-and-effect relationship. For example, a marketing manager might want to explain why profits were affected by fluctuation in exchange rates, or an operations manager might want to explain why an increase in her budget would result in cost savings over the longer term. Often explanations are offered in order to persuade or to sell. In such circumstances it may not be sufficient to ensure that the message is understood. The presenter will need to convince members of the audience that the course of action being advocated is one they should support.

It is a useful discipline to reflect on the purpose of the presentation, to write it down and to refer to it from time to time. If a manager is planning a presentation on the new bonus scheme, she might ask herself whether her objective is to inform a group of salespeople that a new scheme is to be introduced from the first of next month and explain to them how the new scheme will work, or to persuade them to accept the new scheme in preference to existing arrangements. If the objective is to persuade them to accept the new scheme, her presentation is likely to be very different from one merely intended to inform them about its introduction.

Researching the audience Presentations need to be planned with a specific audience in mind. Of critical importance is their status, background and experience. The background and experience of the audience will influence how much they already know about a subject, their level of understanding of technical vocabulary and the extent to which they will be willing to listen to the presentation with an open mind. Past experience of the presenter could also affect the way they interpret what they hear.

In some situations the status of the audience might be important because certain information is restricted. Consequently, a presentation that was originally prepared for the board may need to be modified before it can be given to a group of middle managers or customers.

The size of the audience is also important. How many will be listening: 5, 50 or 500? With large audiences, opportunities for dialogue may be limited and for much of the time the presenter will have to do all the talking, will have to tell the audience what she wants them to hear. With an audience of two or three, the presentation might take the form of a structured discussion rather than a formal speech. Audience size will also have implications for the size of the hall and the kind of visual display that will be appropriate. In a large hall, visual material might have to be projected onto a large screen rather than displayed on a small flip chart.

Defining the content Before preparing the script for a presentation, an essential first step is to decide what information the listener will need if the objective of the presentation is to be achieved. This involves identifying the main factors or categories of information and how they relate. For example, if the objective is to persuade a sales team that a new bonus scheme will be to their advantage, it might be decided that the presentation should include information that will facilitate a comparative review of how the existing and proposed schemes operate.

Discussions with colleagues, brainstorming ideas onto a sheet of paper, and consulting reports might suggest a series of headings such as the target of the scheme (individual or group), the aspects of performance that will be measured (total value of sales, number of new customers), the methods used to calculate the bonus, etc. Not all of the headings generated will be of equal importance and under each heading there might be several ideas and sub-headings that similarly differ in terms of the contribution they can make to achieving the objective of the presentation. Identifying what information is vital, what is important and what is only desirable can ease the task of pruning and editing material, so that, if cuts have to be made, the presentation will still cover all the vital elements. Failure to prioritize material might result in vital material either being omitted or skimmed over quickly, while less important or even irrelevant information (which might be of interest to the presenter) is given too much emphasis.

Structuring the presentation Many factors contribute to a successful presentation. Gage *et al.* (1968), commenting on the differential proficiency of teachers, draw attention to many of the issues identified above and observe that some presenters always get to the heart of the matter with just the right terminology, examples and organization of ideas. Others, however:

> get us and themselves all mixed up, use terms beyond our level of comprehension, draw inept analogies, and employ concepts and principles that cannot be understood without an understanding of the very thing being explained.

Getting us and themselves mixed up reflects a lack of attention to structure. The logical organization of information aids understanding. Most research in this area has been undertaken by educationists. Miltz (1972) found that teachers who were rated as good explainers made presentations that were structured clearly and logically. They itemized elements of the presentation and verbalized the precise nature of the link between the elements. Hargie *et al.* (1981) report that there is a wealth of research into teaching which suggests that the teacher's ability to prepare, structure, organize and sequence facts and ideas with the maximum of logical coherence is related positively to pupil achievement.

Pemberton (1982) suggests that, where the purpose of the presentation is to persuade people to your view, an effective overall structure is to:

1 State the proposition.
2 Anticipate objections and concede possible flaws in the argument. (Even if the presenter decides not to disclose such flaws it is useful to have identified what they might be.)
3 Prove the case. Do this by focusing on the strongest arguments. She argues that quality is better than quantity and cautions against overloading the presentation with too many arguments.

4 Provide practical evidence.
5 End by repeating the proposition.

In abbreviated form this structure involves cueing the audience about what to expect: that is, telling them what you are going to tell them, then telling them, and ending by telling them what you have told them.

Reviewing arrangements On many occasions the presenter will have little choice about venue and the arrangement of seating and other environmental factors. Even so, it can be worth the effort to review the arrangements, test the equipment and note the best place to stand so that the audience has a clear view of blackboards, flip-charts and screens. Where the presenter is in control of the setting, she might consider arranging the seating to minimize distractions. If the audience is able to look out of a large window at an interesting scene, the presenter might find it difficult to compete for their attention. Similarly, if the only entrance to the hall is by the speaker's table, every latecomer will disrupt the presentation. Sometimes it can be fairly easy to change the end of room where the speaker's table is to be located. Seating arrangements can also be manipulated to either encourage or discourage discussion. Seating people in rows makes it more difficult for the audience to assess each others reaction or to interact between themselves, whereas curved rows or horseshoe arrangements makes this easier (see Figure 5.1).

The horseshoe, and to a lesser extent a curved rows arrangement, also encourages interaction between presenter and audience. This is because there are fewer barriers (people) between each member of the audience and the presenter, eye contact between them is easier and individual members of the audience feel less isolated, they are able to assess whether others might

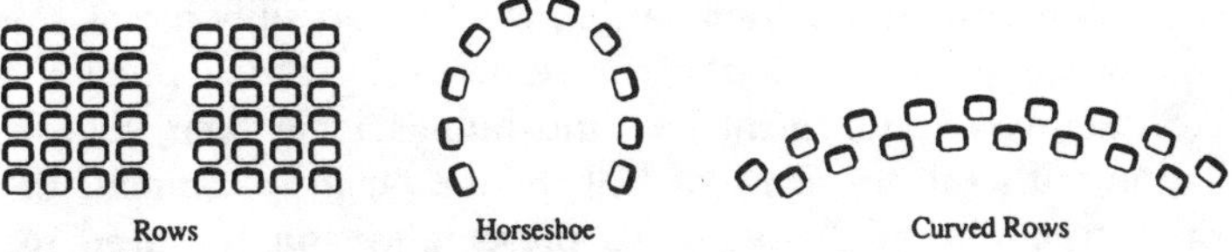

Figure 5.1 Seating arrangements

have the same reaction to what has been said, and therefore they have more confidence to interact with the speaker.

KEEPING THE AUDIENCE'S ATTENTION

The lecturer who is teaching a recreational class at night school is reasonably safe in assuming that the members of her 'audience' are there because they want to be there and because they want to hear what she has to say. This may not be the case for the manager who is making a presentation on the company's new appraisal scheme. The audience may be enthusiastic, neutral or even hostile to the idea of appraisal. Even those members of the audience who are known to be enthusiastic may be preoccupied and not in the ideal frame of mind to listen.

Motivating the audience to listen The presenter has to gain the audience's attention. She has to motivate each person to listen. It is difficult to motivate others to listen if they do not understand what you are talking about. Jay (1972) points to the need for the presenter to 'connect up with the audience.' He uses the analogy of a horse and wagon and suggests that the speaker has to harness the horse of her argument to the wagon of the audience's interest and understanding. If the presenter gallops straight off she may hurtle along splendidly without realizing that the wagon has been left behind. It is important that the presenter starts with material and ideas that members of the audience know and understand before taking them off into unknown territory.

Even if members of the audience understand what is being said, they may not see any good reasons why they should pay attention. What is in it for them? If they are to be persuaded to attend they must be helped to anticipate that the presentation will be useful, interesting or entertaining. It has been suggested that people will not be interested in salvation until they have experienced the fear of damnation, which is possibly the reason why some preachers start their sermons by proclaiming the inevitability of judgement day and familiarizing their congregation with the torments of hell. In the business context, the chief executive might begin his presentation on the need for greater effort by forecasting the possibility of cutbacks and redundancies. Fortunately, inducing a state of fear or unrest is not the only way of capturing attention. The rhetorical question can be used to intrigue or interest the audience. For example:

> What do you think is the major reason why people buy our product?. . . This afternoon I want to share with you the results of our latest market survey and recommend how they should influence our marketing strategy for next year.

Introductions that use rhetorical questions, pose intriguing problems, include controversial statements or simply offer a concise statement of the purpose of the problem in terms that will appeal to the audience, increase the likelihood that the audience will be motivated to attend to the presenter's message.

Keeping their interest Even if the presenter is successful in gaining the audience's attention at the beginning of the presentation, there is no guarantee that people will continue to attend. The shorter the presentation the more likely they are to attend throughout. Ley (1983) reports several studies that suggest that both attending and recall are related to the length of the presentation. It was found, for example, that the more information presented the more patients experienced difficulty in understanding and recalling the instructions given to them by doctors.

Verner and Dickinson (1967) found that learning began to diminish seriously after about fifteen minutes. Various writers suggest that after as little as ten minutes (and in some circumstances this may be an optimistic estimate) attention begins to wane, but as the audience begins to sense that the presentation is reaching a conclusion, attention begins to rise again (Figure 5.2). This has important implications for the presenter. If she structures her message in such a way that key points are presented in the middle, when attention is likely to be at its lowest, the presentation may not have its desired effect. Key points need to be presented when attention is at its highest. This means in the first ten minutes or so, or at the end; or in between, but only when the presenter behaves in a way that will increase the audience's attention.

Attention can be heightened if the presenter breaks up the body of the presentation into logical elements and, as has already

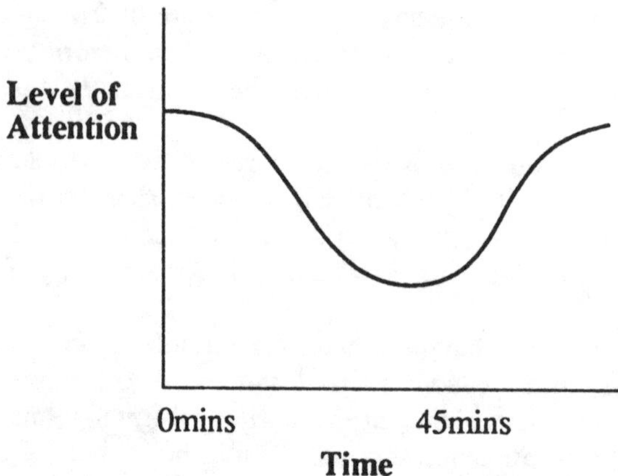

Figure 5.2 The attention curve

been mentioned (see Miltz 1972), signals the end of one element and the start of another:

> 'The third point I want to discuss is . . .'

The effectiveness of this procedure can be increased by offering the audience a framework or structure for the presentation, which they can refer to and use to organize and understand the relevance of the information they receive. The outline of the presentation might be displayed on a flip-chart or a handout so that the 'third point' that is being discussed can be related to the first and second.

Another way of keeping the audience's interest is to anticipate the questions that members might have in their mind at various points in the presentation:

> 'You might be wondering where this is leading. Well . . .'
> 'You could be asking yourself whether the market survey was worth the effort . . .'

Questions can also be useful if you suspect that the audience is losing interest. General questions asked to nobody in particular might fail to evoke a response, whereas targeted questions that offer members of the audience an opportunity to contribute can encourage involvement:

'Mr. Smith. You have been involved in similar projects in the past. Do you think I have missed any major points in my assessment of how the market is likely to react?'
'Mr. Brown. You are the person in the room with the most practical experience. Will the proposal work?'

However, when targeting questions, care must be taken not to embarrass those whose attention may have drifted so much that they could fail to recognize the point of the question if asked and, therefore, could find themselves unable to offer a sensible answer.

Visual aids and demonstrations, which are most frequently used to facilitate understanding, can also be used for impact, that is, to gain the audience's attention. The presenter can anticipate those points where attention is likely to flag and can introduce a chart, slide or practical demonstration to maintain attention. Examples or an amusing story that illustrates a point can also help to maintain interest, as long as the audience can relate to them. Visual aids, demonstrations and stories that are perceived as irrelevant can distract the audience, as can certain gestures and body movements. The speaker who jingles coins in a pocket can be very annoying and the actions of the unconscious nose-picker can either disgust the audience or divert their attention away from the presentation to a consideration of what she might do next.

Not all movements and gestures are distracting. Chapter 3, on listening to non-verbal messages, cites research evidence suggesting that some gestures can improve understanding by, for example, helping to depict spatial relationships, providing emphasis and communicating enthusiasm.

Delivery and the use of words is also important. When most people read a script their voice lacks variety in terms of volume, pitch, timbre, rate, rhythm and inflection. They come across as dull and uninteresting. It is often noticeable that when a presentation is followed by a question and answer session, the presenter's voice changes. It becomes more alive. Two factors account for this. The answers are fresh and unscripted and the presenter uses spoken not written English.

It can be dangerous to attempt a completely unscripted presentation, because the speaker may be tempted to give insufficient attention to the selection and organization of content, might confuse herself as well as the audience and might get lost and 'dry up' part way through. Some kind of script can be very useful, but too detailed a scripting of the presentation can be dangerous. If the presenter writes down everything she wants to say she may write a paper fit for publication rather than a script that is to be spoken. Spoken English is very different from written English. There is also the danger that the speaker might lose her place and miss a section or have to pause while she locates the next sentence. Another problem is that, if the presenter reads a script, she is likely to keep her head down and to have no or little eye contact with the audience.

The important points to remember are that the presenter who drones on in a voice which lacks any variety, who evidences little movement, who avoids eye contact, who provides the audience with few signposts regarding the structure of her message and who introduces no variety into her delivery through visual aids is unlikely to keep the audience involved.

GETTING THE MESSAGE ACROSS

The previous sections of this chapter addressed the presenter's need to prepare and the methods she can use to attract and maintain the audience's attention. This section considers those presentation skills that help to get the message across. Five main categories of presentation skill will be considered. Turney *et al.* (1975) grouped presentation skills under four headings: clarity, examples, emphasis and feedback. A fifth is the presenter's ability to answer questions.

Clarity

As we might expect, there is a wealth of research evidence which demonstrates that clarity is associated with understanding and recall. For example, Soloman *et al.* (1964a, 1964b) found significant correlations between a global factor 'overall clarity of presentation' and performance on a test of factual material. However, for the purposes of training and the development of presentation skills, it is necessary to identify concrete instances of behaviour that make a contribution to greater clarity. Research results point to the importance of four types of behaviour.

1 *Defining technical terms and jargon* This has been shown to be correlated with pupil achievement, which is a good indication that the appropriate use of language can contribute both to understanding and recall.

2 *Explicitness* Reducing the implicit and increasing the explicit information content of a presentation contributes to clarity. An example of implicitness is where the presenter's sentence structure requires the listener to infer complete structures. The greater the use of implicit content, the greater the demand on the listener to fill the blanks. For some audiences there will be little need to 'spell things out', but this will not always be the case. It is all too easy for the presenter to assume an unrealistically high level of knowledge and experience and, therefore, to 'leave blanks' that at least some members of the audience will find it difficult to fill. This point re-emphasizes the need for thorough audience research.

3 *Verbal-fluency* is another important skill contributing to clarity. Hiller *et al.* (1969) reported that verbal-fluency (which they measured in terms of sentence length, number of subordinate clauses and hesitations such as 'uh', 'um', etc.) was significantly different between those who offered effective and ineffective presentations. Hargie *et al.* (1981) suggest that speakers often punctuate what they have to say with sounds such as 'eh' or 'mm' when they are trying to put too many ideas or facts across in one sentence. Short crisp sentences are advocated, with pauses in between them, rather than long rambling sentences full of subordinate clauses.

4 *Avoiding vague expressions* There will be occasions where it is impossible to avoid the use of a vague term. The speaker might not be able to recall a precise term and may have to substitute a less precise one instead, or may not have concrete and specific data to hand. Problems arise, however, when the use of vague expressions becomes habitual. Turney (1972), drawing upon the work of Gage *et al.* (1968) and Miltz (1972), has categorized a sample of vague expressions:

(a) *ambiguous designation* – 'type of thing', 'all of this', 'stuff'.
(b) *negative intensifiers* – 'was not too', 'was not hardly', 'was not quite', 'not infrequently'.
(c) *approximation* – 'about as much', 'almost every', 'kind of', 'nearly'.
(d) *'bluffing' and recovery* – 'they say that', 'and so on', 'to make a long story short', 'somehow',
(e) *indeterminate number* – 'a couple of', 'a bunch', 'some'.
(f) *groups of items* – 'kinds', 'aspects', 'factors', 'things'.
(g) *possibility and probability* – 'are not necessarily', 'sometimes', 'often', 'it could be that', 'probably'.

An audience will rate a presentation high on clarity when the speaker uses appropriate language and defines new terms, when she is explicit, fluent and when vague expressions are avoided.

Examples
There is evidence which suggests that the amount of 'concreteness' in an explanation is related to understanding. One way of avoiding excessive abstraction is to use examples. Examples can offer evidence in support of a statement, and can be used to relate new and unfamiliar concepts to a situation that the audience has already experienced. The selection of examples is important. They need to be ones that the audience can relate to and can use in the way the presenter intended. The use of in-group examples that are not fully explained, for example:

> 'You will remember what happened last year when we tried to persuade Bill to change his mind'

can leave some members of the audience totally confused.

How the examples are used is also important. Turney *et al.* (1975) report that one pattern that has been recommended strongly by some researchers is the *statement – example – statement* rule. An alternative, referred to as the inductive pattern, is for the presenter to offer a series of examples and build from these to a statement or generalization. A marketing manager might try to persuade his executive committee that it would be inappropriate to use price-competition as a way of increasing profits, by offering them a series of examples about what has happened in the past, concluding with the statement that:

> '. . . these examples demonstrate that if we cut prices our competitors will do the same.'

The deductive pattern represents a different approach. It begins with a statement or generalization and is then followed by a series of examples that confirm and add detail to the original statement.

The research evidence about which of these three rules is most effective is inconclusive, but there is little doubt that the audience benefits from discovering self-evident links between statements and examples and, therefore, that the use of examples facilitates understanding.

Emphasis

Some presenters confuse their audiences because they fail to differentiate the wood from the trees. At certain points in a presentation, it may be necessary to call attention to important information while keeping in the background less essential information. If this less essential information is allowed to intrude, the listeners may fail to appreciate the significance of an important point or issue. During the course of a presentation a number of different points might need to become the focus of attention. Therefore, as the presentation progresses the point of emphasis will change. To be effective, the presenter needs to be able to manage the successive emphasis of crucial points. Turney *et al.* (1975) group the sub-skills of emphasis into two categories.

1 *Purposeful variations in aspects of personal behaviour* Reference has already been made to how the presenter can vary behaviour in order to maintain the attention of the audience. Varying behaviour can also focus the audience's attention on specific aspects of the presentation. Examples of how behaviour can be varied to achieve this end include the following:

Verbal markers that highlight main stages in the presentation. They can be used to draw attention to key points so that, in the listener's mind these points stand out, ensuring that the 'figure and the ground', to use a Gestalt analogy, do not merge into one. Similarly, phrases such as 'the important point to remember' may serve to draw attention to certain aspects of the presentation.

Mnemonics can also provide a structure for a sub-part of the presentation and an *aide-mémoire* that will assist with recall. For example, a manager talking to his subordinates about setting objectives might use a mnemonic modelled on the name of the runner Steve Cram to emphasize the essential ingredient of a good objective:

C Challenging
R Realistic
A Achievable
M Measurable

Non-verbal markers, such as pausing, pointing or changing one's voice can also be effective.

2 *Providing information that indicates a basic direction or purpose* This involves structuring the presentation so as to emphasize certain aspects of the message. The presenter can use carefully selected repetition at various points in the presentation. This repetition can take a number of forms. Few people will not have heard Martin Luther King's famous speech in which he kept repeating the phrase 'I've had a dream' to emphasize his main theme. This technique can leave the audience with a 100 per cent recall of the core message and is a form of emphasis that is often used by politicians when they are trying to influence large audiences to remember and accept a core message.

Summaries are another form of repetition. Introductory summaries can be used to alert the audience to important points and the main thrust of the presentation and terminal summaries can be used to re-emphasize selected parts of the presentation.

Feedback
The effective presenter is alert to feedback. The non-verbal behaviour of members of the audience can signal whether they

are interested and involved, and whether they have understood or been convinced by what they have heard. Useful signs of interest are eye contact, facial expression and posture (are they 'on the edge of their seats' or slumped in a corner and nearly asleep?). Statements, questions and requests for clarification from the audience can also be a useful source of feedback on whether the presentation is being understood and perceived as relevant. The presenter might initiate the questioning to obtain feedback. This often happens naturally at the end of the presentation but may also be helpful during the presentation, especially if the presenter suspects that all may not be well.

Answering questions

There will be occasions when the presenter will want to encourage questions in order to vary the pattern of the presentation, maintain attention, promote a feeling of involvement and prevent the audience from feeling steam-rollered. Questions also provide feedback on how the presentation is being received and facilitate clarification and improved understanding.

One way of introducing variety into the presentation is to encourage questions before the end, possibly after each main point has been presented. A danger with this approach is that the presenter may spend too much time answering questions and, as a consequence, may have to severely edit or completely miss out important parts of the message. The audience may also confuse the presenter by asking questions about points that will be covered later in the presentation. Responding to all questions as and when they are asked can destroy a carefully thought-out structure and undermine the clarity of the presentation.

The presenter can discourage the asking of mid-point questions by signalling, during the introduction, that questions would be preferred at the end. If, on the other hand, the presenter had decided to encourage questions before the end she could, in the event of too many questions, move the presentation on by reminding the audience of the time and offering to continue the discussion later:

> 'We only have 20 minutes left. If we could move on after this question I will come back to this point, if we need to, at the end.'

If members of the audience ask questions out of sequence and threaten to undermine the structure of the presentation, they might be persuaded to wait for their answer by being told:

> 'If you bear with me I think you will find that your question will have been answered fully before I finish'

or, more simply:

> 'I will be coming to that later.'

Where questions are reserved until the end there is no guarantee that someone will be ready with a question as soon as the presenter stops talking. It may take a little time for members of the audience to adjust to the possibility of asking a question, and it may also take a little time for them to reflect on what they have heard and to formulate a question they want to ask. There is, however, always the possibility that nobody will be comfortable asking the first question and an embarrassing silence may ensue. One way of avoiding this is to have a chairperson or a friendly plant in the audience who is prepared to ask the first question just to get the 'ball rolling'. Another technique is to propose that the audience divide into small groups to discuss the presentation and identify points that deserve to be challenged, or require clarification or elaboration.

A further problem associated with the question and answer session is the over-eager person who tries to monopolize the presenter's attention. Other members of the audience may become frustrated if their questions remain unanswered. By taking questions in turn and only allowing one question (and possibly one point of clarification) from each questioner, a chairperson can help ensure that the presenter does not ignore parts of the audience. Where there is no chairperson, the presenter might be able to disengage from the persistent questioner by noting:

> 'There seems to be a number of other people with questions. Let me deal with them and, if there's time, we can come back to this.'

People at the back of a large audience may not hear questions asked by those who are sitting near to the front. This problem can be eliminated if the presenter repeats the question so that everybody can relate to the answer.

Sometimes, members of the audience may ask questions in an attempt to destroy the presenter's case or make her look foolish or incompetent. If a presenter suspects that she may be confronted by a hostile questioner, she may deliberately limit the time available for questions by making the presentation longer than scheduled and then offering to deal with questions privately or over coffee.

If she decides, or is faced with no alternative other than to take the questions, every effort must be made to limit damage and to search out opportunities to gain advantage. One way of limiting damage is to be aware of traps that the questioner might try to set. The presenter might ask herself 'why is he asking this question?' A hostile questioner may ask questions that he knows the presenter will find difficult to answer and then try to destroy her case by demonstrating how inadequate the answer was. This kind of trap can be avoided by not attempting to provide an answer. The safest response, if the presenter does not know the answer, is to say so. The rest of the audience might appreciate her honesty. It might also be possible to move the attention away from the hostile questioner by asking the rest of the audience if anybody else can provide an answer (without re-engaging the questioner in eye contact) and then seeking a 'next question' from somebody else.

Sometimes a member of the audience may attempt to put an alternative case or to demonstrate his own competence by making lengthy statements rather than asking questions. Acknowledging the statement and then seeking a question from somebody else can be an effective way of moving the session on:

> 'Yes, I think we need to bear some of these points in mind. May we have the next question please?'

It may not be easy to gain an advantage in the face of a hostile intervention from the audience, but sometimes an opportunity does present itself. Politicians who can make the audience laugh in response to a heckler's interruption often gain such an advantage. Probably the most famous case involved

Harold Macmillan at the UN in New York. Krushchev interrupted his speech by shouting and banging his shoe on the table and Macmillan made Krushchev look very foolish by pausing and then asking the interpreter for a translation. It is not unusual for the hostile questioner to ask questions in order to find fault with the presenter's case without having any credible alternative to offer. If the presenter believes this to be so, she might gain an advantage by turning the question around and asking the questioner for his alternative proposal.

VISUAL AIDS AND DEMONSTRATIONS

Visual aids serve three main purposes. They introduce variety and capture people's attention and interest. They can also aid understanding and assist with recall.

It has often been said that a simple picture can be worth a thousand words. A photograph of people dying on the streets of a third world city can illustrate in seconds a point that might otherwise take minutes to describe. A series of slides showing how an internal combustion engine works can similarly ease the task of explaining and can help the audience remember key points. However, visual aids do have a number of disadvantages. They cost money and they can take a lot of time to prepare, they can divert attention from the main thrust of the presentation, if used inappropriately, and they can go wrong. The bulb may fail in the projector, the plug may fuse, the film may tear or a slide may be lost or projected upside down or at the wrong time. To get the best out of visual aids the presenter needs to plan their use and to have a contingency plan in mind if things do go wrong.

Visual aids can be grouped into a number of broad categories. The first is boards and charts. Flip-charts have the advantage that sheets can be torn off and displayed around the room, whereas the white (or black) board has to be cleared when full. Flip-charts can also be prepared in advance and main points or diagrams can be lightly pencilled in so that they can be quickly reproduced 'live' during the session. The main disadvantage with flip-charts is size. In a large hall it may be difficult to see what is on the chart.

Slides, either overhead projector or conventional 35mm slides, can be projected onto a screen of appropriate size. The main disadvantage with the overhead projector, which the presenter operates herself, is that sometimes people misplace slides or display them the wrong way round or upside down. Frequent pauses while the presenter searches for a lost slide can be very damaging to concentration. Another problem is when the presenter fails to check lines of sight and stands in a position that obscures the view of at least some members of the audience. Similar problems can be associated with conventional 35mm slides. The cassette may be dropped just before the start of the presentation and it may be impossible to re-load the slides in time. Even where there has not been this kind of immediate disaster, some slides may have been loaded upside down and prove difficult to re-load without disrupting the session. If the projector is controlled by a projectionist at the back of the room, there is also the added complication of synchronizing the slides with the script.

Films and videos can be very effective provided they are not over-used and they are not allowed to run for too long. If it is planned to use more than one film or video sequence within the same session, video might offer an advantage over film because it can be much easier to change video cassettes (pre-wound to a required point) than to load and wind on a film.

Demonstrations (for example, using people to show how heavy weights should be lifted or a wind tunnel to illustrate how modifications to the design of a vehicle can affect drag) can be a very effective way of getting a message across, provided that the demonstration works and can be seen by everybody in the audience.

Some general principles associated with the use of visual aids and demonstrations are concerned with the degree of congruence between the spoken and visual message, visibility, complexity and variety.

Congruence with spoken message Visual aids can be used as a substitute for words or to complement what the presenter has said. It can be difficult for the audience to concentrate on what the speaker is saying if this does not fit with the message provided by the visual aid or demonstration. When using slides that contain words, the presenter may need to pause so that the audience has time to read what is on the screen. If the presenter continues to speak, the words used should be the same as those that are on the slide. Additional words can be used if they provide an elaboration or are examples which illustrate the point that is being presented, and if the audience is able to relate the additional words to the message that is on the screen. It can be very distracting for the audience if the presenter uses different words. Do they attend to what is being said or do they read the slide? Similar distractions may arise if a slide or flip-chart is left on display too long. The presenter may have moved on to a new point while the old display in still visible. If the display is an interesting diagram or photographs the audience may be tempted to continue attending to that rather than listening to the next point.

Visibility Care needs to be taken with sight lines. Nobody's view should be obscured. Models and displays should also be large enough to be seen by everybody. This point is closely linked to the next point, complexity.

Complexity Slides and charts need to be kept simple. Graphs, pie charts and bar charts can be a much more effective way of getting the message across than columns of figures, which people may find difficult to read and assimilate. Where slides or flip-charts contain lettering, the impact can be improved by using as few words as possible. Jay (1972) goes so far as to argue that words are not visuals and should be avoided wherever possible.

> If I could engrave a simple sentence on every presenter's heart, it would be this: WORDS ARE NOT VISUALS. How many times have we sat at presentations and seen slide after slide portraying nothing except abstract nouns: OBJECTIVES, OPERATIONS, PREPARATION, PLANNING, PRODUCTIVITY, PROGRESS, RECONNAISSANCE, RECOGNITION, REPORTING, and so on in an endless and utterly unmemorable series.

Jay possibly adopts a rather extreme position. While too many words can undermine the impact of a slide, in some circumstances the presenter may find it helpful to include a series of headings, particularly in those circumstances where he wants to avoid the use of a script but still feels the need for an outline structure to remind him of the main points.

Variety Visual aids and demonstrations can introduce variety, but too much variety can disrupt the smooth flow of the presentation. It can become too bumpy and jumpy, with the presenter switching from blackboard, to slide projector, to flip-chart, to video, to overhead projector. The presenter is more likely to forget which aid comes next and to get things in the wrong order if he is continually switching around rather than steadily working through one pile of overhead projector slides, which he uses at appropriate points in an orderly sequence. Too much variety might result in the presenter not taking sufficient care over sight-lines and talking to the white board or flip-chart rather than to the audience. Thus, although variety has some advantages, it can also lead to problems if it is overdone.

CLOSURE

Presentations have a beginning, a middle and an end. Closure is the management of the end of the presentation. It involves indicating to the audience that the presenter has covered all the material she feels is appropriate. This can be achieved through the use of verbal markers such as:

> 'My final point is . . .'

and by non-verbal markers such as collecting papers together and switching off the overhead projector.

It also involves focusing the audience's attention on the essential features of the material covered and encouraging members to relate this material to the purpose of the presentation, be it to better understand how something works, appreciate why a target was not achieved or be convinced of the advantages associated with a particular course of action. This can be done by offering a selective summary of the main points. After starting the presentation by telling the audience what they were to be told, then telling them, the presenter concludes by telling them what they have been told.

This process can help motivate the audience to future action. For example, a general manager, after summarizing the difficult circumstances facing the company during the next twelve months, might conclude by telling his management team:

> 'We know the problems, we know what needs to be done. Now it is up to you.'

When the speaker has successfully concluded what he or she has to say the transition from the formal presentation to the question and answer session is likely to take place without any uncomfortable silences and without people wondering what will happen next. But it is important to remember that the presentation involves more than a formal speech. It may be just as important for the presenter to pay as much attention to concluding the question and answer session as concluding his own speech. Keep the purpose of the presentation in mind. If it is to persuade a group to adopt a particular course of action it might be better to end with questions from people who are committed rather from those who appear to be hostile to the proposal.

DEVELOPING PRESENTATION SKILLS

One of the most effective ways of developing presentation skills is to make a well prepared presentation to a friendly audience of people who are prepared to offer constructive feedback to the presenter. Appendix 5.1 (p. 122) at the end of this chapter is a rating sheet, which observers can use to structure their observations. Inexperienced raters may find it difficult to attend to all the presenter behaviours covered by the rating sheet. Consequently, the quality of feedback might be improved if the audience were divided into three groups and if the first were asked to concentrate most of their attention on boxes 1–3, the second on box 4 and the third on boxes 5–7. Everybody could also be invited to rate any other aspect of presenter behaviour they have observed. By adopting this procedure the presenter is more likely to receive comprehensive feedback on a wider range of behaviours.

If it is possible to make a video (or even audio) recording of the presentation, the presenter can then rate his or her own behaviour and identify areas for improvement. For the reasons mentioned above, it may be more effective if the presenter observes the recording more than once so that different aspects of his or her behaviour can be attended to selectively on each viewing.

Summary

Most people are required to make presentations or to offer explanations to others. People with poor presentation skills can create a bad impression, can miss opportunities and can foster misunderstandings. This chapter has examined ways in which the presenter can develop more effective presentation skills. Preparation was identified as the essential first step. It was argued that the presenter needed to clarify her objectives, research the audience thoroughly, define and structure the content of the presentation carefully and review the venue and other environmental factors.

Consideration was given to the ways in which the presenter can attract and maintain the audience's attention. A variety of techniques for capturing people's attention were considered, including creating a sense of uncertainty in the mind of the listener (thus motivating her to listen in order to allay her anxiety), the use of rhetorical questions, the posing of intriguing problems, and the use of controversial statements. It was noted that attention often begins to flag in the middle of a presentation and, therefore, the presenter needs to behave in ways that will maintain audience interest. The use of interesting examples, visual aids and demonstrations were a few of the techniques considered.

Five presentation skills that help to get the message across were identified. These were clarity of expression, the use of examples, emphasis, sensitivity to feedback and the ability to answer questions effectively. Attention was focused on specific modifiable behaviours associated with each of these broad skill categories.

It was noted that visual aids and demonstrations can be used to introduce variety and interest into the presentation, to facilitate explanation and promote a better understanding and to provide an *aide mémoire*. The advantages and disadvantages of some of the most commonly used visual aids were considered and several principles associated with their use were discussed.

The importance of drawing the presentation to an appropriate conclusion was also considered. It was suggested that the conclusion should review the key points of the presentation in a way that contributes to the achievement of the purpose of the presentation, be it to inform, explain or persuade.

The final part of the chapter considered ways in which the presenter might develop more effective presentation skills, and a rating sheet was introduced, which identified a number of important presenter behaviours.

Appendix 5.1

ASSESSMENT OF PRESENTATION

Speaker's name ____________________

1. INTRODUCTION	**YES**			**NO**
• **Was a brief, clear introduction provided?**	☐	☐	☐	☐
• **Were the aims defined clearly?**	☐	☐	☐	☐
• **Did the introduction persuade the audience to listen?**	☐	☐	☐	☐

2. CONTENT AND STRUCTURE	**YES**			**NO**
• **Was all the relevant information provided?**	☐	☐	☐	☐
• **Was unnecessary detail avoided?**	☐	☐	☐	☐
• **Was the structure of the presentation clear and logical?**	☐	☐	☐	☐
• **Was the body of the presentation broken down into appropriate elements?**	☐	☐	☐	☐
• **Was the relationship between the elements adequately explained?**	☐	☐	☐	☐
• **Was the presentation easy to follow?**	☐	☐	☐	☐

3. CLOSURE	**YES**			**NO**
• **Was there a concluding summary?**	☐	☐	☐	☐
• **Was it related to the purpose of the presentation?**	☐	☐	☐	☐
• **Did the concluding comments contribute to the achievement of the purpose of the presentation?**	☐	☐	☐	☐

Note
Answer each question by placing a tick (✓) in the appropriate box on the four point scale. The points on the scale are Yes, Largely, Hardly, No.

4. PRESENTATION SKILLS

		YES			NO
a. Clarity of expression					
• Was vocabulary appropriate, were technical terms defined?		▢	▢	▢	▢
• Were explanations explicit/concrete rather than implicit/ abstract?		▢	▢	▢	▢
• Did presenter avoid vague expressions/imprecise terms?		▢	▢	▢	▢
b. Use of examples					
• Were sufficient examples used to illustrate points?		▢	▢	▢	▢
• Were examples relevant to purpose of presentation?		▢	▢	▢	▢
c. Emphasis					
• Did presenter draw attention to key points?		▢	▢	▢	▢
• If so, how?					
i	enumeration (the second point is ...)	▢			
ii	other verbal markers (an important point is ...)	▢			
iii	repetition	▢			
iv	summaries	▢			
v	mnemonics	▢			
vi	visual aids/demonstrations	▢			
vii	non-verbal cues: expressions, gestures, etc.	▢			
d. Sensitivity to feedback		YES			NO
• Did presenter pay attention to non-verbal cues from audience?		▢	▢	▢	▢
• Did presenter ask questions to check understanding, relevance to audience needs, etc?		▢	▢	▢	▢
e. Answering questions					
• Did presenter encourage audience to ask questions?		▢	▢	▢	▢
• Was sufficient time devoted to answering questions?		▢	▢	▢	▢
• Did presenter maintain control during question and answer sessions?		▢	▢	▢	▢
• Were answers related to questions?		▢	▢	▢	▢
• Were answers clear and straightforward?		▢	▢	▢	▢

5. GETTING AND MAINTAINING ATTENTION

- What methods were used to motivate the audience to listen at the start of the presentation?

  i rhetorical questions ☐
  ii the posing of an intriguing problem ☐
  iii controversial statements ☐
  iv concise statements of purpose in terms which appealed to audience ☐
  v other (specify) ____________________

- What methods were used to maintain interest:

  i visual aids used to capture attention ☐
  ii interesting examples and analogies ☐
  iii rhetorical questions ☐
  iv variety in delivery (voice, gestures, pace, etc.) ☐
  v other (specify) ____________________

- At what point(s) in the presentation (if any) did attention appear to flag? ____________________

6. USE OF VISUAL AIDS

YES NO

- Were they well prepared (legible,etc.)? ☐☐☐☐
- Was level of complexity/detail appropriate? ☐☐☐☐
- Could they been seen by everybody? ☐☐☐☐
- Was audience given sufficient opportunity to view/read them? ☐☐☐☐
- Were they effective in:

  . introducing variety and maintaining interest? ☐☐☐☐
  . promoting better understanding? ☐☐☐☐
  . providing an aide mémoire? ☐☐☐☐

7. MANNER OF DELIVERY AND MANAGEMENT OF SESSION

	YES			NO
• Was presenter sure of facts and confident in presenting them?	☐	☐	☐	☐
• Was s/he enthusiastic and committed to message?	☐	☐	☐	☐
• Did s/he speak clearly?	☐	☐	☐	☐
• Was the volume about right?	☐	☐	☐	☐
• Was there sufficient eye contact?	☐	☐	☐	☐
• Was the session well paced?	☐	☐	☐	☐
• Did presenter keep to time?	☐	☐	☐	☐
• Was presenter fully in control throughout?	☐	☐	☐	☐

8. OVERALL ASSESSMENT OF PRESENTATION:Scale 1 - 10 (10 = excellent) ☐

9. COMMENTS

References: Chapter 5

Gage, N. L., Belgard, M., Dell, D., Hiller, J. E., Rosenshine, B. and Unruh, W. H. 1968. *Explorations of the Teacher's Effectiveness in Explaining*, Technical Report No. 4. Stanford, Calif.: Stanford University Centre for Research and Development in Teaching.

Hargie, O., Saunders, C. and Dickson, D. 1981. *Social Skills in Interpersonal Communication*. London: Croom Helm.

Hiller, J., Fisher, G. and Kaess, W. 1969. A computer investigation of verbal characteristics of effective classroom lecturing. *American Educational Research Journal*, 6: 661-75.

Jay, A. 1972. *Effective Presentation*. London: British Institute of Management.

Ley, P. 1983. Patient's understanding and recall in clinical communication failure. In D. Pendleton and J. Hasler (eds), *Doctor–Patient Communication*. London: Academic Press.

Miltz, R. J. 1972. *Development and Evaluatioon of a Manual for Improving Teachers' Explanations*, Technical Report No. 26. Stanford, Standard University Centre for Research and Development in Teaching.

Pemberton, M. 1982. *A Guide to Effective Speaking*. London: The Industrial Society.

Soloman, D., Rosenberg, L. and Bezdek, W. 1964a. Teacher behaviour and student learning. *Journal of Educational Psychology* 55: 23–30.

Soloman, D., Rosenberg, L. and Bezdek, W. 1964b. Dimensions of teacher behaviour. *Journal of Experimental Education* 33: 23–40.

Turney, C., Owens, L. C., Hatton, N., Williams, G. and Cairns, L. G. 1975. *Sydney Micro Skills, Series 2 handbook*. Sydney: Sydney University Press.

Verner, C. and Dickinson, G. 1967. The lecture, an analysis and review of research. *Adult Education* 17: 85–100.

CHAPTER SIX

Helping

To a greater or lesser extent we are all helpers. Some of us work in roles that are concerned almost exclusively with helping others: for example, consultants, social workers and AIDS counsellors. Others, such as personnel managers, systems analysts, priests and undertakers, are engaged in roles that, while not exclusively concerned with helping, involve helping as a major part of the job. However, almost everyone spends some of their time at work (and elsewhere) helping others. This might involve a colleague who requires help to improve her relationship with a major customer, a subordinate who is experiencing difficulties coping with the pressure of work, or a friend who has recently been bereaved.

Sometimes people think of helping as something that is concerned exclusively with assisting others to manage their problems more effectively. However, helping is not only concerned with problems, but also with opportunities. Sometimes, people require help to identify and take advantage of opportunities offered by changed circumstances or potential career moves, or to recognize their own strengths and to exploit them to the full.

Help might be offered informally as part of the normal day-to-day interactions we have with others. A manager might counsel a colleague who is having a difficult time with a new boss, or talk through with somebody how they will cope with working nights when their wife is admitted to hospital, leaving an infirm parent at home. Informal help might also take the form of mentoring. Experienced workers might help their less experienced colleagues to work out the best way of managing unfamiliar assignments. Sometimes, however, help is offered as part of a more formal interaction. In the appraisal interview, appraisers might counsel appraisees about what they could do to improve their performance, or might help them to clarify career goals and identify training needs and development opportunities.

Often the person in need of help (the client) will seek out somebody else to talk to, but self-referral is not the only start point for a helping relationship. A manager might request or even require that one of her subordinates seeks help from a member of the personnel department, the company's medical officer or even an external consultant, depending on the nature of the problem. There may also be occasions when the manager is both the source of referral and the source of help. She might have observed that a subordinate is experiencing difficulties that are threatening the success of an important project but, rather than transferring him to another job or taking control and telling him what to do, she might attempt to help the subordinate to understand the problem and work out for himself what needs to be done to manage it more effectively.

Unfortunately, although lots of people spend a great deal of time trying to help others, those others often find that what they are offered provides little help. In other words, all help is not necessarily 'helpful'. This chapter examines different approaches to helping, identifies key helping skills and outlines the main stages of one approach to helping that has been found to be effective in a wide range of different circumstances.

DIFFERENT APPROACHES TO HELPING

There are many forms of helping relationship. Blake and Mouton (1983) describe the essence of helping as cycle-breaking endeavour. They argue that behaviour tends to be cyclical in character. That is, sequences of behaviour are repeated within specific time periods or within particular contexts or settings. Some of these patterns of behaviour are advantageous to the client or client group, but some do little to promote their interests and may even be harmful. They go on to argue that individuals, groups or larger client systems such as entire organizations may engage in behaviour cycles without explicit awareness or by force of habit, and may not be conscious of the possibility of harmful or self-defeating consequences. They may be aware that things are not going well, but they may not understand why or what they could do to improve matters. Blake and Mouton define the consultant's or helper's function as helping the client to identify and break out of these damaging kinds of cycle.

This cycle-breaking endeavour can take many forms. A doctor might provide a patient with a simplified theory, which explains why people slip their discs, in order to help the patient adopt a safer approach to lifting. A parent may shout at a child, or may even inflict some form of corporal punishment, in order to stop the child running across the road without looking, and a manager may confront a colleague with the consequences of his behaviour in an attempt to help him see how his behaviour upsets others and to identify ways of building more effective relationships.

Blake and Mouton (1983) identify five different kinds of helper intervention:

Prescriptive interventions. These involve the helper in telling the client what to do to rectify a given situation. The helper diagnoses the problem for the client and prescribes the solution.

Confrontational interventions involve the helper in challenging the foundations of the client's thinking, in an attempt to identify assumptions and values that may be distorting the way situations are viewed. For example, the helper might call attention to contradictions in action or attitude, or challenge precedents or practices that seem inappropriate. The objective is to identify alternative values and assumptions that might lead to the development of effective solutions to problems.

Theories and principles interventions involve the helper in identifying theories and principles that are pertinent to the client's problem situation, presenting these to the client and helping the client to learn to use them in developing a better understanding of the situation in an analytical, cause-and-effect fashion. This understanding is then used as a basis for helping the client to identify ways in which systematic change can be secured.

Catalytic interventions involve the helper in assisting the client to collect data that can be used to evaluate and re-interpret the problem situation. It is assumed that deficiencies of information are an important cause of malfunctioning and the objective of catalytic interventions is to help the client arrive at a better awareness of the underlying causes of a problem and to help the client identify what action is required to resolve it.

Acceptant interventions involve the helper in working with the client to help him express those feelings and emotions that impede clear and objective thinking about a problem. The helper listens empathically, withholding judgement, and helps the client to develop for himself a more objective view of the situation. It is assumed that this new level of awareness will often be enough to help clients go on to solve the problem for themselves.

Many people adopt a prescriptive approach to helping. They give advice, they tell the client what to do or maybe even get up and do themselves whatever they believe must be done to solve the client's problem. They behave as though they are sufficiently expert to discern the real needs of the client, and they assume that clients lack the necessary competence to either make a sound diagnosis or design an effective plan for corrective action for themselves. The goal of the prescriptive helper seems to be confined to finding a solution to the immediate problem being experienced by the client.

One danger with this approach is that clients become dependent on the helper. They are not helped to learn how to solve the problem for themselves. Consequently, the next time they experience a difficulty they again have to seek help. Another problem can arise when clients feel that the helper is not as expert as she thinks she is, or if they feel that she is insensitive to their needs. They may react by not cooperating with the helper and by withholding information about the problem. They may also reject the advice or solution offered. However, some clients do respond well to advice offered by prescriptive helpers, especially when they are under great pressure to find a solution and/or when they are at their wits' end. Steele (1969) argues that the needs of both the client and the helper may propel the helper towards exclusive occupancy of the role of expert in their relationship, and that in those circumstances where the client accepts the helper as expert there may be some benefits. But he also identifies some costs. One is the increased dependency, which has already been mentioned, and the other has to do with the helper's neglect of the client's knowledge about their own problem. Even where the client does not attempt to withhold this knowledge the helper may choose to ignore it:

> The client often has great wisdom (intuitive if not systematic) about many aspects of his own situation, and an overweighting of the consultant's knowledge value may indeed cause poorer choices to be made than if there were a more balanced view of that which each can contribute to the situation.

Collaborative approaches to helping, such as the acceptant or catalytic approaches identified by Blake and Mouton (1983), are client-centred and aim to empower the client to manage their own problems or to identify and exploit opportunities more effectively.

Often people feel helpless and unable to manage the problems they are faced with. Seligman (1975) defined helplessness as the psychological state that frequently results when events are perceived to be uncontrollable. Much of the original research was undertaken with dogs, but more recently many researchers have observed learned helplessness in humans. Hiroto (1974), for example, exposed groups of college students to either loud controllable noises, which they could terminate by pressing a button four times, or uncontrollable noises, which were terminated independently of what they did. Another group included in the experiment was not exposed to any noise. All subjects were then tested in a situation in which it was possible for them to exercise control over noise termination. Hiroto found that the groups that had either been subjected to controllable noise or no noise learned to terminate the noise in the later test, whereas subjects who had previously been subjected to uncontrollable noise failed to terminate noises during later tests.

Learned helplessness theory states that when individuals are subjected to events that are uncontrollable (that is, when the probability of an outcome is the same, irrespective of how they respond) they will develop *expectations* of non-contingency between response and outcome. Furthermore it is argued that these expectations will produce motivational, emotional and cognitive deficits.

The theory suggests that the incentive for the client to initiate activity directed towards resolving a problem depends upon his expectation that responding will produce some improvement to the problem situation. If the client has no confidence in his own ability to achieve any improvement, he will not try. Abramson, Seligman and Teesdale (1978) distinguish between universal helplessness, where the client believes that the problem is unsolvable by anyone, and personal helplessness, where the client believes that the problem is solvable (for example, by the helper) but not by himself. The danger with prescriptive approaches to helping is that they can promote a sense of *personal helplessness* in the client and the client may become dependent on the help of others.

Egan (1986) discusses the notion of *empowerment* in the helping relationship. He notes that some clients learn, sometimes from a very early age, that there is nothing they can do about certain life situations. They engage in disabling self-talk (see Ellis, 1974, 1977a, 1977b, 1979) and tell themselves that they cannot manage certain situations and that they cannot cope. Egan's position is that whether clients are victims of their own doing or the doings of others they can and must take an active part in managing their own problems, including the search for solutions and efforts towards achieving those solutions. He also argues that the helper can do a great deal to help people to develop a sense of agency or self-efficacy. The helper can do this in a number of ways: by helping the client to challenge self-defeating beliefs and attitudes about themselves and substituting more realistic beliefs about self-efficacy, helping the client to develop the knowledge, skills and resources they need to succeed, and by challenging them to take reasonable risks and supporting them when they do.

The function of the helper, according to Egan, is to encourage clients to apply a problem-solving approach to their current problem situation and to learn from this experience so that there is an increased probability that they will also apply a problem-solving approach to future problem situations. In other words, his approach is one that is directed towards eliminating feelings of personal helplessness.

Egan is not alone in advocating empowerment as the aim of helping. Reddy (1987) defines counselling as a set of techniques, skills and attitudes to *help people manage their own problems using their own resources*. Hopson (1984) offers a similar definition. He defines counselling as a process that involves helping people to explore problems so that *they* can decide what to do about them.

HELPING SKILLS

The helping relationship is not a special relationship reserved for trained consultants and counsellors. Hopson (1984) argues, for example, that counselling skills are not something separate from other human activities. The behaviours that are bundled together and identified as counselling skills are scattered liberally about us in the community. They include many of the basic interpersonal skills that have already been considered in some detail in earlier chapters (for example, listening). Listed below are some additional skills that are important helping skills.

Empathy is a key skill that builds upon the basic skills discussed elsewhere in this book. It involves letting clients know that they have been understood from within their frame of reference, that the helper can see the world as they see it while remaining separate from it. As noted in Chapters 2 and 3, this involves the helper attending, observing and listening to both verbal and non-verbal messages. The client's non-verbal behaviour can be a rich source of data, especially about feelings. However, although these listening skills facilitate understanding, empathy is only achieved when this understanding is communicated to the client. This communication can be achieved by the helper responding to what has been said, reflecting back to the client what it is that the helper believes the client is thinking and feeling, and then attending carefully to the cues given off by the client, which either confirm or deny the accuracy of these responses. Empathy is a core relationship-building skill. Egan suggests that the client who feels he has been understood feels encouraged to move on and to explore his problems in greater depth.

It can be a useful exercise to observe the extent to which people show empathy when dealing with others. It is all too easy to deny other people's feelings, to belittle their problem. Note how often others take the time to engage in empathic listening and try to assess what this does to the quality of the relationship. And then look to yourself. Without changing the way you normally behave, note how often you communicate empathic understanding. Then consciously change your behaviour. Work at increasing the number of times you show empathy and observe the effect it has. People tend to open up when they feel understood, they become less defensive and not only reveal more of themselves to others but, in the process, often find out more about themselves. The very process of talking openly helps them to reappraise their position. Blake and Mouton (1983), for example, suggest that a person's ability to deal with a problem might be affected by the exclusion of intense emotional reactions from conscious awareness. Talking with an empathic listener may help the client get in touch with and work through these repressed reactions, thus enabling him to take a more objective view of his problem.

Probing has been discussed in Chapter 4. Probes can be used to help the client to explore his problem. Non-directive probes and minimal prompts such as attentive silences, 'and. . .' or 'tell me more' can be used to encourage the client to talk and tell his story. Directive probes such as:

> 'How did you feel?'
> 'What did you do?'

can also help the client clarify his thoughts and think about the problem in more specific terms.

Unless the client thinks about his problem in concrete, operational terms it can be difficult to develop an effective problem management strategy. A person is being concrete in his self-exploration when he identifies and talks about specific experiences, behaviours and feelings that are relevant to his problem. An example of a vague or non-concrete statement might be:

> 'I'm not too happy about things at the moment'

A more concrete statement from the same client might be:

> 'I took up the company's offer of having my own computer and working from home. Sometimes, when I'm working alone (*experience*) I begin to feel quite lonely (*feeling*). I know the feeling will pass, but it makes me restless.'

An even more concrete statement might be:

> 'Sometimes, when I'm working at home alone (*experience*), I begin to feel quite lonely (*feeling*). I even begin to think I don't have any friends – even though I know this isn't the case. I begin to feel sorry for myself (*additional feelings*). Finally, it gets to me so much that I get up and go to the pub (*behaviour*), not to drink my sorrows away but just to be with people.'

The last statement not only includes more information about feelings, it also describes what behaviour occurred as a consequence. The helper can assist the client to be more concrete by encouraging him to talk, thus increasing the chance that more concrete data will be revealed, and by probing to seek clarification.

Egan (1986) offers six suggestions for the use of probes:

1 Keep in mind the purpose of probing, which is to help clients tell their stories, to help them focus on relevant and important issues and to help them identify experiences, behaviours and feelings that give a fuller picture of the problem.
2 Use a mix of directive and non-directive probes.
3 Avoid question and answer sessions (see Chapter 2)
4 If a probe helps a client reveal relevant information, follow it up with an empathetic response rather than another probe.
5 Use whatever mixture of empathy and probing that is needed to help clients clarify problems, identify blind spots, develop new scenarios, search for action strategies, formulate plans and review outcomes of action.
6 Remember that probing is a communication skill that is only effective to the degree that it helps the client.

Giving feedback A client's ability to manage his own problems can be fettered by limited or incorrect perceptions, especially about himself and relations with others. Feedback that offers clients new information about themselves can help them develop alternative perspectives on problems. The Johari window is a model developed by Joseph Luft and Harry Ingham, two American psychologists, which can be used to illustrate the process of giving feedback. An adaptation of this model is shown in Figure 6.1. The client's view of himself is represented by the vertical columns and the helper's view of the client by the horizontal rows.

Nobody knows everything about themselves. What they know is represented by the left hand column. The upper pane, referred to as the *open area*, depicts that knowledge about the self that the client is either willing to or cannot avoid sharing with others, including the helper. The lower pane, referred to as the *facade* or hidden area, depicts that knowledge about himself that the client would prefer not to share and therefore attempts to keep hidden from the helper. As respect and trust develops between helper and client, the client may be willing to reveal more of what he initially attempted to keep hidden. Facades are dropped and real concerns discussed more openly. In terms of the Johari window, the client begins to behave in ways that increase the open area and reduce the hidden area.

		CLIENT'S VIEW OF SELF	
		Things client knows about self	Thing client does not know
HELPER'S VIEW OF CLIENT	Things helper knows about client	**OPEN OR SHARED AREA**	**BLIND SPOT**
	Things helper does not know	**FACADE OR HIDDEN AREA**	**UNKNOWN**

Figure 6.1 The helping relationship

What the client does not know about himself is represented by the right-hand column. This column contains two panes, the blind spot and the unknown, which will be discussed in more detail below.

What the helper knows or does not know about the client is represented by the horizontal rows. The bottom row depicts what the helper does not know about the client. The bottom left-hand pane (the facade or hidden area) can only be reduced when the client decides to share more information with the helper. However, the helper can facilitate this process by behaving towards the client in ways that help him to tell his story. All the relationship building and exploring and clarifying skills that are directly or indirectly referred to in this chapter can help achieve this end. The bottom right hand pane, the *unknown*, depicts knowledge that has not yet been discovered by either client or helper. It was noted earlier that a supportive relationship in which the helper shows empathy towards the client can sometimes enable the client to gain access to information, such as previously repressed emotional reactions, that can help him better understand the issues he is trying to deal with.

The top row of the Johari window represents what the helper knows about the client. The top left-hand pane, already referred to, depicts the knowledge that is shared by helper and client.

The top right-hand pane, the *blind spot*, depicts information which the helper knows about the client but which the client does not know about himself. The helper may have obtained this information in a number of ways, by observing the client's behaviour, by paying careful attention to all he says and by searching for and identifying underlying themes and, sometimes, by reference to external sources of data such as reports from customers, colleagues, etc. By offering the client feedback, the helper is disclosing to the client information about himself that he might otherwise not have access to. In other words, she is revealing to the client information about his blind spots.

Not all feedback is helpful. Given inappropriately feedback can damage the helping relationship and can undermine the client's confidence in his own ability to manage problems effectively. What follows is a set of guidelines for the provision of helpful feedback.

1 *Helpful feedback is descriptive, not judgemental.* To be told that:

> 'You are an arrogant bully'

is less helpful than to be informed that:

> 'Whenever you and I discuss this kind of issue I am left with the feeling that you don't listen to my views and that you attempt to get your way by threatening me.'

The first example is evaluative: the helper is making a judgement about the client's behaviour. The second example is more descriptive. It describes the effect the client's behaviour had on the helper, which might have been precisely the effect the client wanted. He might have decided that the best way to influence the helper was to issue threats. However, this may not have been his intention and the feedback may alert the client to important unanticipated consequences of his behaviour.

2 *Helpful feedback is specific, not general.* To be told:

> 'You never seem to be able to communicate effectively in groups'

offers the client few clues about what he might do differently to improve matters. On the other hand to be told that:

> 'When you were presenting your case to the group last Thursday you spoke so quickly that I couldn't grasp all the points you were trying to make'

provides the client with information that is sufficiently specific for him to determine how he might change his behaviour if he wants to obtain a different outcome at the next meeting.

3 *Helpful feedback is relevant to the needs of the client.* The helper needs to be aware of whose needs she is trying to satisfy when she offers feedback. Sometimes, feedback does more for the helper than for the client. For example, an angry outburst

may help to relieve her frustrations but may do little for the client. Similarly, the provision of sensitive feedback in public may do more to confirm the helper's superiority than to boost the confidence of the client, who may be a new member of the helper's work group.

4 *Helpful feedback is solicited rather than imposed.* In many circumstances people seek feedback. However, although they want to know, they may be fearful of finding out. The helper needs to be sensitive to those cues that indicate whether the other person is seeking feedback and to those cues that signal when he has received as much as he can cope with for the time being. Pushing too hard can trigger a defensive reaction, leading the client to dismiss or ignore further feedback. People tend to be much less receptive to feedback which they feel is imposed than to that which they have sought out for themselves.

5 *Helpful feedback is timely and in context.* Feedback is best given in the context in which the behaviour to which the feedback refers took place, and as soon after the behaviour as possible. The introduction of formalized appraisal systems sometimes encourages helpers to store up feedback for the appraisal interview, whereas it would have been much more effective if it had been offered at the time the problem was observed by the helper. However, accurate behavioural records such as audio or video tape can extend considerably the period over which the feedback is timely; these methods also preserve much of the context and, therefore, are particularly valuable in training situations.

6 *Helpful feedback is usable and concerned with behaviour over which the client is able to exercise control.* Feedback can improve the client's knowledge of how he typically behaves and the effect his behaviour has on others. However, feedback can only help the client secure desired outcomes if it focuses on behaviour that he can do something about. To tell a client with a severe stutter that he is making you impatient, and that he should be quick and say what he has to say or shut up, is unlikely to afford much help.

7 *Feedback can only be helpful when it has been heard and understood.* If in doubt, check with the client to ensure that the feedback has been received and understood.

A checklist for assessing the quality of feedback is offered in Appendix 6.1.

Challenging The goal of challenging or confronting in the helping relationship is to help clients explore those areas of experience, feeling and behaviour that they have so far failed to explore. Blake and Mouton (1983) suggest that confrontational interventions can be among the most effective in reducing the efficacy of defence mechanisms. By challenging the client, the helper can persuade him to face up to contradictions between what he says and does or between how he sees himself and the way others see him. The helper might also challenge the client because she suspects that he distorts reality and uses these distortions to avoid facing up to things. For example, a client might view his subordinate's application for a better job as disloyalty rather than as a timely and appropriate career move, or he may disguise (even from himself) his fear of change as a commitment to the one best and traditional way of doing things.

Egan (1986) suggests that, in its simplest form, a confrontation is an invitation to examine some form of behaviour that seems to be self-defeating, harmful, or both, and to change that behaviour if it is found to be so. He describes confrontation as strong medicine that can be destructive in the hands of the inept. Effective challenges are never punitive accusations. They are invitations to explore contradictions and distortions, or invitations to identify and employ unused strengths and resources. The term 'invitation' cannot be emphasized too strongly. The client who experiences the challenge as a shameful unmasking or some other form of attack will not be receptive to the alternative perspective that the challenge may offer. A likely outcome is that the client who feels under attack will direct his energy towards a defensive action and possibly a counter attack aimed at discrediting the 'helper'. Consider how you might react to the following challenges:

(a) 'Why don't you start being honest. You feel so damn sorry for yourself most of the time that you never even give a thought to the possibility that you might be the cause of most of your own problems. You mope around and never face up to things. Grow up!!'

(b) 'Let me check something out with you. You say that you have been feeling very low because everything seems to be going wrong. You also indicate that there is nothing you can do to change things. Now I'm not sure about this. From what I've observed you appear to behave as if you believe that you can't change things and therefore you don't even try, even in circumstances when you could. For example, you didn't even try to make a case for an increase to your budget at the last managers' meeting. You seem to blame others for your problems but do nothing to change things. Does this make sense to you?'

The second challenge was based on what the client had said and on what the helper had observed. It started by acknowledging the client's point of view, thus signalling that he was understood and that the helper was 'with' rather than against him. It was specific and offered examples. It was also presented tentatively. The phrases, 'I'm not sure about this' and 'does this make sense to you', offered the client the options of accepting, modifying or even rejecting the confrontation without feeling accused by the helper.

Helpful challenges are those that encourage the client to seek greater self-understanding. As well as being based on accurate empathy and presented tentatively, they must also be made when the client is in a fit state to respond. To paraphrase Egan, a confused and disorganized client might be further disoriented by a challenge that adds to his confusion.

Core Values The behaviour of effective helpers appears to be influenced by certain core values. Rogers (1958) identified these as unconditional positive regard for the client (i.e. respect) and genuineness.

Respect Egan (1986) and Reddy (1987) elaborate the core value of unconditional positive regard or respect to include:

Being 'for' the client. This involves the helper behaving in a manner that indicates that she is 'with' or 'for' the client in a non-sentimental caring way. If the client feels the helper might be against him he is unlikely to put his trust in her or reveal anxieties, weaknesses or specific information that he fears could be used against him.

Signalling that the other's viewpoint is worth listening to. This reflects the helper's willingness to commit herself to working with the client. It also suggests a minimum level of openness to the other's point of view. Without this openness, empathic listening is impossible. Too often, even when we go though the motions of asking the other for his viewpoint, we are not really committed to listening. For example, a parent, before visiting her wrath upon a child, might ask for an explanation of his behaviour, but even though she asks she may not really expect to receive a satisfactory explanation and, therefore, may not prepare herself to listen to what the child has to say. However, Reddy (1987) cites an example in which the parent realizes at the last minute that what the child has to say is important. From his perspective the behaviour in question makes perfect sense and deserves praise, not punishment. The effective helper needs to respect the client's point of view and needs to clearly signal this respect if the client is to be encouraged to work with the helper.

Suspending critical judgement. The helper needs to keep an open mind and avoid reaching premature conclusions. This does not mean that the helper should signal approval of everything she hears or observes; rather, she should communicate that she understands the client's point of view. Reddy (1987) suggests that communicating understanding in this way can help the client to change. Rather than pushing him into a position that he may resist, by suspending judgement and trying to understand the other's viewpoint the helper can offer the client the opportunity to explore his position and give him the freedom to change his view. According to Reddy, suspending judgement and keeping an open mind does not come naturally, because we have been conditioned to persuade others to our point of view. At school there is nearly always a debating society, but rarely a listening club. It may be that we often fail to keep an open mind because if we listen we may end up agreeing, and if we agree we may appear to have lost. However, the aim of the helping relationship is not to win. Suspending judgement encourages the client to believe that the helper is 'for' him and has his interests at heart.

Working with the client as a unique individual. This involves being willing to support each client in his or her uniqueness and not relating to them as just another 'case'. It requires the helper to personalize the helping process and tailor it to the needs, capabilities and resources of each client.

Respecting the client's right to determine his own fate. The role of the helper in the collaborative helping relationship is to help the client develop a sense of agency or self-efficacy rather than to promote a state of dependency and a feeling of helplessness. This implies an attitude, on the part of the helper, that the client does have the resources necessary to manage his problems more effectively. The helper's role is to facilitate the development of these resources. It is not the helper's role to take over the client's problems and prescribe solutions. If the client opts for a course of action, which the helper feels does not offer the best way forward, she might encourage the client to challenge his chosen solution, but ultimately the helper needs to respect the client's right to determine his own fate.

Assuming the client is committed to the goal of managing problems more effectively. It has already been noted that some clients may not have referred themselves for help and might engage in the helping relationship with some reluctance. However, their initial reluctance to work with the helper does not necessarily imply that they are not committed to finding ways of managing their problems more effectively. Egan (1986) suggests that respectful helpers will assume the client's goodwill and will continue to work with the client until this assumption has been clearly demonstrated to be false. A client who recognizes that the helper respects him and is oriented to his needs is more likely to engage positively in the helping relationship than one who observes little evidence of any respect.

Genuineness is important in the helping relationship. If respect for the client is faked, and if such attitudes as openness and interest in the client are not genuine, then there is a high probability that this will be detected by the client and that it will seriously damage or even destroy the helping relationship. Being genuine involves being honest, sincere and without facade. It involves a refusal to take on a stylized helper role. Egan defines it as a value that can be expressed as a set of behaviours that includes being oneself, being open, spontaneous, assertive and consistent.

STAGES IN THE HELPING PROCESS

Many people think of helping in terms of empathic listening or giving feedback. They lack an overview of the process and tend to concentrate their efforts on one aspect of the helping relationship. The acceptant mode of helping, for example, focuses on the provision of empathy and passive support in order to help clients develop a new level of understanding. It is assumed that this awareness will enable them to move forward, without any further help, and manage their problems more effectively. While this might be the case for some clients, there will be others who will not know what to do with this new awareness; they will require help to establish goals and to develop action plans.

Blake and Mouton (1983) suggest that most helpers tend to develop one style of intervention and rely on it exclusively: they may be purely acceptant, purely catalytic, confrontational and so on. Egan cautions against such a narrow approach to helping. His model draws together ideas and techniques from a variety of theories to produce a three-stage integrative approach to problem management. He argues that helpers should not be 'stage-specific specialists'. They should be competent in all aspects of the helping process because they are all interdependent. The helper who specializes in confrontation may be a poor confronter if her confrontations are not based on an empathic understanding of the client. He also suggests that few helping skills are specific to particular stages. Most are applicable throughout the helping process.

Egan presents his model as a cognitive map that can be used to assist the helper to understand the nature of her relationship with the client and provide her with a sense of direction. While it is a stage model, it does not assume that helping will necessarily involve a sequential progression through each of the three stages. The helper might move backwards as well as forwards throughout the model because, for example, while planning for action the client may raise new concerns that have to be clarified and understood before the problem can be resolved.

The three-stage helping model presented here is based upon Egan's integrative approach to problem management. The first stage is concerned with identifying and clarifying problem situations and unused opportunities, the second with goal setting and the third with action.

Stage 1 Identifying and clarifying problem situations and unused opportunities

This first stage is important because problem situations cannot be managed or unused opportunities developed until clients are able to identify and understand them. Egan (1975) originally presented this process of identification and clarification as one that involved two steps. He referred to them as the inward journey and the outward journey.

The inward journey is concerned with helping clients tell their stories and develop a subjective understanding of their problems. It focuses on how the client sees things. No attempt is made, at this stage, to persuade clients to consider alternative ways of thinking about their problems. The helper assists clients to clarify their problem situations *from within their own frames of reference*. She does this by attending and responding in ways that help them to explore their own feelings, attitudes and behaviours and to consider what it is that they do or fail to do that has a bearing on their problems. It is important that the helper empathizes with clients, that she shows that she understands what they are saying and how they are feeling from within their own frames of reference. The helper may also have to nudge clients into dealing with concrete and specific issues and feelings, if they are to clarify and better understand their problem situations. Vague generalities provide a poor foundation for the generation of strategies to develop unused opportunities or manage problem situations.

Some people find it easy to share their thoughts with a helper, whereas others feel reluctant to talk about their problems. The effective helper has to be good at listening and drawing people out. Relationship building plays a central role in this phase of the helping process. Strong (1968) defines helping in terms of a social influence process. He goes on to suggest that helpers need to establish a power base and then to use it to influence clients. This is clearly what happens in prescriptive helping relationships, where clients define helpers as experts and bow to their expertise. However, in the collaborative helping relationships advocated here, the helper must be careful to avoid using her ability to influence in ways that will increase the clients' feelings of powerlessness. Nonetheless, where clients trust the helper and believe that she is 'on their side' and is working 'for' them, they will be more likely to share sensitive information about themselves and, in the next phase of stage one, to be receptive to suggestions from her that point to alternative ways of looking at their problems. However, where the helper is seen to be untrustworthy, incompetent and not 'for' them, clients will be much more likely to reject any feedback offered by the helper and to react defensively to any attempt by her to influence their thinking by introducing alternative frames of reference.

The outward journey is concerned with helping clients identify blind spots and develop new perspectives. While the inward journey focused on helping clients to clarify problems from within their own frames of reference, the outward journey focuses on the development of a more objective assessment. Old and comfortable frames of reference may keep clients locked into self-defeating patterns of thinking and behaving, and the helper may need to help them identify blind spots and develop alternative frames of reference.

There are a number of ways in which the helper can persuade clients to consider their problem situations from alternative perspectives. As they tell their stories, the helper may draw attention to themes:

> 'You have mentioned several times, in several different ways, that you feel uncomfortable when you have to manage people

who have more paper qualifications than you. Is this the way you see it?'

She might also draw attention to what appears to be the bigger picture:

'The problem doesn't just seem to be that your new boss is a woman, your resentment also seems to be directed at a number of your male colleagues.'

During the 'outward journey' the helper needs to show what Egan refers to as advanced empathy, to communicate to clients an understanding not only of what they say but also of what they imply, what they hint at and what they convey non-verbally. In this phase the helper might also begin to constructively challenge clients in those situations where their old frames of reference appear to be preventing them from identifying better ways of managing their problems.

Stage 2 Goal setting: developing a more dearable scenario
Insight is seldom sufficient, however interesting it may be. The helping relationship aims to promote problem managing *action*. Egan (1986) suggests that assessment for the sake of assessment, exploration for the sake of exploration or insight for the sake of insight are close to useless. The first stage of the helping process, identifying and clarifying problem situations and unused opportunities, can only be judged to be effective to the extent that it helps clients construct more desirable scenarios in terms of realistic and achievable goals.

This might involve identifying those aspects of the problem that are to be tackled first. Some problems are too big or too complex to be tackled in one go. If clients set unrealistic goals for themselves they are unlikely to succeed, and failure may reinforce their feelings of helplessness. The identification of realistic and achievable goals is more likely to lead to success and to the promotion of a feeling of self-efficacy. For example, if a problem were identified in terms of:

'The quality of my working life is deteriorating'

it might be more difficult to identify achievable goals than if it were broken down into sub-problems such as:

> 'I am overworked';
> 'My subordinates don't get along with each other and I am surrounded by conflicts';
> 'I spend too much time away from the office and home';
> 'In my absence problems multiply and nobody seems to care';
> 'My boss and I have different priorities so I am reluctant to ask him to keep a watching brief in my absence';
> 'I seem to have been doing the same old thing for far too long'.

This process not only helps clients identify what a more desirable scenario would look like, but also points to the possibility of selecting alternative scenarios. For example, should the client work at being away less or at building a better relationship with his boss so that fewer problems will arise during his absence?

Clients may need help to think through and anticipate the consequences of opting for different scenarios and to identify specific priorities for action if their chosen scenario is to be realized.

Stage 3 Helping clients act

Stage 2 was concerned with goals. Stage 3 is less concerned with goals (*ends*) and more concerned with the *means* for achieving these ends. It involves identifying different strategies for action and selecting and implementing the strategy that offers the greatest promise of success. Egan (1986) illustrates the importance of stage 3 with the example of Kate who, on New Year's Eve, decides to lose twenty pounds only to find, some time later, that she had actually gained five pounds. Her lack of success might be attributed to several factors. First, her goal was not expressed in terms of specific behaviours, such as exercising more or eating less. Second, she failed to think through what losing weight would require in terms of personal commitment and what factors might affect her level of commitment, and, finally, she failed to think through how she was going to accomplish her goal. She failed to identify an action programme.

One aspect of the helper's role is to guide clients away from convergent thinking (there is only *one* cause for the present difficult situation, only *one* solution if matters are to be improved or only *one* strategy for achieving that solution) to divergent thinking. In stage 3 of the helping process this means encouraging the client to identify and evaluate alternative strategies. Techniques such as brainstorming and synectics can be a useful way of identifying different ways of achieving goals, and the chosen route may well end up comprising a combination of ideas derived from different strategies.

The force-field approach Force-field analysis offers one approach to systematically searching out viable courses of action. It is a method, based on the work of Kurt Lewin, for identifying the psychological and social forces that affect a person's behaviour.

If the client can be helped to define realistic problem management goals in terms of the behaviours that would be most desirable, and the behaviour that would be least desirable he will have identified the two extreme points in a force-field. His current behaviour is likely to be somewhere in between these two points and usually will not vary very much towards one or other extreme.

If we return to the example of Kate. She might have defined her goal in terms of eating less than 1000 calories a day compared with her current consumption of 1500. During the last few months her calorie consumption might have changed very little, maybe increasing marginally, but not approaching anything like the worst scenario of 2000 or the best of 1000. This equilibrium level of consumption of about 1500 is maintained by a set of driving forces (pushing for the lower level of 1000 calories) and a set of restraining forces that work against the achievement of this goal. These forces can be within the client: for example, Kate might constantly eat between meals because she always feels hungry. Alternatively, some forces might be part of her social environment. Her house-bound mother might express her affection for her daughter by investing a lot of her time in the preparation of elaborate meals, and Kate may feel compelled to eat them in order to avoid hurting her mother's feelings. Both of these are examples of restraining forces that hinder the achievement of her goals. A driving force might be the desire to wear her sister's dress at a forthcoming dinner dance, but it might be too tight for her at the moment (see Figure 6.2).

The force-field approach fits well with Egan's integrative approach to problem management. When the client has identified and clarified the problem in concrete terms and determined what a more desirable state of affairs would look like he can specify, again in concrete terms, one goal or a related set of realistic goals. This provides the framework within which he can undertake a force-field analysis. The client can be encouraged to list all the restraining forces that are keeping him from his goal and all the driving forces that are helping him reach his goal. At this stage he should be encouraged to list as many as possible and to make no attempt to list them in order of importance.

As the next step the client reviews these two lists and identifies those forces that seem to be the most important and that he might be able to do something about. When the key forces have been identified, the client can review each one in more detail. For each key restraining force he might think about all the possible action steps that he could take to reduce the effect of the force. Similarly, for each key driving force, he might think about all the possible action steps that could increase the effect of the force. At this stage it can be useful to list as many action steps as possible without worrying too much about how practical or effective they would be. The aim should be to be as creative as possible. Brainstorming can sometimes help.

Having generated a wide range of ideas the client then needs to review them to identify those that seem most promising, bearing in mind such practical considerations as the availability

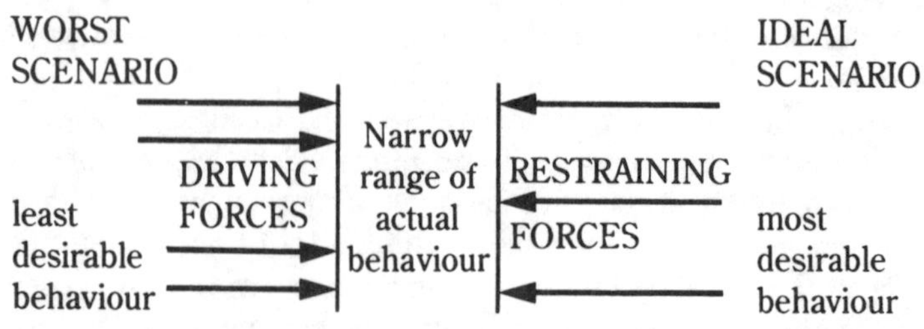

Figure 6.2 The force-field

of people, time and other resources. It is very important at this stage that the helper does not impose her own values. The client's commitment to the action plan is crucial and, therefore, he must select action steps that are in keeping with his own values.

The final phase involves reviewing the chosen action steps from the point of view of how they might be brought together to fit into a comprehensive and workable action plan. It may be necessary to modify or eliminate items that do not fit in with the overall plans. It might also be necessary to add new steps that will round out the plan.

Sharing the helping model with clients

Egan (1986) presents his model as a cognitive map to give direction to the helper when she is interacting with the client. However, he also raises the interesting question, how much should the client be told about the model the helper is using? In his opinion clients should be told as much about the model as they can assimilate, on the grounds that they, like the helper, will also have a cognitive map that will give them a sense of direction and that, if they know where they are going, they will get there faster.

Blake and Mouton (1983) offer support for this view. They argue that a very effective intervention strategy, the theories and principles approach, involves communicating a theory to clients in a way that enables them to take in the main concepts and then evaluate them against their natural way of dealing with a situation. Clients can use this evaluation to identify their own self-defeating patterns of behaviour and replace them with more effective theory-indicated ways of behaving.

Blake and Mouton argue that theory can help clients change their behaviour in a number of ways. It offers them a *sense of perspective*, which can motivate them to think through the longer term implications of what they do. This often causes them to re-assess the efficacy of their normal, possibly impulsive, ways of responding. Theory can also affect *motivation*. It offers a model of excellence that clients may aspire to reach. It can also have an effect on *creativity* in that clients might become more curious about what they observe and more imaginative in their search for solutions. Finally, it has implications for *autonomy*, insofar as theory increases the clients' capacity for self-direction.

Summary

To a greater or lesser extent we are all helpers in the sense that we all relate with others and attempt, at least occasionally, to help them manage their problems or develop unused opportunities more effectively. It was noted, however, that all help is not necessarily helpful. One danger is that, possibly unwittingly, the helper may end up making clients more rather than less helpless. This can happen when the helper undermines the clients' confidence in their ability to manage problems and when they end up becoming more rather than less dependent on the helper.

The function of the helper is to encourage clients to adopt a problem-solving approach to current problems and to learn from this experience so that they can adopt a similar approach to the management of other problem situations.

This chapter draws heavily on some of the basic interpersonal skills discussed in earlier chapters and highlights four skills that are particularly relevant in the context of helping relationships. These are empathy, probing, feedback and challenging. The importance of two core values, respect and genuineness, were also discussed in the context of their impact on the behaviour of helpers. A set of guidelines for the practice of empathy was presented earlier in this chapter, and a checklist for assessing the quality of feedback is offered in Appendix 6.1.

The final section of the chapter presented a three-stage model of helping that provides the helper with a cognitive map and a sense of direction when she is working with clients. The first stage of the model is concerned with identifying and clarifying problems and unused opportunities, the second with goal setting and the third with action.

Appendix 6.1

CHECKLIST FOR ASSESSING THE QUALITY OF FEEDBACK

Note whether the feedback is:

Descriptive	☐	☐	Judgemental
Specific	☐	☐	General
Relevant to client's own needs	☐	☐	Irrelevant to client's needs
Focused on behaviour client can control	☐	☐	Focused on behaviour client cannot control
Solicited	☐	☐	Imposed
Timely	☐	☐	Delayed
Checked for understanding	☐	☐	Not checked for understanding

References: Chapter 6

Abramson, L. Y., Seligman, M. E. P. and Teesdale, J. D. 1978. Learned helplessness in humans: Critique and performulations. *Journal of Abnormal Psychology,* 87, 1: 49-74.

Blake, R. R. and Mouton, J. S. 1983. *Consultation: a Handbook for Individual and Organization Development.* Reading, Mass.: Addison-Wesley.

Egan, G. 1975. *The Skilled Helper: a Model For Systematic Helping and Interpersonal Relating*. Belmont, Calif.: Wadsworth.

Egan, G. 1986. *The Skilled Helper: a Systematic Approach to Effective Helping*. Belmont, Calif.: Wadsworth.

Ellis, A. 1974. *Disputing Irrational Beliefs (DIBS)*. New York, Institute for Rational Living.

Ellis, A. 1977a. The basic clinical theory of rational-emotive therapy.

In A. Ellis and G. Grieger (eds), *Handbook of Rational–Emotive Therapy*. Monterey, Calif.: Brooke/Cole.

Ellis, A. 1977b. Rational-emotive therapy. Research data that supports the clinical and personality hypotheses of RET and other modes of congruitive behaviour therapy. *Counselling Psychologist,* 7, 1: 2-42.

Ellis, A. 1979. *New Developments in Rational-Emotive Therapy*. Monterey, Calif.: Brooke/Cole.

Hiroto, D. S. 1974. Locus of control and learned helplessness. *Journal of Experimental Psychology*, 10,2: 187-93.

Hopson, B. 1984. Counselling and helping. In C. I. Cooper and P. Makin, *Psychology for Managers*. Leicester: British Psychological Society.

Lewin, K. 1951. *Field Theory in Social Science*. New York: Harper & Row.

Reddy, M. 1987. *The Manager's Guide to Counselling at Work*. London: British Psychological Society/Methuen.

Rogers, C. R. 1958. The characteristics of a helping relationship. *Personnel and Guidance Journal,* 37: 6-16.

Seligman, M. E. P. 1975. *Helplessness*. San Francisco: W. H. Freeman.

Steele, F. I. 1969. Consultants and detectives. *Journal of Applied Behavioural Science*, 5, 2: 193-4.

Strong, S. R. 1968. Counselling: an interpersonal influence process. *Journal of Counselling Psychology,* 15: 215-24.

CHAPTER SEVEN
Influencing

Many people working in organizations experience problems when attempting to influence others. Sometimes the source of difficulty is perceived to be rooted in a particular relationship or sometimes it is experienced as a more general inability to exercise influence.

People react to these perceived problems in different ways. Some give up trying. They accept the impossibility of introducing any significant change and become apathetic and passive. Some respond by trying harder. They devote more energy to influencing others and achieving results, but when things do not go their way their frustrations surface in the form of abrasive and coercive behaviour. They continue to push their ideas, but they become aggressive and behave like the proverbial bull in the china shop, upsetting others and creating unnecessary resistance to their proposals. The most effective people, however, seem to be those who expect to experience resistance to their attempts to influence others and get things done, but nevertheless keep on taking initiatives, carefully selected initiatives, in ways that eventually tend to produce the results they desire.

This chapter attempts to identify what it is that makes some people more effective than others. It looks at the kind of initiative they take and what they do to increase the likelihood that their initiative taking will be successful.

Two approaches to influencing are examined. The first focuses on assertiveness and examines those behaviours which help an individual stand up for her rights and communicate important messages to others. The second adopts a more macro perspective and considers influencing as a political process.

Proactivity and influence

Most organizations, with very few exceptions, are having to compete harder than ever. Within the present lean and aggressive environment the successful organization has to behave strategically. It must be creative and take risks. Playing it by the book, reacting to situations according to well-tried traditional practices, is no guarantee of survival and growth. Reactive management must give way to proactive management. The organization must question established practice, take initiatives and innovate. This can only happen when individual managers, professionals and other employees are themselves proactive and are committed to getting things done and overcoming unnecessary barriers to goal achievement.

Proactive people appear to behave as if they are continually asking themselves the question 'What do I need to do to bring about the state of affairs I desire?' Three characteristics seem to differentiate them from others:

1 *They appear to have clear ideas about what it is they want to achieve.* They recognize that they cannot achieve everything and that some ordering of priorities is necessary. A common cause of wasted effort is the spreading of resources too thinly across too many projects, coupled with a poor ordering of priorities.

2 *They pay attention to what needs to happen if they are to bring about the state of affairs they desire, and invest their time, energy and other resources accordingly.* It is all too easy for people to focus initiative-taking on those areas they enjoy and where they feel competent and comfortable, and devote less attention to other areas that may be equally, or even more, critical. For example, an engineer may enjoy taking initiatives in technical areas but invest little effort in initiative-taking to secure the resources necessary to pursue the work of her group or to ensure that it will be welcomed by possible users.

3 *Finally, they possess a set of skills to do with influencing others and the exercise of power.* Not only do they know what they want and what needs to be done to achieve it,

but they have the ability to actually implement plans and push their projects forward.

Influencing others

Some people, even many of those who occupy senior positions in organizations, seem to find it difficult to influence others. They do not find it easy to ask others to do things and they seem unable to refuse requests, even unreasonable requests, that others make of them. They feel powerless when it comes to bringing about a state of affairs that they desire. It is possible to identify a number of different styles of interacting with others, which range along a continuum from non-assertive to aggressive (see Figure 7.1).

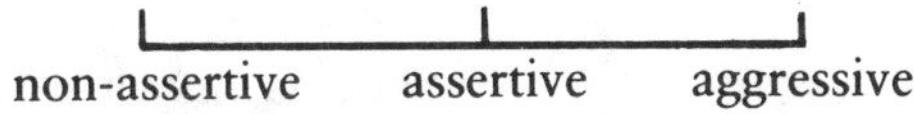

Figure 7.1 The non-assertive – aggressive continuum

People who are non-assertive find it difficult to express their needs and influence others. For example, even though they may be allergic to cigarette smoke, they are the kind of people who would be reluctant to tell colleagues working in the same office that their smoking makes life uncomfortable for them, and they would find it even more difficult to ask them to stop. If they ever do express their honest feelings they tend to do so in an apologetic way. Phrases like '. . . but it really doesn't matter' and non-verbal behaviours such as low eye contact, soft voice and submissive postures signal to others that what has just been said is not really important.

Assertive people express their needs and stand up for their own rights, but do so in ways that respect the rights of others. They are unlike the many non-assertive people who are so preoccupied with the need to avoid conflict that they fail to let others know where they stand on issues or what they hope to achieve. An assertive interpersonal style involves communicating clearly with others, stating one's own position in a confident manner, avoiding phrases that devalue the message and using appropriate non-verbal behaviours that signal to others that they should pay attention to the speaker's point of view.

People who adopt an aggressive style of interacting with others tend to be those who are determined to win, regardless of what happens to the other people involved. They often express their feelings and pursue their needs at the expense of others, and they fail to pay attention to what it is that others value. In behavioural terms aggressive people tend to talk loudly, look angry and use phrases which abuse, blame or undervalue others. In the short term aggressors often win, but, because they do so at the expense of others, in the longer term their aggressive style tends to foster opposition and resistance.

Think about your own interpersonal style Consider the hypothetical situations presented in Figure 7.2 and identify the response that most nearly reflects the way you would deal with each situation.

Now think about four or five recent occasions when you wanted to change somebody else's behaviour or refuse a request. For each incident place a checkmark at the points on the non-assertive – aggressive continuum which best describes your response.

	situation	non-assertive	assertive	aggressive
1.	If you were allergic to cigarette smoke and shared an office with a smoker, would you:	say nothing and suffer in silence	tell your colleague about your allergy, explain the consequences of his smoking for you and politely ask if he would refrain from smoking in the office.	get angry, tell him that he is inconsiderate and uncaring and demand that he stops smoking immediately
2.	If your boss asked you for help when you were busy trying to meet an important deadline, would you:	seethe inside but shrug your shoulders, mutter something about being a bit busy and agree to help	tell her about the important deadline, apologise and refuse immediate assistance but offer to help her as soon as you are free	complain that she is always interfering and demand to be left to get on with your own work

Figure 7.2 Ways of responding to a situation

non-assertive	assertive	aggressive

Ask yourself whether the way you behaved produced the outcome you wanted and consider whether you are satisfied with your interpersonal style.

ASSERTIVENESS

During the last twenty years many books and hundreds of research studies have been published on the topic of assertiveness and assertiveness training. The evidence clearly supports the view that assertion skills are related to interpersonal effectiveness in conflict situations. Schroeder, Rakos and Moe (1983) identified seven different classes of assertive response, which they grouped under the two headings positive and negative expressiveness. The focus of attention here will be the negative or conflict assertion skills which include:

Expressing unpopular or different opinions: 'I disagree with Jim's proposal that we should settle the pay claim at 8 per cent. I think we should hold out for a better deal.'

Requesting behaviour changes: 'I feel that I am being kept in the dark when you don't keep me informed about customer complaints. From now on I would like you to provide me with a daily report.'

Refusing requests: 'No, I will not change the date of your appraisal interview.'

People who are able to express their rights by using these kinds of assertive responses are more likely to influence others and achieve desired outcomes than those who are unable to assert their rights in such ways.

One reason why some people do not assert themselves and, therefore, find it difficult to influence others is because they have a high need for approval and acceptance, and fear that if they stand up for their rights others might reject them. Consequently, they are reluctant to refuse requests, express unpopular opinions or request behaviour changes. Assertive behaviour is not without risks. It may be necessary to risk dissention and accept some level of conflict if established relationships are to be changed and the assertor is to become more influential. However, these risks can be minimized if the person who wants to stand up for her rights and influence others has a well-developed set of asserting skills.

Assertion skills

The skills of asserting can be grouped under three headings:

1 Content skills – what the assertor says.
2 Non-verbal skills – how the assertor looks and sounds.
3 Social interaction skills – the way the assertor behaves in the process of the interaction, including escalating, persistence, and the management of defensive reactions.

Content skills

Effective assertion messages tend to be *brief and direct* statements. Rambling, non-specific or ambiguous responses are much less effective because they are open to misinterpretation. It has been found that the more assertion messages are elaborated the greater the danger that side-issues will intrude and undermine the impact of the message.

Effective assertion messages are also *respectful.* They express the assertor's concerns without blaming or attacking the other. Respectful messages are more effective because the non-judgemental statements they contain are less likely to elicit a defensive reaction. The other person is more likely to receive the assertion as a new input, which offers a different perspective on the reasonableness of their requests or on the consequences of their behaviour, rather than as an attack. This new input may encourage the recipient to re-evaluate his behaviour and may motivate him to take steps to modify his relationship with the assertor.

If a person asserts her rights without paying attention to the rights of others she is more likely to encourage resistance and she increases the risk of damaging her relationship with the other person. According to Rakos (1979), the assertive expression of rights is more effective when it is presented as part of a process that involves a chain of behaviours, some proceeding and some following the actual assertion. He argues that prior to emitting the assertion the assertor should engage in whatever behaviours might be necessary to determine the rights of *all* the people involved, and she should develop a verbal and non-verbal response repertoire that will enable her to influence the other's offending behaviour without evaluating his 'worth' . She should also consider all the potential negative consequences that others might experience as a result of the assertive response. He suggests that after emitting the assertive response the assertor should elaborate her assertion in a way that makes it more acceptable to the other.

Recent research evidence (e.g. Woolfolk and Dever 1979; Romano and Bellack 1980 and Pitcher and Meikle 1980, reported by Rakos 1986) suggests a number of ways in which standard assertive messages can be elaborated and made more acceptable without undermining their potency. They include:

Offering a non-defensive, honest explanation of the need to assert oneself. 'I cannot change the date of your appraisal interview because I have to visit the factory in Germany next week.'

Offering an empathetic statement that recognises the effects on other parties. 'I cannot change the date of your appraisal interview. I know you will be disappointed because you have been invited to attend the project review meeting.'

Offering a short apology for the consequences. 'I cannot change the date of your appraisal interview. I'm sorry because I know it will mean that you will have to miss the project review meeting.'

Attempting to identify a mutually acceptable compromise. 'I cannot change the date or time of your appraisal interview, but would you like me to ask Graham if he could start the project review meeting in the morning?'

Praising or offering another positive comment directed towards the other person. 'Graham told me that he had invited you to the project review meeting because of the contribution you made towards getting the project back on schedule. I'm sorry I cannot change the date of your appraisal interview.'

Developing a verbal response repertoire Many people are unable to assert themselves because they find it difficult to formulate appropriate assertive responses. In conflict situations they feel under pressure and cannot think what to say. As a result, they either say little or nothing and engage in flight behaviour, or they let their frustrations and anger get the better of them, become aggressive and engage in fight behaviour.

Anticipating the need to assert and preparing appropriate assertion messages can help overcome these problems. Bolton (1986) offers a simple formula for constructing assertion messages, which can be very effective in those circumstances where the assertor desires to change the behaviour of another. He suggests that assertive responses should include a non-blaming description of the behaviour that is being confronted, a disclosure of the assertor's feelings and a clarification of the tangible effect the other's behaviour has on the assertor. This formula takes the form:

> *When you* (a non-evaluative description of the other's behaviour)
> *I feel* (disclosure of assertor's feelings)
> *Because* (clarification of effect)

Although this three-part assertion message formula might seem rather mechanistic and its structure might not be appropriate for all situations, it has been found that writing down and assessing the likely impact of alternative assertion messages can help people develop their assertive response repertoire. This kind of practice makes it more likely that when the assertor eventually confronts another, even though she may be under pressure, she will speak with precision and convey precisely the meaning she wants to convey.

Describing the other's behaviour. Some of the issues that assertors might need to pay attention to when formulating non-evaluative descriptions of behaviour have already been mentioned. Writing them down can help the would-be assertor to differentiate between direct respectful responses such as:

'When you are late for project review meetings . . .'

from fuzzy, imprecise and judgemental responses such as:

'When you are selfish and waste other's time . . .'

Disclosure of feelings. Writing down how she feels about the other's behaviour can help the assertor to formulate statements that accurately communicate her feelings. Bolton argues that the genuine disclosure of feelings can increase the potency of the assertion by making the recipient aware of the assertor's affective response to his requests or behaviours. However, he cautions against overstating or understating feelings. If the assertor feigns stronger emotions in the hope that she will be more convincing, her pretence may be detected, thus undermining her efforts to influence the other. On the other hand, understating the intensity of her feelings will deprive the other of important data that could motivate him to change his behaviour.

Clarifying effect. Bolton also argues that if the assertor can convince the other that his attitude or behaviour has concrete and tangible effects, such as unnecessarily costing the assertor money, harming her possessions, consuming her time, causing her extra work, endangering her job and/or interfering with her

Behaviour description	**Disclosure of feelings**	**Tangible effects**
When you are late for project review meetings	I feel frustrated	because my time, and that of others, is wasted while we wait for you
When you make last minute changes to production targets	I feel *very* annoyed	because I have to work late and do not see my children before they go to bed

Figure 7.3 Three-part assertion messages

effectiveness, then the probability of change will be even greater. Figure 7.3 offers some examples of the kind of three-part assertion message advocated by Bolton.

Non verbal skills

The potency of an assertive response can be influenced by paralinguistic characteristics, such as volume, firmness of delivery and inflection, and non-verbal behaviours, such as facial expression, eye contact, gestures and posture.

The research on volume (see Rose and Tryon 1979) indicates that assertive people speak louder than non-assertive people, but not as loud as aggressive people. Findings suggest that non-assertive people speak at a level of 68 dB, assertive at 76 dB and aggressive at 84 dB. Lay people, when asked to judge whether others are assertive, point to the importance of inflection as well as volume. Although the research evidence presents a fairly complex picture on this, there does seem to be agreement that intermediate levels of inflection are associated with greater impact. Firmness of delivery is another paralinguistic characteristic associated with assertiveness. These research findings are supported by Alberti and Emmons (1975) who, in their book *Stand Up, Speak-Out and Talk Back: the Key to Self-Assertive Behaviour*, argue that the voice is the most valuable resource for assertive communication. They stress the need to use inflection to emphasize precisely those parts of the message that require emphasis and volume to attract the attention of others. Get control of your voice, they suggest, and you will have harnessed a powerful tool for developing your assertiveness.

Research on facial expression (McFall *et al.* 1982) points to the importance of mouth, eyebrow and forehead cues. It has been found that an uncontrolled fidgety mouth, wrinkled forehead and constantly moving eyebrows undermines the potency of an assertive response. There is also evidence (Kolotkin *et al.* 1984) that, although smiles generally have little impact on the evaluation of the potency of an assertive response, they do detract from a woman's evaluation of the impact of female assertors. Eye contact is also important. Assertive people tend to engage in more eye contact than non-assertive people, but this contact, especially when the assertor is talking, tends to be intermittent. The fixed stare tends to be associated with aggressive behaviour.

Gestures have been found to enhance the impact of assertive responses. Extraneous or restrained movements tend to undermine impact, whereas smooth and steady arm movements while speaking and inconspicuous non-fidgety gestures while listening increase the impact of assertion messages. In terms of posture, a similar pattern can be detected. High impact is associated with purposive movement while speaking and little movement while listening. Effective assertors tend to face the other squarely and adopt an upright posture. Stooped or hunched posture and shrugging and squirming movements seriously undermine the impact of any attempt to be assertive.

Social interaction skills

Under this heading special attention is given to three aspects of asserting: escalation, persistence and the management of defensive reactions.

Escalation Rimms and Masters (1979) suggest that the initial assertion should be what they refer to as the minimal effective response. Common sense supports this view. The aim of the assertive response is to encourage the others to reassess the reasonableness of their behaviour and to consider modifying it so as not to infringe the rights of the assertor. The more intense the initial assertive response is, the less likely the recipient is to perceive it as an invitation to reassess his position and the more likely he will be to interpret it as an attack that threatens his own rights. The most effective sequence appears to be to start with an assertion that the assertor perceives to be the minimal effective response (MER). If this proves to be ineffective, the way forward is to gradually escalate the intensity of the assertion messages issued. Intensity can be increased by changing both the verbal and non-verbal content of the assertion. Rakos (1979) illustrates the principle of escalation with the example of a salesman selling a product that the assertor does not want.

Minimal effective response 'No thanks, I'm not interested.'
Escalation 1 'No, I told you I'm not interested. Good day.'

Escalation 2 'I am *not* interested' (louder volume and firmer delivery).
Escalation 3 'I told you I am not interested. If you do not leave immediately I will contact your supervisor and register a complaint against you.'

The impact of the escalation may be lost if the assertor allows herself to get sidetracked onto other issues. For example, an encyclopedia salesman might attempt to sell his product by suggesting that encyclopedias will help children with their school work, and he might try and divert the assertor by asking whether she is concerned about her childrens' education. To maximize the impact of her assertion the assertor needs to avoid being sidetracked and she needs to persist with her core message:

'I'm not interested in purchasing encyclopedias.'

Another form of escalation involves the assertor becoming increasingly explicit about the nature of the change she is seeking to achieve. There is a body of opinion that suggests that the initial assertion message should not specify the desired change. For example, Bolton's *When you . . . I feel . . . Because . . .* formula does not present the other with a solution but leaves him free to offer one that satisfies both his and the assertor's needs. Attempts to impose a solution might satisfy the needs of the assertor at the expense of the other. Assertion messages that do not back the other into a corner may be more effective, because they are less likely to provoke a defensive response and counterattack. However, there may well be occasions when the recipient either offers no solution or one that the assertor judges to be unsatisfactory. Therefore, she needs to escalate by becoming increasingly explicit about what she wants. For example, an initial assertive message might be:

'My steak is cold'

If this does not elicit a satisfactory response, it may be necessary to escalate it by being more explicit about the consequences this has for the assertor:

> 'My steak is cold and I cannot eat it.'

If this still does not work, the only way forward might be for the assertor to tell the other what she wants him to do about it.

> 'My steak is cold and I cannot eat it. Please bring me another.'

Persistence It is sometimes necessary to reassert several times before the recipient will respond as desired. One reason for this is that the recipient's defensiveness may get in the way of his hearing and understanding what the assertor has said. Too often assertors fail to get what they want because they give up too soon. They fail to persist.

Managing defensive reactions The assertor can minimize the effect of defensive reactions by reflectively listening to the other's response. Reflecting skills have been considered in detail elsewhere (Chapter 2). They are effective because, when the other person's defensive response is reflected back with respect, it gives him confidence that his views have been recognized and understood. Reflecting skills are especially important when the assertor is attempting to change an ongoing relationship. Simply repeating the core assertion message, even though effective when judged in terms of securing specific behaviour changes, may hurt the other and damage the relationship. Reflective responses can help minimize feelings of hurt, anger or disappointment.

An example might illustrate this point. A young product engineer may feel that, if she is to progress, she needs to break free of her mentor and demonstrate to herself and others that she is ready to assume more responsibility. However, she might value her relationship with the person who has unstintingly given of his time and taught her much of what she needed to know to make a success of her early career. Her initial assertion, therefore, might contain both elements of praise and explanation to make her expression of rights more acceptable.

> *Assertion* 'Jim, you've given me a first class apprenticeship, but I think the time has come for me to begin to stand on

my own two feet. I think it is time to end our regular daily meeting.'

However, what Jim hears might be that Chris is rejecting him. He might not be conscious of her need for independence or her feeling that it is time to prove herself to others. Therefore he might reply:

Response 'So you don't think an old hand like me has anything useful to offer any more. You think I'm past it.'

If Chris recognizes Jim's concerns about rejection she can respond to them by offering a reflective response before going on to reassert her need for independence.

Reflective response and re-assertion 'You feel I don't value your advice because I think you are out of touch with new developments. That is not the case. I want to break off the daily meetings because I feel it is time I took more responsibility for my own work.'

Bolton's view is that effective asserting hinges on a rhythm of asserting and reflecting.

'Shifting between these two different roles is the most demanding interpersonal skill we teach. After asserting most people forget to listen. When the other person makes her defensive response, they clobber her with another confrontative statement and a battle ensues . . . Other people get stuck in the listening role and neglect to assert.'

Blocks to assertiveness

It has been argued that sometimes people do not assert themselves because they are afraid that by so doing they will damage important relationships. The first part of this chapter has focused attention on a number of skills that can help individuals to stand up for their rights in ways that will limit the risk of such damage. Another reason why people do not stand up for their rights is because they believe that, if they assert themselves and attempt to influence others, their influence attempt will be unsuccessful. They feel powerless. It has already been noted in Chapter 6 that if people expect that a given behaviour will not lead to desired outcomes they are unlikely to engage in that behaviour. The first part of this chapter has also considered a number of ways in which the impact of assertive responses can be increased, thus increasing the probability that the desired outcome will be achieved.

The final part of this chapter switches attention to a different set of factors, which can influence the probability that an attempt to influence will be successful. It will consider influencing as a political process.

INFLUENCING AS A POLITICAL PROCESS

Most people do not work alone. They are members of complex organizations. Many people working in organizations are less influential than they might be because they do not fully understand the nature of organizational life. One widely held assumption people make is that organizations are well-integrated entities within which everybody works harmoniously together in order to achieve a set of shared goals. It is assumed that decisions are made logically and rationally, and that people select the alternatives that maximize the achievement of these shared goals. Little attention seems to be given to self-interest and to the competing personal goals of organizational members.

An alternative view of organizations is that they are political organisms within which individuals and groups attempt to influence each other in the pursuit of self-interest. Decisions and actions result from bargaining and negotiation between people who have different goals. Often they represent a compromise, they are the result of explicit or implicit working agreements that interested parties are prepared to live with, at least temporarily. When preferences conflict, it is the power and influence of the individuals and groups involved that determines the outcome of the decision process, not logic and rational argument.

The acquisition and exercise of power and influence can be viewed as a political process. Some people are too political, in the sense that they pursue their self-interest without paying any attention to the rights of others or to the survival and growth of the organization. Their aim is that they should win. Others are too passive and accepting, and fail to contribute as effectively as they might to the organization's survival and growth. These non-assertive people may react to events, but rarely, if ever, engage in proactive behaviour to bring about the kind of changes that they think are desirable. However, there is a middle ground. There are people who acquire power and exercise influence in order to bring about what they perceive to be a more desirable state of affairs, and they use their power and exercise influence in ways that do not unnecessarily deny others their rights.

The acquisition and exercise of power and ingluence

A person can increase her ability to influence others by paying attention to herself, to others, and the kind of relationship they have.

Developing the capacity to satisfy others' needs First, the individual needs to look to herself. She needs to ensure that she is professionally competent. People who are incompetent or possess obsolete skills may be seen by others as irrelevant because they have little to offer. Such people are unlikely to be able to influence others. To develop and maintain a power base, people need to invest time and effort in maintaining existing areas of professional competence and/or in developing new ones. In some organizations, resources are not readily available for these activities, whereas, in others, personal growth and management development are an important part of the organizational culture. However, irrespective of the organizational support available, the individual can take steps for herself to ensure that she remains professionally competent.

In order to be in a position to exercise influence, a person not only needs to be competent, she needs to be seen by others to be competent. Therefore, she needs to pay attention to her own and her department's reputation. Account is more likely to be taken of people who are known to be motivated, competent and capable of making an effective contribution.

Assessing others' dependence The influencer will also benefit from taking stock of the information and resources she provides (see Pettigrew 1972). She needs to know how important these are to others and to the achievement of their goals, and she needs to assess how readily they can obtain what she has to offer from alternative sources. This appraisal will provide some indication of how dependent others are on her. This is vital information because, as Emerson (1962) so clearly stated, power is inherent in any relationship in which one person is dependent upon another.

> it would appear that the power to control or influence the other resides in control over the things he values, which may range all the way from oil resources to ego support. In short, power resides implicitly in the other's dependence.

Increasing others' sense of dependence In order for a person to exercise power, other people have to be aware of their dependence upon that person. She can make others aware of their dependence in a number of ways. For example, she may threaten to withhold some vital product or service. However, such heavy-handed measures may frighten the dependent others and provoke them into initiating a thorough search for alternative sources which, if successful, could reduce their dependence on her, or into seeking out counter-dependencies, which they may use against her as bargaining points. Neither of these responses is unreasonable, indeed, as will be noted below; in certain circumstances they are to be encouraged. However, there is a danger that coercive, bullying-type attempts to raise awareness may promote the kind of win–lose climate that could easily deteriorate into one where everybody loses. The objective of any awareness-raising exercise must be to raise an awareness of dependency, but to do so within a climate that supports the ideal of mutual help and co-operation.

The person who, through her interaction with others, can convince them that they need the information or other resources that she controls can increase her influence over them. (Whether or not she actually controls or is the only available source of that resource is less relevant than the impression she manages to create. However, as you will see later in Chapter 8, on negotiating, some people are less comfortable than others with bluff and concealment. They feel bluff involves unfair manipulation.) The influencer's ability to 'define reality' for others and convince them that they are dependent on her, especially when this is a true reflection of reality, is probably one of the most effective ways of enhancing her power in practice.

Assessing own dependence In order to acquire and exercise power it is not sufficient for a person to ensure that she is competent, has a good reputation and that others are aware of the extent to which they are dependent upon her. She also needs to pay attention to her dependence upon others and she needs to identify who the significant others are, both inside and outside the organization, who can help or hinder the achievement of her goals.

Minimizing own dependence She might reduce her dependence on others by searching for alternative sources of required resources, thus minimizing her reliance on any one individual or unit. She may also challenge established working agreements where she suspects that others are exercising power over her because of dependency relationships that may have prevailed in the past, but which no longer reflect the current situation. As available resources, market conditions or any number of similar factors change, so also do the nature of dependency relationships and, therefore, the distribution of power.

Once the 'others' that a person is dependent on have been identified, she needs to build direct or indirect links with them. Such links can serve a number of purposes. For example, if one of the 'significant others' is responsible for allocating a scarce resource, it may be helpful if the person who is seeking to exercise more influence can communicate with the resource allocator and present the case why she should be the one to whom it should be allocated. Often, important projects are starved of resources simply because people are unable to communicate with important decision-makers. Another benefit from building links is that the influencer might identify information or resources that the others require and that she can provide, thus establishing a basis for negotiation and trade.

One of the intangible resources others can offer a person is support. 'Important others' may be able to influence individuals or groups who are inaccessible to the person wanting to exercise influence, or they may be able to champion her cause to a much wider audience than she could ever reach on her own. Sponsorship of this kind is typically a reciprocal relationship. The sponsor gives support but expects something, maybe loyalty, in return. By seeking and accepting sponsorship, people unavoidably become dependent on others and, therefore, vulnerable to their influence attempts.

Negotiating advantageous agreements Most working agreements within work organizations and other social systems are based on some degree of reciprocity or interdependence. The effective influencer is likely to be the kind of person who is aware of this and able to assess, realistically, what it is that she can offer to others and what it is that she needs from them. She will be able to set this alongside an equally realistic assessment of what they have to offer her and what they need from her. She is also the person who can use these assessments to negotiate the best working agreements and bargains for herself and her department.

The ineffective influencer tends to be the person who constantly enters into explicit or implicit agreements that are to her disadvantage. Not only does this ensure that she is exploited and unable to fulfil her own goals, it means that she is unlikely to be able to adequately fulfil her role in the organization and contribute to its success. For example, if the production director consistently exploits senior marketing managers and always forces her will on them without taking account of the long-term market implications, or if product engineering has weak leadership and is always ignored by production management, then this could have important consequences for the organization's survival and growth.

It is not necessary to erode the power of one organizational member to enhance that of another. Interactions within organizations do not occur within the fixed framework of a zero-sum

('I win, you lose') game. More political awareness and greater participation in the negotiation of a new organizational order and in the establishment of new working agreements up, down and across the hierarchy might best be viewed in the context of an increasing-sum game (win-win). Effective participation in the political process can lead to a better definition of organizational problems and to the generation and implementation of more successful solutions.

The effective manager is less likely to feel that the system gets in her way and frustrates her attempts to manage. She is more likely to have a clear idea of what she wants to achieve, to believe in her own ability to manage events and get things done, to be clear about how best to invest her time and energy and, possibly most important of all, to possess a well-developed set of assertion and political skills.

IMPROVING YOUR ABILITY TO INFLUENCE OTHERS

This chapter has looked at influencing from two perspectives. The first has to do with interpersonal style and face-to-face behaviour. Those behaviours that help a person express her views, especially when these are different or unpopular, request others to change their behaviour, or refuse unreasonable requests have been discussed, and some of the factors that inhibit assertive behaviour, such as the need to be liked and expectations about outcomes, have also been considered. The second perspective has to do with the acquisition and exercise of power. Assertive behaviour is much more likely to influence outcomes when the assertor is seen by others to be relatively powerful.

It was noted at the beginning of this chapter that some people experience difficulty influencing particular individuals or groups, whereas others are dissatisfied with their ability to influence in most situations.

Where the need is to improve your ability to influence in specific situations, one way of identifying important influencing skill deficiencies is to undertake a personal audit. Think about those situations in which you are *satisfied* with your ability to influence others and, using the checklists provided in Appendices 7.1 and 7.2, build a profile of your successful influencing style. Next, think about those situations in which you are *dissatisfied* with your ability to influence, repeat the procedure and build a profile of your unsuccessful style. Compare the two profiles and look for differences in your behaviour. Differences between the two profiles might point to changes that could help you achieve desired outcomes in those situations where you typically fail.

A weakness with this approach is that different situations might demand a different approach. In other words, an influencing style that works in some situations might not be effective in all situations. An alternative approach, therefore, is to compare your unsuccessful profile with the profile of somebody who, in the same situation, tends to be consistently more successful. This approach can also be used when you want to identify ways of improving your ability to influence in a range of different situations. Observe others who have this ability and compare their profiles with your own.

Often people are reluctant to assert themselves because they assume that they have a weak power base. Sometimes this may not be the case. They may be unaware of their potential ability to influence because they have never attempted to consciously assess how dependent they are on others and to compare this with the extent to which these others are dependent on them. Thinking about relationships in terms of relative dependencies can point to ways in which the balance of power might be changed in your favour, and can radically change expectations about the probable outcome of any attempt to assert your rights and influence others. Nonetheless, there are still people who are aware that they occupy potentially powerful positions yet who experience difficulty in influencing others. This is often because they do not assert themselves. Developing assertion skills involves diagnosing the most important areas for skill development, identifying new behaviours and practising them in low-risk situations.

Appendix 7.1

ASSERTION SKILLS CHECKLIST

Note the use of the following assertion skills when attempting to express unpopular or different opinions, request behaviour changes or refuse requests.

1. CONTENT SKILLS

Are assertion messages:

brief and direct	☐	or rambling and ambiguous	☐
respectful	☐	or blaming and judgemental	☐
empathic*	☐	or blunt	☐

* if assertion messages are empathic do they:

offer an explanation of need to assert	☐
offer a short apology	☐
recognize effect on other	☐
attempt to identify a compromise	☐
offer praise to other	☐

2. NON-VERBAL SKILLS

is voice	soft ☐☐☐ loud	
is inflection used to emphasize message?	Yes ☐	☐ No
is delivery firm?	Yes ☐	☐ No
is facial expression controlled?	Yes ☐	☐ No
eye contact	high ☐	☐ low
	intermittent ☐	☐ staring
is posture square and upright?	Yes ☐	☐ No

3. SOCIAL INTERACTION SKILLS

Escalation:

Is initial response a minimum effective response? Yes ☐ ☐ No

If the initial response is ineffective is the intensity of successive responses gradually increased? Yes ☐ ☐ No

Do the assertion messages become more explicit in terms of required outcome? Yes ☐ ☐ No

Focus:

Does the assertor avoid being side-tracked and stick to the core message? Yes ☐ ☐ No

Persistence:

How many times does s/he assert before giving up? ☐

Management of defensive reactions

Does the assertor listen to the other's reply? Yes ☐ ☐ No

Before re-asserting does the assertor reflect back the other's response? Yes ☐ ☐ No

Appendix 7.2

CHECKLIST FOR THE ACQUISITION AND EXERCISE OF POWER

1. DEVELOPING THE CAPACITY TO SATISFY OTHERS' NEEDS

Have you invested enough effort in maintaining relevant skills, keeping well informed, being professionally competent?	Yes ☐ ☐ No
Have you promoted your reputation?	Yes ☐ ☐ No

2. ASSESSING OTHERS' DEPENDENCE ON YOU

Have you taken stock of what others want from you?	Yes ☐ ☐ No
Have you attempted to identify alternative sources of supply and/or substitutes?	Yes ☐ ☐ No
How important to others is the resource you provide?	Yes ☐ ☐ No

3. INCREASING OTHERS' DEPENDENCE ON YOU

Have you raised others' awareness of their dependence on you?	Yes ☐ ☐ No
Did you do this in a way that minimized the threat to others?	Yes ☐ ☐ No
Have you attempted to persuade others that what you offer is necessary and only available from you?	Yes ☐ ☐ No

4. ASSESSING YOUR DEPENDENCE ON OTHERS

Have you taken stock of what you want from others?	Yes ☐ ☐ No
Have you built links with significant others?	Yes ☐ ☐ No

5. MINIMIZING OWN DEPENDENCE ON OTHERS

Have you sought alternative sources of supply and/or substitutes?	Yes ☐ ☐ No
Have you sought to develop interdependencies with significant others?	Yes ☐ ☐ No
Have you challenged or reassessed established relationships?	Yes ☐ ☐ No

References: Chapter 7

Alberti, R. and Emmons, M. 1975. *Stand Up, Speak-Out, Talk Back: the Key to Self-Assertive Behaviour,* New York: Pocket Books.

Bolton, R. 1986. *People Skills.* Sidney: Prentice-Hall of Australia.

Emerson, R. M. 1962. Power-dependence relations. *American Sociological Review* 27: 31–41.

Kolotkin, R., Wielkiewicz, R., Judd, B. *et al.* 1984. Behaviour components of assertion: comparison of univariate and multivariate assessment strategies. *Behav. Assess.* 6: 61–78.

McFall, M., Winett, R., Bordewick, M. *et al.* 1982. Non verbal components in the communication of assertiveness. *Behaviour Modification,* 6: 121–40.

Pettigrew, A. M. 1972. Information control as a power resource. *Sociology,* 6: 2, 187–204.

Pitcher, S. and Meikle, S. 1980. The topography of assertive behaviour in positive and negative situations. *Behaviour Therapy,* 11: 532–47.

Rakos, R. 1979. Content consideration in the distinction between assertive and aggressive behaviour. *Psychological Report* 44: 767–73.

Rakos, R. 1986. Asserting and confronting, in O. Hargie (ed.) *A Handbook of Communication Skills.* London: Croom Helm.

Rimms, D. and Masters, J. 1979. *Behaviour Therapy: Techniques and Empirical Findings,* 2nd edn. New York: Academic Press.

Romano, J. and Bellack, A. 1980. Social validation for a component model of assertive behaviour. *Journal of Consulting and Clinical Psychology*, 48: 478–90.

Rose, Y. and Tryon, W. 1979. Judgements of assertive behaviour as a function of speech loudness, latency, content, gestures, inflection and sex. *Behaviour Modification,* 3: 112–25.

Schroeder, H.E., Rakos, R. and Moe, J. 1983. The social perception of assertive behaviour as a function of response class and gender. *Behaviour Therapy* 14: 534-44.

Woolfolk, R. and Dever, S. 1979. Perceptions of assertion: an empirical analysis. *Behaviour Therapy* 10: 404-11.

CHAPTER EIGHT
Negotiating

We are all negotiators. Negotiation is a process of joint decision-making in which people with different preferred outcomes interact in order to resolve their differences. It can be an explicit process when, for example, we bargain with a supplier over the price of a component, seek to establish a new rate for a job with a group of workers, or argue for an increased budget with our boss. However, it can also be an implicit process through which the nature of our relationships with others is determined. We all have many demands on our time, so if a colleague calls for assistance we have to weigh the costs and benefits of helping out. Failure to help the colleague to achieve her desired outcome might provoke her to reappraise her priorities and offer us less assistance in the future when we seek help. Generous support, on the other hand, might cement an alliance that could be mutually beneficial. Much of the give-and-take of everyday life represents a process of negotiation. Some people are better negotiators than others and, consequently, are more successful in terms of achieving their desired outcomes.

Negotiation is not necessarily a win–lose process: that is, it need not involve one party seeking to improve its lot at the expense of the other. Often negotiation can be a win–win process, through which an agreement can be reached that helps both parties to achieve their preferred outcomes. This chapter aims to help you develop a better understanding of the process of negotiation and will consider collaborative as well as competitive strategies. It will also help you to identify the skills you need if you are to become a more successful negotiator.

The questionnaire presented in Figure 8.1 has been designed to help you assess your views about negotiating. Think about

1.	Is the aim to achieve:	a. ☐	the best result for all involved?
		b. ☐	the best deal for you/your department/company?
2.	Is it most helpful to know about the:	a. ☐	opposing negotiator's personal style?
		b. ☐	his/her company's policy towards customers/suppliers?
3.	Do personal feelings influence the outcome of a negotiation:	a. ☐	frequently?
		b. ☐	rarely?
4.	When you are selling is it best to ask:	a. ☐	a price much higher than you expect to get?
		b. ☐	a price reasonably close to the one you feel will eventually be agreed?
5.	If you were buying how would you feel if you made an offer a long way below the asking price:	a. ☐	comfortable?
		b. ☐	very uncomfortable?
6.	During a negotiation is it best to:	a. ☐	"stay firm" and refuse to make any concessions?
		b. ☐	try to open up the negotiation with an early concession?
7.	If you decide to make a concession is it best to:	a. ☐	offer very little and make only the smallest concession?
		b. ☐	make a generous concession to get things moving?
8.	Do you believe that making a large concession will:	a. ☐	weaken your position?
		b. ☐	encourage the other party to reciprocate?
9.	Do most people respond to threats by:	a. ☐	giving way and conceding?
		b. ☐	making counter threats?
10.	Which should you do most in a negotiation:	a. ☐	listen?
		b. ☐	talk?

Figure 8.1 Negotiation questionnaire

your answers as you read this chapter. It might be useful if you complete the questionnaire a second time when you have read the chapter, so that you can note any changes in your views.

A simplified model of negotiation: targets, limits and opening bids

When people begin to negotiate they normally have some idea about the level of benefit they hope to secure. This is their *target* outcome. They also have some idea about the level of benefit below which they will not go. This is their *limit*. A settlement can only be achieved when the limits which each party brings to the negotiation coincide or overlap. In the situation represented by Figure 8.2 a settlement is not possible.

The buyer seeking to purchase a component from a supplier refuses to pay more than £1.50 per unit. This is her limit, maybe because her company cannot afford to pay more or because she is aware of an alternative supply at £1.50. The supplier refuses to sell at anything less than £2.50, possibly because he can get a better price elsewhere or because to drop his price further would result in a loss.

A settlement is possible in the situation represented by Figure 8.3 because the buyer is prepared to pay up to £3 a unit and the supplier, if pushed, will sell for as little as £1.50. The relative skill of the two negotiators will determine what the settlement price will be. If the supplier (seller) is the more skilled negotiator,

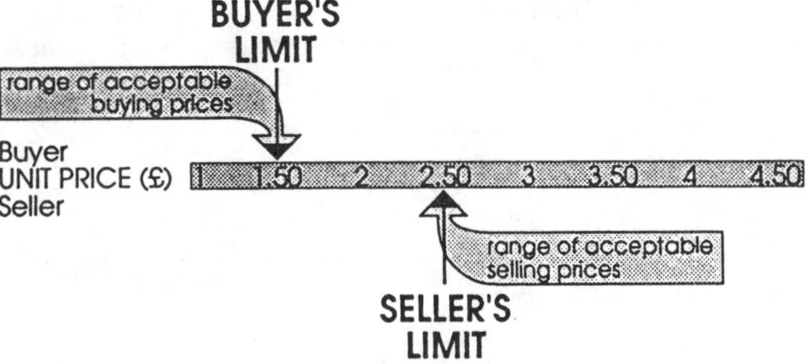

Figure 8.2 Settlement not possible

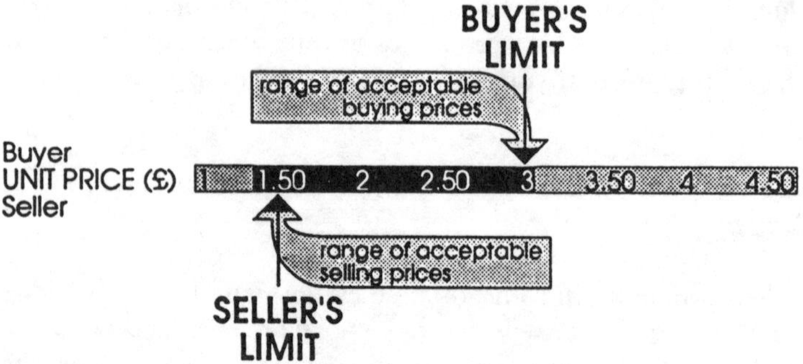

Figure 8.3 Overlapping limits offer possibility for settlement

the price is likely to be towards the £3 limit of the buyer, or vice versa.

Skilled negotiators attempt to discover their opponents' limit. To push an opponent beyond his limit will lead to a breakdown in the negotiation. The competitive negotiator seeks to secure an agreement as close to her opponent's limit as possible, thus maximizing her own benefit. To achieve this outcome, skilled negotiators need to know how to research their opponent's case before coming to the negotiating table and, during the negotiation, must be skilled at probing and listening, so that all available information is gathered and can be used to maximum advantage.

Opening bids are important. Unskilled negotiators can weaken their position considerably by making inappropriate opening bids. If the buyer's opening offer is £2 (that is, 50p above the seller's limit of £1.50, see Figure 8.4), it will be almost impossible for the buyer to revise her offer downward towards

Figure 8.4 Buyer's opening bid

£1.50, even though she may learn, later, that the supplier is selling to a competitor at this lower price. This emphasizes the importance of researching your opponent's case before making your opening bid.

The normal convention in negotiations is that the opening bid does not represent the final position and that some concessions will be made. However, each party attempts to convince the other that their opening bid is in fact very close to their limit and that they have little or no room to make concessions. The supplier, in Figure 8.5, by opening with an offer to sell at £4, attempts to convince the buyer that her offer to purchase at £2 per unit is totally unrealistic. If the buyer is convinced that it will be impossible to conclude an agreement at £2, she is likely to revise her offer and move towards her limit of £3 in search of a settlement.

Skilled negotiators are able to employ tactics that help them to convince their opponents that they must concede if an agreement is to be reached, and are able to counter similar tactics when these are employed against them. These tactics will be explained in some detail later in this chapter.

Given negotiating conventions, and knowing that some concessions will probably have to be made, most skilled negotiators make opening bids beyond their target. If the buyer's opening bid of £2 also represented her target (see Figure 8.6) there would be a strong likelihood that the final settlement would yield less than her target benefit (that is, she will probably end up paying more than £2).

If the supplier's target price is £2.50, by opening with a bid of £4 he leaves himself room to concede and still achieve his target

Figure 8.5 Seller's opening bid

Figure 8.6 Bidding at or beyond target outcome

outcome or better. The factors that need to be taken into account when deciding on an opening bid will be considered below.

Stages in the negotiation process

There is more to negotiating than bidding and counter-bidding. Some of the important stages in the negotiation process which will be explored in this chapter are:

(a) preperation
(b) climate setting
(c) choice of strategy
(d) definition of opening bids
(e) bargaining
(f) settling

PREPARATION

Anticipate the need to negotiate. Preparations take time and often a negotiator's case is weakened because she does not have the time to prepare adequately. The area manager of a petrol company that is looking for a new site for a filling station knows that at some point she will have to negotiate with the owners of land. Two possible sites might be identified. At this stage an analysis of traffic-flows, the proximity of other filling stations and similar considerations could facilitate the calculation of profit, which in turn could help determine the *maximum* rental or purchase price that would be commercially viable for each site (that is, the petrol company's 'limit' for each site). The acquisition of knowledge about alternative uses for these sites and the profits these activities might generate could also provide some idea about the kind of bids competitors for these sites might make.

This knowledge can provide vital clues about the site owner's bargaining power and 'limit' (determined by the maximum alternative bid). Usually this kind of information cannot be acquired overnight, so it pays to think ahead.

It is important, at the outset of a negotiation, to have a clear idea about what is wanted and, therefore, what needs to be negotiated. Rarely are negotiations concerned with only one variable such as price. Someone buying a car may also need to agree colour, delivery charges, road fund licence, delivery date, payment terms, etc.

It is not unusual for someone to feel she has negotiated a better deal on price from another garage, only to find that the car is delivered with only a six months' road fund licence, no radio/cassette player, interior mats, mud flaps, etc., all of which she thought were part of the standard product.

Buying and selling a car offers a relatively simple example. Buying and selling a business presents a more complex situation, especially if the business is a 'know-how' business such as public relations, because what the buyer is wanting to acquire is the know-how and contacts of key staff. This kind of deal often involves some provision that locks in key people. If the aim is to retain the services of the previous clients, the basis for an agreement might involve what is often referred to as an 'earn out'. The price that is offered for the company is not a straight price but a target figure, say £20 million, which will be paid if the company that is being acquired meets certain profit objectives over a period, say five years. The sellers are required to stay on and manage the company over this period for the new owners. If the newly acquired company is less profitable, the final price paid will be reduced. In this way, the sellers are motivated to manage the company as profitably as possible. Negotiators in this kind of situation might be concerned about the final price, the profit levels that will have to be achieved to obtain their price, the period of the 'earn out', how much will be paid up front and how much each year, the interim profit levels that will trigger staged payments, the penalties for failing to achieve target profits, etc. It might also be important to negotiate how much freedom to manage the previous owners of the acquired company will have. 'Interference' from the new owners might make it more difficult to achieve target profit levels. After the takeover, it could be very difficult to keep the new owners at arm's length, unless this has been negotiated in advance. The more complex the deal, the more thought has to be given to the variables that need to be negotiated.

Preparation not only involves thinking through *what* it is that the negotiator wants to achieve but also *how* she is going to achieve it. Part of this preparatory analysis must involve some consideration of what the opponent wants and what concessions he would value.

However, part of the preparation should also involve some research into how the opposition is likely to go about getting what he wants. Often managers encounter the same opponents in successive negotiations: for example, when negotiating with union officials. In other cases it might be possible to talk with other negotiators who have previously encountered the opponent. Predictions about how the opposition is likely to behave can help the negotiator plan an effective strategy. Trying to collaborate with an opponent the negotiator cannot trust and who, she knows from past experience, will attempt to wring every last drop of benefit from her is unlikely to yield the kind of outcome she desires. In these circumstances, she might have no alternative but to be fiercely competitive.

CLIMATE SETTING

People's behaviour can be interpreted in many different ways. An enquiry from someone the negotiator knows and trusts might be interpreted very differently than one from a stranger or someone she does not trust.

When strangers meet, first impressions can be very important. If one party creates the impression that they are unsure of their ground, believe that they themselves have a weak case, that it is important for them to reach an agreement or that they are anxious to settle quickly, they will encourage the other party to believe that they have the stronger case. The other party might then make high demands, stand firm and push the first party into making substantial concessions.

If, on the other hand, the first party appears confident and launches into an attack immediately, the other party may be pushed into a defensive position or provoked into making a counterattack. However, this kind of win–lose climate is not inevitable. If the negotiators are able to present themselves as people who are genuinely seeking a mutually beneficial agreement, then the possibility of a collaborative negotiation exists.

The social encounter model presented in Chapter 4 (p. 63) also applies in the context of a negotiation. The nature of their encounter influences how the negotiators interpret each other's behaviour and how they will respond.

When negotiating, especially with strangers, it is easy to get drawn into a competitive interaction where one party seeks to maximize his or her benefit at the expense of the other. Careful management of the initial encounter might increase the possibility of discovering a common purpose and establishing the trust that is necessary for collaborative negotiation. Responding immediately to the other party's competitive thrusts will, almost inevitably, eliminate this possibility and encourage, at least initially, a competitive climate for negotiations. Scott (1981) emphasizes the importance of not being drawn in this way if the negotiators would prefer to test the possibility of a collaborative relationship. He advocates the introduction of neutral topics, which can provide the space necessary for the parties to assess each other's aims and intentions.

A brief example might illustrate this point. If the supplier opens with:

> 'Welcome, how are you?'

and receives a reply from a potential customer such as:

> 'Fine thanks, how are you? I hear things are a bit difficult for your company at the moment.'

the supplier has to decide whether this reply represents a real concern for her wellbeing or is an attempt to gain a bargaining advantage by demonstrating that the customer suspects the supplier is desperate for work. Instead of replying with an equally competitive statement designed to counter this view and undermine the buyer's position, such as '*Difficult is an understatement, we have so much work in the pipeline that we are having to take a hard look at the kind of orders we can accept*', the supplier might decide to test the customer's intention by responding:

> 'Maybe we can talk about that later. Did you have a good journey?'

The customer can then choose to respond competitively and follow up his initial comment with '*Oh, fine. Tell me, what kind of order would you need from me to avoid the need to lay people off?*' or provide evidence that the opening statement was a genuine enquiry about the supplier's wellbeing by responding to her cue to talk about 'difficulties' later and replying:

> 'Fine, apart from the road works near Woking. At one point I thought I would be late.'

Scott (1981) suggests that talking about procedures can offer a relevant but neutral topic that provides a useful context for testing and moulding the climate. Under this broad heading of procedure Scott includes:

(a) *purpose*: for example, is the negotiation to be concerned with the clarification of evidence, achievement of an agreement in principle, an agreement in specific detail, a review of progress, etc.?
(b) *agenda* for the meeting: topics, order, etc.
(c) the *time* available.
(d) *introductions* of the people involved in the negotiation.

As the negotiation begins to unfold each negotiator will provide the other with clues that indicate their desired outcome and preferred approach, and also with information about their negotiating skills and experience. Careful listening and gentle probing in the early stages of the negotiation will help each negotiator judge whether there is any common ground and shared goals. An initial assessment of the other's attitude might also be possible, thus providing some basis for deciding what would be the most appropriate negotiating strategy to adopt.

CHOICE OF STRATEGY

Negotiators decide what to do on the basis of their expectations about how the others will respond. The outcome of a negotiation depends upon how accurately the negotiators diagnose the situation that confronts them and the skill with which they choose and enact appropriate moves. This has much to do with the choice of negotiating strategy.

Morley (1984) suggests that one way to view negotiation is as a struggle. This approach emphasizes concealment and competitive tactics. An alternative view of negotiation is as collaboration, a process in which parties make sacrifices rather than demand concessions in the pursuit of some overriding goal. The basis of these two approaches is reflected elsewhere. Strauss (1978) divides negotiations into those that are competitive and those that are collaborative. Scott (1988) presents two contrasting styles, which he labels competitive and constructive. Pruitt (1981) discusses competitive and co-ordinative negotiating tactics and the concept of integrative bargaining. He defines integrative bargaining as the search for mutually beneficial agreements. These might involve working towards novel outcomes that could produce considerably greater benefits for both parties than a straight compromise.

Negotiators with a high need to win are likely to favour competitive strategies, especially if they feel that they are in a strong bargaining position. Experimental evidence also suggests that in those situations where negotiators feel that they have to satisfy tough constituents (for example, members of their union or work group), they will adopt a more competitive approach. Competitive strategies are also likely to be adopted where one or both parties do not trust the other's intentions, where they feel that their opponent will exploit them and where they expect the other to only make concessions when forced.

Skilled negotiators are more likely to favour collaborative strategies when two basic conditions are satisfied. The first concerns trust. It would be unwise to adopt a collaborative strategy unless some measure of trust exists between the parties. This is because collaborative negotiation tends to involve the disclosure of information about goals, priorities and limits that a competitive opponent could use to his or her advantage. Collaborative negotiation also tends to involve offering concessions in the hope that they will be reciprocated. This could weaken a negotiator's position by projecting a 'soft' image, both to other negotiators and to constituents.

The second condition for the effective use of a collaborative strategy involves the nature of the benefit associated with possible outcomes. When the reward structure encourages the belief that a mutually beneficial exchange and outcome is possible, a collaborative approach to negotiation is likely to be more attractive. This could be the case when, for example, each party controls resources that would cost little to give up but would have high value for the other, or when all parties believe that a problem-solving approach to negotiating their difference might lead to a more beneficial solution than could be achieved through a win–lose competitive approach.

OPENING BIDS

Whatever strategy is adopted, some consideration needs to be given to opening bids. In competitive negotiations, however, bidding and bargaining tend to assume greater importance than in collaborative negotiations.

In collaborative negotiations the most important stage tends to be climate-setting, during which common ground and key differences are identified and, at least to some extent, explored, thus laying the foundations for a constructive discussion. In collaborative negotiations it is important to open with a realistically high bid but to avoid concealment and bluff. If discovered, concealment and bluff will undermine the collaborative climate and push the negotiation towards being more competitive.

Opening bids tend to be influenced by various factors. These include the negotiator's desire to protect her limit from detection, to provide room to trade concessions and to challenge the opponent's expectation regarding the likely outcome of the negotiation.

The aim of challenging expectations is to persuade the other party that the target outcome they hope to achieve is one that yields an unrealistically high level of benefit. In the example presented earlier in this chapter (and reproduced in Figure 8.7), the buyer's opening bid of £2 was above the seller's limit of £1.50 and only 20 per cent (50p) below the seller's target of £2.50. The chances are that this bid provided less of a challenge to the seller's expectation than the seller's counter bid to supply at £4, a bid that was 100 per cent greater than the buyer's target price of £2. While the supplier's opening bid of £4 might have shocked the buyer into revising upwards the target price she would have to pay, there is also the danger that it might have been so high (it was above the buyer's limit of £3) that the buyer would see little hope of reaching an acceptable settlement and would therefore break off negotiations.

A guiding principle, when constructing opening bids, is to remember that negotiators who ask for little usually reach an agreement, but one which yields little benefit for themselves. Negotiators who demand too much may fail to reach any agreement at all. Those who make *realistically* high demands are the ones who have the best chance of obtaining the greatest benefit.

The normal relationship between initial demand and outcome is illustrated in Figure 8.8. It is worth remembering that if a negotiator's initial demand is too low the other party may believe it is too good to be true and ask 'what's wrong with it?' If a prospective buyer expected to pay £25,000 for a canal barge and she is offered one for £700, she is likely to worry

Figure 8.7 Using bids to challenge target outcomes

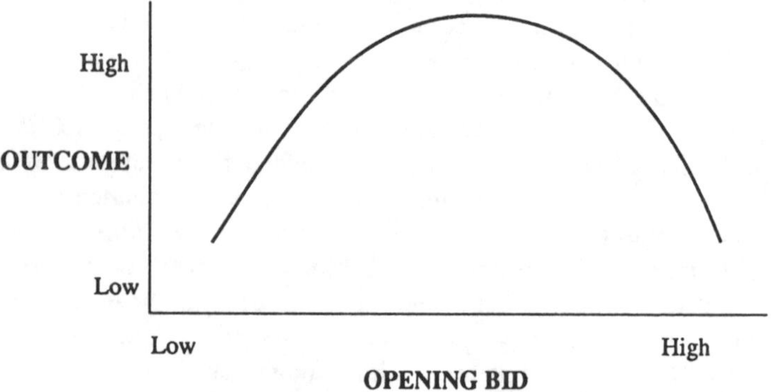

Figure 8.8 The relationship between opening bid and outcome

about whether the hull is rotten or whether something else is wrong with it. She might also have a similar reaction if, after making an initial high demand, say £29,000, the seller offered large concessions in rapid succession.

People, especially where they expect to engage in a competitive negotiation, are more likely to value an outcome if they have had to work hard for it.

BARGAINING: COMPETITIVE TACTICS

While competitive negotiating tactics have been labelled and presented in many different ways (see Karrass 1974, Scott 1981, 1988), the work of Pruitt (1981) has made the greatest contribution to the framework used here to discuss some of the most important competitive tactics.

1 Demonstrating a commitment to hold firm

One aim of many competitive tactics is for the negotiator to convince the other party that she is determined to hold firm and will not give ground. If agreement is to be reached it is the other party who will have to concede most. This can be achieved in a number of ways:

(a) Indicating that 'the cupboard is bare', that there is no room to concede The essence of this move is to convince the other

party that the current offer is very near the negotiator's limit, and that there is no room for manoeuvre. A travel agent might attempt to convince a customer that, if he insists on using a certain credit card to pay for his air ticket, the commission will be so high that it would be impossible for her to consider a discount. She might even quote commission rates and margins to reinforce her point.

(b) Demonstrating a limited mandate to negotiate A variation on the above tactics is to convince the other party that the mandate the negotiator has been given allows little or no room to negotiate certain variables. For example, the negotiator might claim that she is bound by company policy, which is only to offer goods for sale at list price. The mandate tactic can also be used to make it appear that it is not the negotiator who is being difficult but some third party, thus helping her to appear firm without creating personal resentment.

(c) Conceding slowly Small concessions, offered slowly, are more likely to reinforce a firm image than large concessions or a series of small concessions, offered in rapid succession.

(d) Resisting the other party's persuasive arguments or threats An example of this tactic is to counter the opponent's attempt to impose time pressure by asking him if he can suggest a good hotel, thereby demonstrating that time is may be less important to you than to him.

2 Imposing time pressure

The objective of tactics listed under this heading is to persuade the other party to concede by increasing the perceived cost or risk of continued negotiation.

(a) Imposing deadlines to dramatize the likelihood of breakdown There are various ways in which a negotiator can attempt to convince the other party that the negotiation could break down without agreement unless he or she is prepared to concede. For example, a diplomat might declare that she has to catch the 4 o'clock flight because she has been recalled to London, or a buyer might state that the deal must be concluded before the

end of the financial year, otherwise the available funds will be lost.

(b) Making preparation to leave Collecting papers together and packing a briefcase, standing up and looking around for a coat are all strong signals that, unless some concessions are forthcoming, there is little point in continuing the negotiations.

(c) Making it costly to continue negotiating Examples of this tactic are legion. A company trying to agree a claim for damages or divorced parents fighting over the custody of a child might attempt to increase the cost of continuing negotiating for the other party by initiating expensive legal proceedings. This kind of tactic is more effective when one party can more easily afford these extra costs than the other.

(d) **Dragging out the negotiation** Pruitt (1981) suggests that this tactic is often embodied in the familiar routine of consulting with higher ups. He offers the example of a car salesman who keeps a customer waiting 20 minute while he checks with his boss to see if he can offer a marginally better price. Customers who value their time may capitulate after such a delay.

Dragging out negotiations can be a very effective technique when the cost of lost time is high: for example, when it is important to reach agreement about the delivery of perishable vegetables or the completion of work for an important deadline.

3 Reducing the other's resistance to making concessions

This involves (1) attempting to shift the other's limit in the direction favoured by the negotiator; (2) attempting to lower the other's expectations (target) regarding the overall level of benefit that can be achieved from an agreement; and (3) attempting to convince the other party that he has underestimated the value of the concessions he has been offered and overestimated the value of the concession he might be willing to make. A number of tactics can be used to achieve these objectives:

(a) Opening bids The way in which opening bids can be used to influence aspirations has already been illustrated above (see Figure 8.7). Other tactics include:

(b) Undermining the other party's case This can be done by questioning the assumptions on which the opponent's case is based. For example, when negotiating the number of established posts in a hospital, a negotiator might question the assumption that certain duties can only be performed by professionally qualified staff. A negotiator might also gain some advantage by questioning the facts of an argument and questioning the conclusions drawn from the facts. If the other party can be convinced that his case is weak there is a greater likelihood of his making concessions.

To use this tactic effectively the negotiator needs to be skilled at asking questions and listening. The more she can persuade the other party to talk the more information he is likely to give away, thus revealing inconsistencies and omissions and disclosing weaknesses that further undermine his case.

(c) Persuasive argument The most persuasive arguments are those that convince the other party that the way forward proposed by the negotiator has advantages for him. Advocacy of this kind is most effective when the negotiator is able to empathize with his opponent's point of view, understand his needs, even some of those that may not be directly related to the issue being negotiated, and frame arguments that go as far as possible towards satisfying them. For example, an employer wanting to acquire tighter control over the hours worked by her employees might persuade the union to consider the introduction of flexi-time, which could have many advantages for union members, in the full knowledge that flexi-time would involve workers having to clock on and clock off.

(d) Feints Feints represent a special case of persuasive argument. The basis of this tactic is to focus attention on an unimportant issue, making the other party believe that it is critical, and then concede on this issue in order to divert attention away from what is really a much more important issue for you. In exchange for giving away something that

the other party believes is very important to you, he might be persuaded to reciprocate with a concession on what he thinks (possibly incorrectly) is a less valuable issue. The other party is happy because he has been persuaded that he has received a large concession from you in exchange for something worth very little. You are happy because you have not been pressed to concede an important variable and may have received a valuable reciprocal concession.

(e) Threats Threats involve the declared intent of imposing some sanction if the other party refuses to concede: for example, the threat to strike unless a new wage rate is agreed, or the threat to go elsewhere for a product or service and hinting that an alternative might be found that is better, cheaper or more reliable.

Threats are likely to be most effective when the party issuing the threat is seen to have the power to impose it. However, he must also be seen to have the will to carry it out. Consequently, whether previous threats were implemented will influence how seriously current threats are regarded. The perceived cost of fulfilling a threat will also have some impact. In those circumstances where the cost of carrying out a threat is seen to be greater than the benefit it will produce the less likely it will be that the threat will be believed. In circumstances where all parties are aware that it will cost very little to follow through and implement a threatened sanction, the perceived probability of the threat being carried out will be high.

(f) Promises Promises offer a reward for conceding. A promise can be distinguished from a straight concession by its conditionality. 'If you do this *then* I will do that'. It is a reciprocal concession. Nothing is given away until the other party concedes. Whether promises will be believed will be influenced by the same kind of considerations that determine the effectiveness of threats.

4 Improving the relationship with the other party or improving the other's mood

There is ample evidence that people tend to help those people they like, identify with or depend on. Knowing this, a skilful negotiator may attempt to make others like her, with the objective of increasing the likelihood that they will make concessions to help her. Tactics which attempt to achieve this end include:

(a) Being warm and friendly, agreeing with the other party, whenever possible, and appearing to value his opinion. These are all behaviours that will encourage the other party to develop a positive attitude toward the negotiator.

(b) Doing favours for the other party is likely to generate a feeling of indebtedness and dependence as well as to encourage the other party to like the provider of favours. Being told by a negotiator that it took her hours to convince her boss that he should consider a contractor's tender, even though it was submitted one hour after the deadline, makes it more difficult for the contractor to squeeze her too hard and increases the likelihood that the contractor will be persuaded to relax his demands a little.

(c) Behaving in accordance with the other's values The other party is more likely to identify with someone who shares his values than with someone who offends them. For example, a company negotiating an agreement in some Islamic countries may find that male negotiators are better received than female negotiators.

(d) Choosing a pleasant setting for the negotiations Helpfulness can be induced by being in a good mood. Many factors can affect mood. One is the setting for the negotiation. A negotiator who is visiting a client might decide that the relaxed atmosphere of a restaurant might be more conducive to a productive negotiation than meeting in the client's office where he will be subject to interruptions, competing demands for his attention and the many immediate irritations that may be a feature of his working environment.

(e) Temporarily substituting a 'more reasonable' negotiator This is a variation of the good guy/bad guy tactic. The contrast between the two negotiators might encourage the other party to enjoy a sense of relief during the bad guy's absence. His mood

might be improved and he might feel that it would be productive to make progress in the negotiation, to a conclusion if possible, before the bad guy returns. He might be less fearful of being exploited by the good guy, he might even feel that it would be useful in the long run if the 'other side' could be persuaded that the good guy was the better negotiator. Therefore, he could feel that a concession on his part might not be too damaging and would help to get the negotiation moving.

Creating opportunities to take time out and think

It is difficult to anticipate every move in a negotiation. Sometimes an unexpected opportunity presents itself or an opponent makes a move that puts the negotiator under pressure. At times like these it can be useful for the negotiator to create the space to think through what to do next. This can be done in a number of ways. The most obvious is to ask for a recess in order to 'take stock' or consult with constituents. However, the negotiator may wish to take time out without making this obvious to her opponent. A more covert approach is to ask an irrelevant question. While the other party answers, the negotiator can do her thinking. A similar technique is to offer a summary, but to deliberately mis-state the other party's position. He will demand the opportunity to clarify where he stands, again creating a breathing space.

Resistance and retaliation

In some cases competitive tactics appear to produce the desired effect whereas in others they provoke retaliation. Pruitt (1981) suggests that the reaction of the other party to the use of competitive tactics is influenced by the 'heaviness' of the bargainer's efforts to influence. Heaviness, in this context, refers to the extent to which negotiators put pressure on the other to the point of creating a feeling of resentment. Making 'if–then' promises or attempting to influence the other by improving the relationship normally does not produce a feeling of resentment. Making threats and imposing time pressures, on the other hand, are examples of tactics that are more likely to generate such feelings. When a party regards the other's behaviour as heavy-handed, the probability that he will offer resistance is increased. This resistance is most likely to develop into active retaliation when the pressured party judges her bargaining power to be equal to or greater than the other's. Retaliation is even more likely when a negotiator is aware of being observed by his constituents. There is also evidence that where the resentment is very strongly felt some people will be prepared to retaliate even when they believe that their chances of winning are small or non-existent. They would prefer to go down fighting rather than let the other win. In these circumstances the win–lose competitive relationship deteriorates into one that can best be described as lose–lose.

BARGAINING: COLLABORATIVE TACTICS

Collaborative negotiation involves the search for a mutually beneficial agreement. It involves more openness and a greater willingness to offer concessions than competitive negotiation. Consequently, it involves higher risks. The tactics a negotiator might choose to employ will be determined by the extent to which she feels she can trust the other party. Pruitt (1981) has identified some high and low risk negotiating behaviours.

High risk collaborative tactics

The negotiator may offer a large concession to the other party in the hope that this will be reciprocated. This kind of move is high risk because, if it is not reciprocated, the negotiator will have seriously weakened her position.

Lower risk tactics

Where a negotiator wishes to collaborate but is unsure whether she can trust the other, she might favour the kind of move that is reversible, disavowable and covert. These moves minimize the risk of image loss (appearing 'soft'), position loss (offering concessions that cannot be taken back) and, to a lesser extent, information loss (providing information that a competitor might use to his advantage). Some examples are:

(a) Signals and hints Signals can be used to suggest a willingness to make a concession or reciprocate if the other concedes. Early signals tend to be more ambiguous so that they can be more easily disavowed, thus enabling the signaller to avoid image loss if the other party does not reciprocate. An amorous young man

might smile at a female colleague. If she returns his smile he might seek an opportunity to get very close to her. If she does not move away he might initiate some physical contact, he may touch her hand. If she delays slightly before withdrawing it, he might feel reasonably confident in risking a more direct approach and invite her out for the evening. The initial use of ambiguous sign language, followed by more noticeable signals, enables him to minimize the risk of being rejected. If the initial smile had not been reciprocated or if she had physically distanced herself as soon as he sat close to her, he could have maintained the earlier working relationship and denied any suggestion that he was hoping for anything more.

When negotiating a pay deal, the parties involved might use gestures or phrases to hint that a concession may be possible if the other party would also be willing to move. This kind of tactic can be particularly useful partway through a negotiation, to test whether there is any possibility of moving from what, so far, might have been a competitive confrontation towards a more collaborative interaction. For one party to directly introduce this possibility could be very risky. The opportunities offered by indirect communication minimize such risks.

(b) Messages transmitted through intermediaries can be used in the same way. A colleague might suggest to a manager that the person she had been negotiating with would be willing to agree the transfer of staff she wanted if he could feel confident that she would not block his application for an increased computing budget. If she felt unable to offer this assurance, the negotiation could continue as if no concession had been offered. On the other hand, if she were to inform the intermediary that she would agree not to oppose the other manager's application, he might feel confident enough to directly propose the compromise next time they met.

(c) Informal problem-solving sessions These can take place over lunch, on the golf course, in the lift or on the telephone. Because they are discussions that occur outside the framework of the formal negotiation they provide the opportunity to informally explore possible moves. Such discussions tend to be very tentative and liberally peppered with 'what if' type statements.

Often they are secret, away from the eyes of constituents and even fellow negotiators. This approach has been used very effectively on many occasions to find a way out of a seemingly deadlocked situation. Because such discussions take place outside the formal negotiations, if they fail to produce an agreement the negotiators are able to return to the bargaining table without prejudice and continue from where they left off.

(d) Small concessions, followed by larger ones if reciprocated If the initial concession is not reciprocated, relatively little will have been lost. If, on the other hand, it produces movement, it might lead to further concessions and eventual agreement.

The other party's response to concessions

As mentioned earlier, the normal convention is that the opening bid does not represent the final position. It is anticipated that agreement will be reached, irrespective of whether the climate of negotiation is competitive or collaborative, after a process of trading concessions.

Concessions are most likely to be reciprocated when the negotiator offering the concession has a 'firm' image. A firm image is promoted by resisting the other party's threats and creating the impression that movement will not be achieved easily.

When the negotiator has a 'soft' image, concessions are more likely to be interpreted as a sign of weakness. Instead of reciprocating, the other party may be encouraged to stand firm and press for even more concessions. Thus, where one party is seen to be relatively soft (that is, to have a weaker bargaining position), there is a greater chance that the negotiation will become competitive. However, if as a result of a competitive phase of negotiations both parties come to realize that the other is unlikely to give way, there is the chance that the negotiators might begin to adopt a more collaborative approach in the hope of finding agreement.

SETTLING

The final stage of the negotiating process involves recognizing when the other party is ready to settle and making or accepting a proposal that will form the basis of an agreement. It is important to make sure that the agreement is defined in sufficient detail to ensure that it will be implemented, as intended, by both parties. In some cases a verbal summary will suffice, but often ratification in writing, and sometimes in legal detail, may be required.

IMPROVING YOUR ABILITY TO NEGOTIATE EFFECTIVELY

A useful start point is to train yourself to observe and recognize what is happening during a negotiation. The negotiation tactics observation record shown in Figure 8.9 can provide a useful framework for recording your observations. If you have the opportunity to observe other parties negotiating, use the record sheet to keep track of what is going on. Maybe you could accompany a relative or friend when they go out to purchase a new car. Alternatively, you might be present during a negotiation at work. Try and identify some situations where you can sit back and observe what is going on. Accurate observation is more difficult when you are actively involved in the negotiations, so start by observing others.

When you have begun to develop some skill in keeping track of what is going on and identifying the tactics that people employ, you might decide to switch the focus of your observation onto yourself. Immediately after a negotiating session, think through what happened. After a while you will be able to build up a profile of your normal negotiating style. Consider whether you favour certain tactics and ignore others. Try and identify your typical approach. Are you inclined towards being competitive or collaborative?

Once you have built up a picture of how you behave typically you might consider different ways of behaving that could help you to achieve a more satisfactory agreement. At this stage begin to plan the 'how' of a negotiation. Think through the strategy and tactics. Try and anticipate how the other party might behave, what tactics they could employ, how they will react to your moves.

The 'what' of a negotiation also requires careful planning. Be clear about your target outcome. Ensure that you have taken account of the main variables that this will involve (product specification, price, delivery, payment terms, etc.). Think about your ultimate fall-back position. What is the limit you must not go beyond. Seek out clues that will help you identify what your opponent's target and limit are likely to be. Even though you will only be able to make a subjective assessment of what the other party's target, limit and key variables are, this assessment will provide a useful basis for planning your own strategies. Decide on the most appropriate opening bid.

The negotiation preparation sheet presented in Figure 8.10 provides a useful *aide mémoire* for recording key planning information. Assess the importance of each variable for all the parties involved in the negotiation. It can be less costly if you offer concessions on your low priority variables and more beneficial if you can persuade the other party to concede on the variables that are most important to you.

Personality factors

Do not underestimate the importance of personality factors. Some people have a strong need to win. They may enjoy the cut-and-thrust of competitive bargaining and have few scruples regarding concealment and bluff. Others may have an equally strong need to be liked, and a well-developed sense of 'what's right' and 'fair play'. Such people may feel uncomfortable doing or saying anything that might upset another. They may, for example, be reluctant to ask a high price or to make an offer that is considerably below what they believe the other expects to receive. There are even some people who would only feel comfortable if they were to open a negotiation by asking for their target outcome, leaving themselves with absolutely no room to trade concessions and achieve their target.

It can be helpful to know as much as possible about your opponents. What kind of assumptions do they make about negotiating? Do they see it exclusively in terms of a win–lose competition or are they prepared to consider the possibility of a win–win collaborative activity? At a different level, are they likely to ask probing questions? Can they be easily put off? How persistent are they? Researching your opponent in this way can be extremely useful when deciding which negotiating tactics to employ.

By the same token, know your own strengths and weaknesses. Are you easily put off? If your opponent fails to answer a probing

1. Did you observe any of the following competitive behaviours?

APPEARING FIRM

No. of times used

a. demonstrating impossibility of concessions (cupboard is bare) a. ☐

b. demonstrating limited mandate to concede b. ☐

c. offering only very small and infrequent concessions c. ☐

d. resisting the other's threats d. ☐

IMPOSING TIME PRESSURE

a. imposing deadlines to dramatise the likelihood of breakdown a. ☐

b. making preparations to leave b. ☐

c. making it costly to continue negotiating c. ☐

d. dragging out the negotiation d. ☐

REDUCING THE OTHER'S RESISTANCE TO MAKING CONCESSIONS

a. high opening demands a. ☐

b. undermining the other's case b. ☐

c. persuasive argument c. ☐

d. feints d. ☐

e. threats e. ☐

f. promises f. ☐

IMPROVING THE RELATIONSHIP WITH THE OTHER PARTY, OR THE OTHER'S MOOD

a. being warm and friendly a. ☐

b. doing favours for the other party b. ☐

c. behaving in accordance with the other's values c. ☐

d. choosing a pleasant setting for the negotiation d. ☐

e. substituting a 'more reasonable' negotiator e. ☐

2. WAS NEGOTIATOR HEAVY HANDED? i.e. put pressure on to the point of creating resentment

Yes ☐ ☐ No

What did negotiator do to create resentment? ____________________

____

If threats were used did they result in: concessions? ☐ counter threats ☐

If concessions were made did the other party

match those concessions? ☐
hold firm? ☐

Did you observe any of the following reactions to competitive pressure?

a. conceding too much, too fast ☐

b. backing down in the face of threat ☐

c. failing to mount a vigorous defence of own demands ☐

d. showing lack of confidence/disclosing weak power base ☐

e. appearing anxious about possible breakdown in negotiations ☐

Did you observe any of the following collaborative behaviours?

HIGH RISK

a. large unilateral concessions to encourage reciprocal concessions ☐

b. unilateral proposals for a compromise solution ☐

LOWER RISK

a. signals/hints ☐

b. messages transmitted through intermediaries ☐

c. informal problem-solving discussions (e.g. over lunch) ☐

d. small concessions, followed by greater ones if reciprocated ☐

Figure 8.9 Negotiation tactics observation record

My target ______________	Their target ______________
My key variables PRIORITY	Their key variables PRIORITY
__________ ▢	__________ ▢
__________ ▢	__________ ▢
__________ ▢	__________ ▢
__________ ▢	__________ ▢
__________ ▢	__________ ▢
__________ ▢	__________ ▢
My limit ______________	Their limit ______________
My opening bid ________________________	

Figure 8.10 Negotiation preparation sheet

question, would you repeat the question and then stay silent until she answered. Or would you ask an 'easier' (and from your point of view less satisfactory) question, suggest an answer for her, or simply move on? This kind of self-analysis may help you develop a more effective approach to negotiating.

Summary

The aim of this chapter is to help you develop a better understanding of the process of negotiation and to help you identify the skills you need if you are to become a more successful negotiator.

Negotiation has been presented as a process with six main stages: preparation, climate-setting, choice of strategy, definition of opening bids, bargaining, and settling.

Preparation involves thinking through not only *what* you want to achieve but *how* you are going to achieve it. Climate-setting is a period of exploration and impression management in which each negotiator 'sniffs over' the other in an attempt to determine the best way to proceed. The impression each presents to the other can be very important in moulding the way the other will react. Climate-setting is closely related to the next stage, choice of strategy. Special attention has been given to the prerequisites for a collaborative strategy. While it is not unusual for these not to exist at the outset of a negotiation, particularly between strangers, conditions can change and they can emerge later, possibly prompting a subsequent change in strategy. Opening bids have been shown to serve a number of functions, but their role in challenging the opponent's expectations received most attention. As a guiding principle it was suggested that negotiators who make realistically high opening bids gain greatest benefit. Bargaining tactics have been considered in some detail and a Negotiating Tactics Observation form has been presented to help you construct a profile of your negotiating style. Finally, the importance of settling was underlined if a negotiated agreement is to be achieved and implemented successfully.

Throughout this chapter attention has been paid to many important negotiating skills. Underpining these are some generic skills, which are important in most kinds of interpersonal relationship such as listening, questioning, testing understanding, etc. These skills are dealt with in more detail elsewhere in this volume.

References: Chapter 8

Karrass, C. L. 1974. *Give and Take*. Chicago: World Book Co.

Morley, I. E. 1984. Bargaining and negotiation. In C. L. Cooper, and P. Makin (eds), *Psychology for Managers*. London: BPS and Macmillan.

Pruitt, D. G. 1981. *Negotiation Behaviour*. New York: Academic Press.

Scott, B. 1988. *Negotiating*. London: Paradigm.

Scott, W. P. 1981. *The Skills of Negotiating*. Aldershot: Gower.

Strauss, A. 1978. *Negotiations: Varieties, Contexts, and Social Order*. San Francisco: Jossey-Bass.

CHAPTER NINE
Working in groups

Groups provide an important context for work activity. Boards of directors, management committees, planning groups, project teams, task forces, quality circles, safety committees and autonomous work groups are but a few of the many different kinds of group within which organizational members have to work. Handy (1985) estimates that, on average, managers spend 50 per cent of their working day in one sort of group or another and senior managers can spend 80 per cent.

The ability to work effectively with a group of other people, either as leader or member, is an important interpersonal skill.

Sometimes groups are very productive. They are valued because they create ideas, make decisions, take action and generate commitment in ways that might otherwise be difficult to achieve. On the other hand, groups can be anything but productive. They can waste time, make poor decisions, be ridden with conflict and frustrate their members.

The first part of this chapter identifies some of the main factors that influence group effectiveness and highlights the role group interaction processes can play in promoting better group performance. The second part of the chapter focuses on interaction processes and presents an approach to developing a range of diagnostic and action skills that can be employed to improve group effectiveness.

DETERMINANTS OF GROUP EFFECTIVENESS

One of the most promising models of group effectiveness, in terms of offering a basis for diagnosing strengths and weaknesses in groups, is that advanced by Hackman (1987). Hackman identifies three criteria for assessing group effectiveness. The first deals with the actual output of the group. He argues that group output should meet or exceed the performance standards of the people who receive and/or review it. He proposes this criterion rather than some more 'objective' index of performance because, in his opinion, what happens to a group tends to depend most on how its performance is viewed by these key people. The second criterion deals with the state of the group as a performing unit. The social processes used in carrying out the work of the group should maintain or enhance the capability of members to work together in the future. A group would not be very effective if, in the process of achieving an acceptable task output, members ended up fighting or not trusting each other and it destroyed itself. The third criterion deals with the impact of the group experience on individual members. He argues that the group experience, on balance, should satisfy rather than frustrate the personal needs of group members.

Hackman's model is attractive because it embraces this broadly based measure of effectiveness and because it focuses on variables that are powerful (that is, they make non-trivial differences to how a group performs), and, at least potentially, can be managed. He attempts to explain why some groups perform better than others by proposing that effectiveness is a joint function of:

(a) the level of *effort* group members expend collectively on carrying out the task,
(b) the amount of *knowledge and skill* members bring to bear on the group task,
(c) the appropriateness to the task of the *performance strategies* used by the group in its work.

Asking questions about effort (e.g. are members working hard enough?), knowledge and skill (e.g. do members possess the required knowledge and skill and are they using it effectively?) and performance strategies (e.g. has the group developed appropriate ways of working on the task?) can provide valuable data about how well the group is performing. Hackman's model examines the various features of a group and its context, which can lead to an improvement in its level of effort, its application of member knowledge and skill, and the appropriateness of its performance strategies. The framework adopted here to explore some of the main factors contributing to group effectiveness is based on Hackman's model.

Effort

A number of factors can influence the amount of effort group members expend on carrying out the task.

Task design The design of the task can have an enormous impact on member motivation. Handy (1985) points to the importance of task salience and task clarity. Hackman (1987), extrapolating from the model of individual task motivation developed by Hackman and Oldham (1980), suggests that group norms encouraging high effort are likely to emerge when the task is challenging, important to the organization or its clients, is 'owned' by the group and when it generates regular feedback on how group members are performing. Task design, therefore, provides an important part of the foundation upon which long-term group effectiveness can be built. It could even be argued that a well-designed task is a necessary (although probably not sufficient) condition for effective performance: so much so that improvements in the quality of group interaction processes are unlikely to do much to compensate for a very poorly designed task, except in the short term. Thus, although task design will not receive much attention in this chapter, its implications for group effectiveness must not be underestimated.

Reward system Closely linked with task design is the organizational reward system. Where the reward system provides groups with challenging performance objectives and reinforces their achievement, effort will be higher than where objectives are not clear, lack challenge or where the level of performance achieved by the group appears to have no consequence.

Group interaction processes Group interaction processes can have an important influence on the level of effort members will expend on the task. People can develop process skills that will minimize what Hackman (1987, following Steiner 1972) labels the inevitable 'overhead costs' that must be paid when group members perform tasks. Coordinating member activities takes time and energy away from productive work. In some groups these overhead costs are much higher than in others, because members lack the process skills to ensure that activities are coordinated efficiently.

As well as minimizing coordination losses, skilful management of the group process can limit certain kinds of motivational loss. As groups increase in size, the amount of effort invested by each member tends to decline. Latane, Williams and Hoskins (1979) refer to this as 'social loafing'. In a larger group, people may feel less responsible for the task outcome or feel that they can hide behind others and get away with less preparation than would be possible in a smaller group or if they were doing the task alone.

The quality of group interaction process can have other motivational consequences. For example, it can exaggerate or reduce considerably the motivational losses that tend to arise as a result of the way conflict is managed in the group. Deutsch (1949) emphasized the importance of those behaviours, such as mediating, which help to 'maintain' the group in good working order (see below).

Hackman also argues that, where individuals do not value membership of the group, their investment of effort is likely to be low, even if the task is well designed. On the other hand, where people identify themselves strongly with their team, this commitment will encourage them to work hard in order to make their team one of the best. The aim of many team-building exercises is to cultivate this sense of team spirit.

Knowledge and skill

Group composition A group will not be able to perform effectively if it does not have access to the resources it requires to complete its task. Knowledge and skill are key resources.

The availability of task-relevant expertise is largely determined by group composition. Unfortunately, all too often the composition of a group is determined by factors such as seniority or personal preference rather than ability. It might also be decided to assign certain people to a group because they represent the interests of various constituents, rather than because of their knowledge and skill. This kind of consideration has implications for group size.

Group size Many groups in organizations are larger than they really need to be because additional members are recruited for 'political reasons'. Large groups composed in this way can be effective in so far as their representative membership can help ensure that their output will be well received; however, the quality of the output of large groups may be inferior to that of small groups. A number of factors may account for this. Large groups encourage social loafing (see above) and can adversely affect participation rates: some people find it much more difficult to contribute within a large group. This can be important for two reasons. First, because there is a tendency for those who make the biggest contribution to exercise most influence and vice versa (Handy 1985), and, secondly, because the people who do not contribute may deprive the group of relevant knowledge and skill.

Group interaction processes Hackman (1987) draws attention to two other factors that, given the group's composition, can influence the availability of knowledge and skill to all members. The first concerns the weighing of member contributions. Hackman argues that the knowledge and skill of group members can be wasted if the group solicits and weighs contributions in a way that is incongruent with members' expertise: for example, giving more credence to contributions from certain people because of their age or status, even if they do not possess the most task-relevant expertise. The second he labels 'collective learning'. There can be a synergetic effect when members of a group interact in a way that helps them to learn from each other, thus increasing the total pool of talent available to the group.

The interpersonal skill of group members can influence the extent to which the task-relevant expertise, discussed above, is applied to the work of the group. Some people lack the interpersonal competence necessary to work with others on a common task and can seriously undermine the group's ability to perform effectively. It is within this context that the work of Belbin (1981) and Deutsch (1949), discussed later in this chapter, is of importance.

Performance strategies

Performance strategies are often taken for granted and never questioned. As a result, people sometimes work hard to little effect because the way their group has set about its task is not as productive as it might be. According to Hackman, the likelihood that a group will employ a task-appropriate performance strategy is increased when three conditions are satisfied. These three conditions are discussed under two headings.

Availability of information One of these conditions concerns the availability of information for group members to use when assessing the situation and evaluating alternative strategies. The organizational context within which some groups perform may offer easy access to needed information. Other groups may have to operate in an environment where information is so limited that it may be difficult even to determine the criteria that will be used to assess the quality of their output. Faced with this kind of environment, groups may either react passively and accept this state of affairs as something that they cannot influence, or deliberately allocate resources to the task of changing the environment in order to increase the likelihood that it will yield required data.

Group interaction processes A second condition concerns the extent to which group interaction processes encourage the use of available information. Hackman argues that the performance strategy is more likely to be appropriate to the task when group norms exist that support both an explicit assessment of the performance situation and an active consideration of alternative ways of proceeding with the work. Before starting work, some groups always allow a little time to check out what the task is and how they should proceed. They may also, from time to time, take stock of how things are going and consider whether they should change the way they are working. Other groups, however, tend to plunge straight into the task and never give a second thought to performance strategy.

A third condition involves the existence of group interaction processes that, on the one hand, foster creativity and, on the other, help the group minimize slippage on strategy implementation. Greater creativity will increase the likelihood of members generating new ideas and improved ways of proceeding with the work. However, this is unlikely to occur in those groups where there are strong pressures for conformity and where the expression of deviant ideas is discouraged.

Many factors can contribute to 'slippage' but one variable, which has much to do with both the appropriateness of the chosen strategy and the way in which the chosen strategy is implemented, is the quality of decision-making.

One of the most widely discussed problems associated with group decision-making has been described by Janis (1982) as 'groupthink'. Groupthink occurs when the pressure to reach a consensus interferes with critical thinking, thus inhibiting the appraisal of possible alternatives. Janis has identified eight symptoms of groupthink:

1 Invulnerability: Members become over-optimistic and assume that the group's past success will continue.
2 Stereotyping: Members ignore disconfirming data by forming negative stereotypes which discredit the sources of such information.
3 Rationalization: Members find rationalizations which explain away evidence which threatens their emerging consensus.
4 Illusion of morality: Members believe that right is on their side and tend to be blind to the moral implications of their policy.
5 Pressure: Members are discouraged from expressing doubts too forcefully.
6 Self-censorship: Members keep quiet about misgivings and try to minimize their doubts.
7 Mindguards: Members protect the group from being exposed to disturbing ideas.
8 Unanimity: Members screen out the possibility of divergent views as soon as the most vocal members are in agreement.

Groups that experience problems with decision-making, such as those described by Janis, are more likely than others to choose an inappropriate strategy in the first place and then to make poor decisions about how the chosen strategy should be implemented. The decision-making procedures adopted by a group are an important element in its overall performance strategy. Different decision-making procedures will be discussed in some detail later.

The importance of group interaction processes and interpersonal skills

The first part of this chapter has drawn attention to some of the main factors that influence group effectiveness and has highlighted the role group interaction processes can play in promoting better group performance.

It has been shown that the quality of group interaction processes can influence the 'overhead costs' associated with coordinating group activity, the motivational losses that can occur through either 'social loafing' or conflict management, and the synergetic gains that can be derived from high levels of commitment to the group. All these factors can have a direct effect on the amount of *effort* that group members will expend on carrying out the task.

The amount of *knowledge and skill* members bring to bear on the task can also be influenced by the quality of group interaction processes. Attention was focused on participation rates, the weighting of member contributions and the benefits of collective learning. Furthermore, the process skills of group members were shown to effect the extent to which task-relevant skills are actually applied to the task.

It has also been shown that the quality of group interaction processes can have implications for the *appropriateness of the performance strategies* used by the group. Behaviours that support situation scanning and strategy planning, foster creativity, improve decision-making and minimize slippage in strategy implementation can have an important impact on group effectiveness.

The second part of this chapter will take a closer look at group interaction processes and will suggest ways in which either the group as a whole or individual group members can develop skills that will increase group effectiveness.

IMPROVING GROUP PERFORMANCE: DIAGNOSTIC AND ACTION SKILLS

One way to improve the effectiveness of a group is to improve the diagnostic and action skills of its members. In Chapter 1 the football analogy was introduced to illustrate this point. It was noted that players use their diagnostic skills to understand what is going on and, at half time, share their diagnosis with other members of the team. They do this in an attempt to understand what, in the first half, they might have done differently to secure a better result and what, in the second half, they need to attend to if they are to improve their performance. It was also noted that players develop and use action skills such as marking, running with the ball, passing and shooting. These are the skills that, given their diagnosis of what needs to be done, enable them to intervene and take the action required to secure desired goals.

Although the development of diagnostic and action skills can improve the effectiveness of work groups, all too often the culture that characterizes many of these groups emphasizes the *task* (what the group has to do) and ignores the *process* (how the group works together in order to accomplish the task). Consequently, in practice, little effort is invested in the development of process (i.e. diagnostic and action) skills.

Returning to the football analogy for the moment: although many players might engage eagerly in a post-match discussion of the process, how the game was played, their diagnosis may be far from accurate. The players may have poor diagnostic skills. They may be highly subjective in their review and attribute lack of success to their opponents' foul play, fail to recall many of their own shortcomings and only see themselves in an unrealistically favourable light. Even when they want to be objective when making their analysis, they may experience difficulty reaching a sound diagnosis because they lack an awareness of what kinds of behaviours and relationships are important and deserve attention.

The first part of this chapter addressed this issue and identified a number of problems that detract from group effectiveness. This second part offers some suggestions about those aspects of group behaviour that might deserve attention, presents a range of diagnostic tools that can be used to help determine what is going on in the group and indicates the kind of action that might be necessary to improve matters.

The first step in making a diagnosis is to observe what is going on, to collect data. If we try to observe a group of people working together, we quickly realise that so much is happening that it is impossible to pay attention to everything at the same time. The task can be made much easier if the observer focuses attention on just certain aspects of how the group is working together. What follows is an introduction to several approaches to group observation that can be used as a basis for diagnosis.

Frequency and duration of communication

Chapple (1940) believed that the most important characteristic of an individual's interaction could be measured along a dimension of action–silence. Using a machine that he called an interaction chronograph, he conducted many studies that were based largely on recordings of the frequency and duration of speeches and silences. Social scientists and trainers who have followed in Chapple's footsteps have concentrated on observing only the pattern of interaction (for example, who communicates, how often, how long and with whom?) without any reference to the verbal or emotional content of the communication.

The frequency of communication can be measured by simply placing a check mark against each group member's name every time he or she says something. A crude measure of duration can be obtained by repeating the procedure every 10 seconds until the speaker has stopped talking. This data can be summarized to show who spoke most often, who made long speeches and who tended to rely more on short contributions. For example, Figure 9.1 shows that David hardly spoke at all, whereas Victoria and Liz both made ten separate contributions; however, Victoria made much longer speeches than Liz.

Recording participation rates for each five-minute period can provide data about how the pattern of participation changed over the course of the meeting. Figure 9.1 indicates that while James participated fairly frequently throughout the first ten

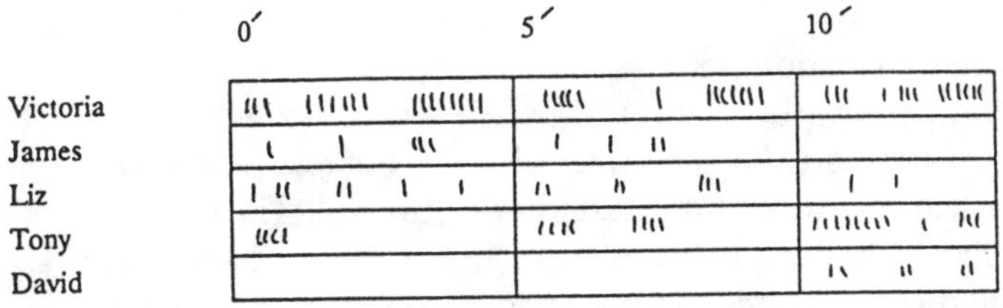

0′ 5′ 10′

Victoria
James
Liz
Tony
David

Figure 9.1 Frequency and duration of communication

minutes of the meeting he said nothing during the final period, whereas David made no contribution until the last five minutes.

Simple analyses of this kind, undertaken by an observer who subsequently shares her findings with the group, can point to a number of important issues. For example, it might be found that some quiet members have relevant contributions they wish to make, but are experiencing difficulty in breaking into the conversation. A remedy might be for some other members of the group to assume a 'gatekeeper' role, checking from time to time whether quiet members wish to contribute. Alternatively, it might be found that quiet members do not contribute because they lack confidence or fear attack. This kind of problem might be overcome if the group were more encouraging and accepting of member contributions. It is possible, of course, that people who are seen to be quiet are not quiet at all. The observer may report that they actually do make a number of contributions that are not heard or are ignored by others. Should this be the case, it may be useful to consider whether this is because past experience has taught others that what they have to say is not worth listening to or because the group, for various reasons, is disinclined to give proper weight to 'deviant' opinions or to contributions, whatever their worth, from certain kinds of member: women, engineers, juniors in rank, age or tenure.

Bearing in mind the research findings already reported (that those who talk most often exercise most influence), it might be helpful to enquire whether those who do most of the talking are those who have most to contribute in terms of knowledge, skill and experience. If not, consideration may be given to the promotion of norms and procedures within the group, which will both lead to a more effective sharing of air time and to the discovery of those who possess relevant knowledge, skill and experience.

Communication patterns

It might also be useful to observe who talks with whom. Data can be recorded in a number of ways, but one relatively straightforward method is illustrated in Figure 9.2. The observer draws a line from the speaker to the recipient, with the arrow indicating the direction of communication. In practice, this may not be as easy as it might appear because it is not always clear to whom

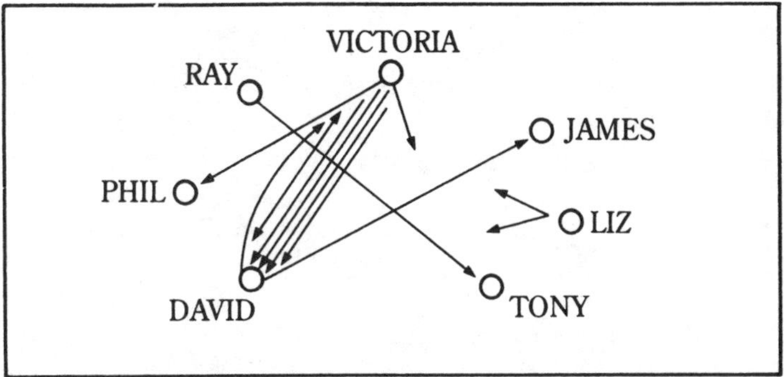

Figure 9.2 Communication patterns

a remark is addressed. Body posture and direction of gaze can help determine this, but on some occasions a remark may not be aimed at anybody in particular, but addressed to the group as a whole. This can be recorded by a line which ends in the middle of the circle. Arrows at each end of a line can be used to indicate that the initiator of a message received an immediate response from the recipient. Because observation charts of this kind soon become congested it may be necessary for the observer to use several charts and then aggregate the results.

The interaction patterns revealed by this kind of analysis may provide many clues about how the group is working together. They may indicate whether the group is united in its efforts, or whether various subgroups and cliques are operating to propagate particular views and influence decision-making. Attention may also be focused on certain aspects of the group's performance strategy. For example, in situations where a quick decision is required and where the appropriate way forward will be fairly obvious once certain information has been shared, the interaction pattern often referred to as the 'wheel', shown in Figure 9.3a, may be appropriate.

This pattern can sometimes be observed in formal committees where the majority of all communications are addressed to the chairman. Groups adopting this wheel pattern tend to reach decisions much more quickly than those who adopt the 'all channel' pattern shown in Figure 9.3b. If, however, the group needs to reach a creative solution to a complex problem, it may find that the 'wheel' is considerably less effective than

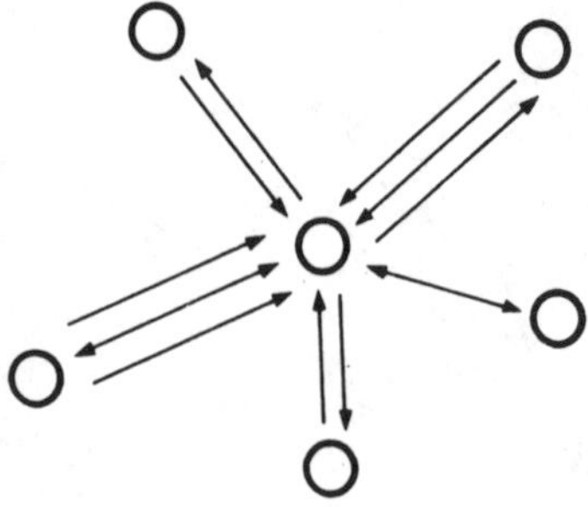

Figure 9.3a Wheel pattern

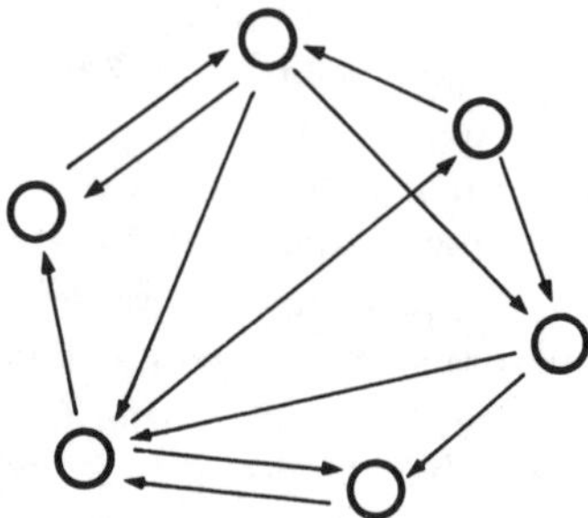

Figure 9.3b All channel pattern

the 'all channel' pattern. Research evidence suggests that 'all channel' patterns are most likely to produce the best solution when the group is faced with a complex open-ended problem. All channel interaction patterns may also be more appropriate in those circumstances where it is necessary for the group to reach a consensus.

It is important to stress, however, that interaction patterns only provide clues as to what might be going on in a group, and great care must be exercised when interpreting findings. The interaction pattern, for example, between Victoria and David in Figure 9.2 shows that Victoria tends to address most of her communications to David. She may talk mostly with David because he tends to support her ideas and she identifies him as an ally. On the other hand, she may address many of her messages to him because he is the person from whom she expects most opposition and she feels, therefore, that the best way forward is to confront him first in order to judge the strength of the opposition she may face.

The apparent target of a communication is not the only aspect of interaction that deserves attention. Eye movements that precede and follow a communication can also be a rich source of data. Paying attention to such glances can help unearth important relationships. Ray may glance at James before talking to Tony and then again at James when he has finished speaking. This may indicate that James is an important 'other' for Ray: a boss or informal leader, an opponent, or possibly someone who might be hurt by what he has to say.

Speakers often look to leaders for permission to speak or for feedback on what was said. They may also look towards possible opponents for their reaction. Observing the pattern of such glances over a period can reveal alliances. If Ray, Victoria and Liz all glance at James, and Phil and Tony look towards David, this may signal the existence of two subgroups, at least when certain issues are being discussed.

Interaction patterns highlight the existence of relationships. However, knowledge about the content of communications may be required if the nature of these relationships is to be understood or predicted with any confidence.

Role functions

Another way of analysing how a group is working is to examine member behaviour in terms of its purpose or function. Belbin (1981) has produced research evidence that identifies eight key team roles that need to be exercised in a group if it is to be effective. He also found that each was associated with a particular type of personality. The roles he identified were:

Chairman, the person who is a good judge of people, who recognizes where the team's strengths and weaknesses lie, and coordinates and controls the work of members, making the best use of the team's resources in order to achieve group goals.

The chairman tends to be the kind of person who is calm, self-confident and controlled.

Shaper, the person who offers dominant task-leadership and tries to galvanize the group into action. She tends to be outgoing, impulsive and impatient when seeking to impose some shape or pattern on group discussions or the outcome of group activities.

Plant, the person who is the major source of original ideas and proposals: very intelligent, often introverted and usually more interested in fundamental principles than practical detail.

Resource-investigator, the person who, rather than being the originator of ideas, is someone who picks up ideas and information from others, especially from outside the group, and develops them. This kind of person tends to be an extrovert, an enthusiast and a good communicator. She performs as the group's diplomat, salesman or liaison officer.

Monitor-evaluator, the person who is serious-minded, prudent and, unlike the shaper or resource-investigator, has a built-in immunity from enthusiasm. She is able to stand back and evaluate ideas and suggestions so that the team is better placed to take balanced decisions.

Company worker, the person who turns concepts and plans into practical working procedures. She is methodical, trustworthy, efficient and willing to do what has to be done, even if it is not intrinsically interesting or pleasant.

Team Worker, the person who supports and builds on other people's strengths and underpins their weaknesses. She tends to be skilled at listening to others, facilitating communications within the group and dealing with difficult interpersonal situations.

Completer-finisher, the person who is motivated to finalize anything that is started, and to do so with thoroughness. Her relentless follow-through is important, but not always popular.

Belbin (1981, pp. 153–7) presents a useful self-perception inventory, which provides a profile of the roles a person typically performs, based on responses to a set of questions that explores how the respondent normally behaves in certain situations. One problem sometimes associated with this kind of approach is that people may not actually behave in the way that they think they do. Nonetheless, Belbin's work has some important messages for both team composition and interpersonal skills training.

Morton Deutsch (1949), in conjunction with his research on cooperation and competition in groups, which he conducted in 1947, was one of the first to develop a system for categorizing role functions. He argued that members of an effective group must perform two kinds of function, one concerned with completing the task and the other with strengthening and maintaining the group. More recently, Hackman (1987) echoed this view when he argued that unless group members possess certain interpersonal skills the task-relevant expertise that exists within the group might not be applied effectively to the task.

Task functions If a group is to be successful in terms of completing its task, members must define the problem/task and suggest possible ways forward, share facts and opinions relevant to solving the problem or completing the task, elaborate and clarify ideas, challenge and evaluate proposals, make decisions, etc. Difficulties may arise if some members push their own views but fail to pay attention to those held by others, if vaguely stated proposals are left unclarified, if some members push for a decision before the problem has been explored fully or alternative solutions debated, or if the group loses its sense of direction and wastes time on irrelevant business.

Maintenance functions Just as a machine has to be maintained if it is to remain in good working order, so a group demands regular maintenance if it is to be effective when working on task issues. Quiet members may require encouragement if they are to make a proper contribution, those who have withdrawn and 'taken their bat home' after an argument may require help if they are to reintegrate with the group, and people who are unhappy with the way the group is being managed may find it difficult to continue working on the task until some of their concerns have been explored.

Based on the work of Deutsch, several methods for observing and categorizing role functions have been developed. These methods have the advantage that they avoid self report bias. An observer categorizes the behaviour of group members as it actually occurs rather than relying on members to report, at some later date, how they thought they behaved.

The category set presented here draws heavily on earlier work but focuses attention on those role functions which the author has found most useful when observing groups. There are eleven task roles and five maintenance roles:

Task roles

1 **Initiator** Defines a group problem: proposes tasks or immediate objectives: suggests a new procedure or a different approach to solving the problem.

2 **Information seeker** Asks for information and facts relevant to the problem being discussed, seeks clarification of suggestions.

3 **Opinion seeker** Asks for opinions, seeks clarification of values pertinent to what the group is undertaking or of values in a suggestion made.

4 **Information giver** Offers facts or generalizations that are 'authoritative' or related to own experience.

5 **Opinion giver** States opinions or beliefs.

6 **Elaborator** Expands and explores ideas, offers examples or provides a rationale for suggestions made previously. Tries to envisage how an idea or suggestion would work out if adopted by the group.

7 **Evaluator/critic** Evaluates or questions the 'practicality', logic, facts or the procedure of a suggestion or some aspect of the group's discussion

8 **Coordinator** Shows or clarifies the relationship among various ideas, tries to pull ideas and suggestions together or tries to coordinate the activities of members of the group.

9 **Decision Manager** Prods the group to decision, sends up 'trial balloons' to test group opinions.

10 **Recorder** Records the progress of the discussion, records decisions, acts as the 'group memory'.

11 **Supporter/follower** Offers positive support for an argument or proposal, or signals a willingness to go along with an idea.

Maintenance roles

1 **Encourager** Praises, argues with and accepts the contribution of others in a way which encourages them to participate more fully in the group.
2 **Gatekeeper** Attempts to keep communication channels open by inviting contributions or proposing procedures that will enable everyone to contribute.
3 **Mediator** Attempts to reconcile disagreements or attempts to relieve tension by jesting or pouring oil on troubled waters.
4 **Compromiser** Operates from within a conflict in which her idea or position is involved. Offers to compromise or holds back from escalating a conflict.
5 **Standard setter** Suggests and defends standards for the group to achieve in terms of output or procedures.

This category set is not exhaustive, because it only includes behaviour that helps the group to work effectively. Some behaviour is more concerned with the satisfaction of individual needs and is dysfunctional from the point of view of group effectiveness. Benne and Sheates (1948) discuss a number of such roles. For example, the aggressor, a person who attacks others, jokes aggressively or shows envy towards another's contribution by trying to take credit for it, or the playboy, a person who makes a display of his lack of involvement in the group by trivializing the task and distracting others by fooling around. Although it can be helpful to draw attention to these kinds of dysfunctional behaviour, the focus of attention of the category set presented here is functional group behaviour.

A necessary first step for diagnosing role behaviour in groups is the collection of data. Role functions can be recorded using the matrix presented in Figure 9.4. The observer places a check mark in the appropriate cell each time a member of the group performs one of the functions listed. The data generated by this procedure can then be used in a number of ways.

The overall performance of the group can be reviewed by noting the kinds of behaviour observed for the group as a

MEMBER'S NAME / ROLE					
INITIATOR					
INFORMATION SEEKER					
OPINION SEEKER					
INFORMATION GIVER					
OPINION GIVER					
ELABORATOR					
EVALUATOR/CRITIC					
COORDINATOR					
DECISION MANAGER					
RECORDER					
SUPPORTER/FOLLOWER					

ENCOURAGER					
GATEKEEPER					
MEDIATOR					
COMPRISER					
STANDARD SETTER					

Figure 9.4 Role functions

whole. An initial analysis might focus on the balance between task and maintenance behaviours. Although task behaviour normally predominates, in some very task-oriented groups there may be no evidence of any maintenance functions being performed, a state of affairs which, over the longer term, could threaten the ability of the group to continue working effectively.

Within each of the broad task and maintenance categories the low incidence or complete absence of particular role functions might point to areas of group functioning that deserve attention. For example:

(a) If nobody performs the evaluator/critic role, there may be a danger that the group will arrive at the kind of ill-considered solutions illustrated earlier, when the phenomenon of groupthink was discussed (see p. 214).
(b) If nobody performs the coordinator role, the discussion may lack focus, related issues and underlying themes may

go unrecognized, members may either duplicate or fail to undertake necessary preparatory or follow-up work and the group may fail to 'pull together'. Consequently, the overhead costs, discussed earlier (p. 210), might be unnecessarily high.

(c) If nobody acts as decision manager, the group might miss decision points and the discussion might drift from topic to topic before any decisions have been made. Alternatively, the group might rush into decisions before all the relevant facts have been considered or alternative solutions examined. These kinds of behaviour can also create problems of coordination (thus increasing overhead costs) and can lead to the adoption of inappropriate performance strategies by the group.

(d) If nobody acts as mediator, conflicts may go unresolved, members may withdraw psychologically from the group or, possibly more damaging, may pursue hidden agendas to get back at the other party, thus producing motivational losses or the diversion of effort to activities that detract from group effectiveness.

(e) If nobody performs the gatekeeper role, people who have a contribution they wish to make may remain silent and the group may be deprived of a potentially important contribution in terms of task-relevant expertise.

An individual's behaviour can also be audited to review the kind of contribution he or she normally makes to the work of the group. Particular attention can be focused on the range of role functions performed. Some people confine themselves to a narrow range of behaviours, whereas others have a wide repertoire at their disposal. Another focus for analysis might be the appropriateness and/or timeliness of the behaviour in terms of its consequences for group effectiveness. Returning to the football analogy, there is little advantage in being expert at shooting the ball and scoring goals if you fail to recognize the difference between your own and your opponents' goal. A wide range of action skills can increase a person's effectiveness, but only if they are applied appropriately. A good mediator, for example, may have a low tolerance for any kind of conflict and, on some occasions, by intervening to smooth things over, may inhibit the exploration of important differences in the group. Similarly, a compromiser may be too ready to let go of a good idea if pressured by a more assertive member. If the person good at mediating had not mediated and the compromiser had not compromised, the group, in the examples presented, might have accomplished its task more successfully.

If a member is unhappy with his or her own performance, an audit of the role functions performed might suggest alternative ways of behaving.

The dedicated 'devil's advocate', the person who always sees the problems and pitfalls that others appear to overlook, may find that many of her contributions tend to be ignored by the rest of the group. The evaluator/critic role is essential, but if it is the only role a person performs it may be rendered ineffective. Performing other roles and making a wider range of contributions can help avoid the negative consequences sometimes associated with the label 'group critic'.

The person who is happy to offer the group information or opinions, but never seeks ideas from others, may find that she is less effective than she could be. Such a person might consider achieving a better balance between giving and seeking both information and opinion.

Although the diagnostic techniques outlined here are important, they are not sufficient if group members are to begin to work together more effectively. Members need to be able to intervene, to take the action needed to improve matters. This involves the development of action as well as diagnostic skills. If quiet members need encouragement, somebody needs to recognize this need and intervene to satisfy it. If a member recognises a need for better coordination, she must be able to either intervene and perform the coordinator role herself or persuade somebody else to do so.

A group can be strengthened and can work more effectively if members:

(a) become more aware of the wide range of role functions that need to be performed;
(b) have the ability to observe which roles functions are being over-used or neglected and to identify what changes are necessary;

(c) possess the necessary skill to modify their own behaviour in order to provide needed role functions.

Practice makes perfect. One approach to developing the skills necessary to perform a wider range of role functions is to identify those role functions most neglected and to deliberately seek out opportunities to practise them. Just as some people seek to widen their vocabulary by choosing a new word each day and finding at least five opportunities to use it, so the group member can widen her repertoire of role functions by practising under-used behaviours until they become second nature.

Interpersonal style and group climate

In order to identify the underlying dimensions of interpersonal behaviour, Hare (1982) reviewed the development of different approaches to the observation of behaviour and the various studies that factor analysed the results of such observations. The four dimensions that emerged as important are presented in Figure 9.5. They are dominant versus submissive, positive versus negative, serious versus expressive, and conforming versus non-conforming. These dimensions can be used to identify an individual's interpersonal style or to describe group climate.

Relating these dimensions to the role functions presented above, we might expect that dominant group members would engage most frequently in such behaviour as initiating, giving information and opinion, evaluating and decision-managing, and less frequently in such behaviour as compromising and mediating.

Positive members may be more sensitive to the need for maintenance functions than are negative members. In particular, we might expect the positive member to seek information and opinion in an encouraging way, to act as a gatekeeper when necessary, and to avoid unnecessary conflict and confrontation.

Serious members are more likely to engage in group-oriented functional behaviours rather than in the individually oriented dysfunctional behaviours that can often be observed in groups (see Benne and Sheats 1948). Although serious members are likely to be very task-oriented, this will not prevent their paying attention to group maintenance requirements if the failure to do so would impede task accomplishment. Expressive members, on

DOMINANT versus SUBMISSIVE

Dominant	1 2 3 4 5	Submissive
Assuming autocratic control or seeking status in the group by making direct suggestions or by giving opinions which serve to guide group activity. (Also measured by total talking rate.)		Showing dependence by asking for help, showing anxiety, shame and guilt, or frustration,laughing at the jokes of a dominant person.

POSITIVE versus NEGATIVE

Positive	1 2 3 4 5	Negative
Seeming friendly by showing affection, agreement or by asking for information or opinion in an encouraging way.		Seeming unfriendly by disagreeing, showing antagonism, or diffuse aggression.

SERIOUS versus EXPRESSIVE

Serious	1 2 3 4 5	Expressive
Giving information or opinions which indicate serious involvement in the task.		Giving support to others regardless of task performance or showing tension release through joking or other evidence of flight from the task.

CONFORMING versus NON-CONFORMING

Conforming	1 2 3 4 5	Non-conforming
Seeking to be guided by the group norms.		Acting in ways that are clearly different from the majority. Urging anarchistic values.

Figure 9.5 Dimensions of interpersonal style (based on Hare 1982).

the other hand, are likely to evince much less concern for the task. They are likely to be more committed to the achievement of personal goals within the context of the group.

Conforming members are likely to be very aware of and guided by group norms and to engage in behaviour that will preserve traditional attitudes and practices within the group. However, should group opinion begin to move, the conforming member may decide to go along with the change in order to protect her place in the group. The conforming member is less likely than the non-conforming member to engage in evaluative or critical behaviour or to propose initiatives that are out of line with group thinking. The non-conforming member, on the other hand, is much less likely to compromise her views simply to preserve group solidarity or to protect her position as a member.

Hare's four dimensions of interpersonal style might provide the individual who is seeking to improve her effectiveness in groups with a set of useful benchmarks, which can be used as a basis for experimenting with and developing more effective interpersonal/communication styles. For example, someone who is dissatisfied with the amount of influence they have may decide to experiment with new behaviours, observe the consequences and, if the desired outcome is achieved, modify their interpersonal style to incorporate the new behaviour. A person who, using Hare's dimensions, assesses herself towards the submissive end of the dominant versus submissive scale may attempt to exercise more influence by experimenting with more assertive behaviours, such as taking initiatives, expressing opinions, talking more in the group and engaging in many of the behaviours discussed in Chapter 7. Alternatively, if she sees herself as a very friendly and agreeable person, she may decide to experiment with more negative behaviours, agreeing less and challenging more. Paying attention to the other two dimensions might also suggest ways of exercising more influence. She could behave in a more serious way, joking less and being more clearly involved in the task, or conforming more by seeking to accomplish the task in ways that are acceptable to the group.

If the group as a whole is perceived to be ineffective it might be worth considering whether this is because too many people are trying to dominate and power struggles get in the way of the task (dominant v. submissive), because the atmosphere is overly negative and not conducive to cooperative effort (positive v. negative), because members evidence little commitment to the task and are too flippant in their approach (serious v. expressive), or the group lacks discipline and co-ordinated effort (conforming v. non-conforming).

Performance strategies

How a group organizes itself will have an important impact on how successful it will be in completing its task. Hackman (1987) argues that one of the key factors that will increase the likelihood of a group employing a task-appropriate performance strategy is the existence of a group norm, which supports explicitly an assessment of alternative ways of proceeding with the task. Too often the possibility of adopting an alternative performance strategy is never considered. The routine is accepted as the inevitable. Even the purpose of the group can escape scrutiny and, in extreme cases, some members may not know why they are there or may have completely different views to those held by their colleagues about the nature of the task confronting them.

When observing a group at work, is it worth asking whether the members have developed an approach to work that is fully appropriate for the task being performed? Note whether performance strategies are ever discussed explicitly, or whether anyone ever initiates a review of how well the group is performing.

Many of the problems noted above can be avoided if members at least recognize the need to clarify group purpose and consider alternatives before selecting a performance strategy (a process that is likely to manifest itself through initiator, elaborator, evaluator and standard setter roles). At a fairly mechanistic level this may involve members of a board of directors deciding the kind of item to be included in the agenda (a reflection of purpose) and then, in terms of performance strategy, deciding about the information they should receive prior to a meeting, the preparatory work they should undertake, the procedures that should be employed during the meeting for exploring issues and making decisions, and the steps to be taken to ensure that board members take the necessary action to implement decisions after the meeting.

More generally, the legitimacy of paying attention to such issues as clarifying purpose, identifying expertise, defining acceptable risk, promoting creativity and generating ideas, weighing alternatives, and gaining commitment to decisions needs to be established if the group is to be effective. One aspect of performance strategy that deserves a more detailed discussion is decision-making.

Decision-making

Group decision-making is often ineffective because group members do not possess necessary information or task-relevant expertise and/or because they fail to behave rationally. These information deficits and irrational behaviours impair decision-making by distorting the way problems are defined, influencing the nature and range of alternative solutions that are generated, and by influencing the way the group evaluates and chooses between the available alternatives.

Reference has already been made to the way that social pressures for conformity can result in irrational behaviour that leads to what Janis (1982) has described as groupthink. The consequence is often poor decisions, because little effort is given to the procurement of new information, only a handful of alternatives are considered, and those that are considered are evaluated inadequately. There is also a strong tendency for group members to maintain things as they are and give little attention to contingency planning.

Harvey (1974) has identified a related process, which he has labelled the Abilene paradox. This concerns the group's inability to manage agreement. He points to the tendency for some groups to take action that is in contradiction to the desires of all of its members. The underlying dynamics of the paradox appear to be that while, individually, group members know what needs to be done to solve the problem, they are reluctant to take whatever action is required. This reluctance stems from the fear that their action will be disapproved of by others and that this disapproval will result in rejection. Consequently, each individual refrains from confronting others with their view of reality. It is each individual's failure to confront which results in the group's making decisions that nobody agrees with. Each member goes along with and even actively contributes to bringing about a decision, because she believes that everybody else agrees that this is the best way forward. The reality is that everybody agrees that it is *not* the best way forward, but everybody behaves in a way that makes it impossible for this agreement to come to light.

Another phenomenon worthy of mention is the tendency in some groups for members to make decisions that involve a higher level of risk than they would normally be inclined to accept if they were personally responsible for the decision. Stoner (1968) found that although individuals favoured relatively safe decisions that offered the prospect of moderate pay-offs, many groups tended to favour relatively risky decisions that offered the prospect of higher pay-offs. Several explanations have been advanced to account for this, including the possibility that the people who are inclined to take risks are more influential in group discussions than conservative people, that risk taking is regarded as a desirable cultural characteristic, especially in some organizations, and that this characteristic is more likely to be expressed in group settings, and that responsibility for a group decision can more easily be attributed to others if something should go wrong.

Although in some groups a failure to confront and non-assertive behaviour can be problematic, in others a major source of difficulty is overly aggressive behaviour and the attempt by some members to impose their view on others. This manifests itself in win–lose approaches to decision-making, a consequence of which can be that members invest a great deal of their time and energy in promoting and defending their own or their allies' preferred solution, and in attacking and undermining others. Ensuring that one's preferred solution is adopted can assume a much greater importance in the eyes of group members than ensuring that the best solution is chosen. This kind of approach to decision-making can have enormous costs in terms of group cohesion, esprit de corps and member commitment to group decisions.

This brief review of some of the factors that can undermine the effectiveness of group decision-making procedures emphasizes the importance of ensuring that the group adopts appropriate performance strategies, especially in relation to decision-making. One of the factors that might be considered when evaluating the efficacy of decision-making processes is the range of alternative solutions that the group typically generates: a feature of groupthink is that only one or a small handful of (often similar) alternatives are considered. Another is the way that the group weighs and evaluates alternative solutions. All four of the phenomena discussed above (groupthink, the Abilene paradox, risky-shift, and aggressive win–lose battles) evidence weaknesses that are associated with the way alternatives are evaluated. The availability and use made of relevant knowledge and expertise is also important.

Decision-making procedures

Murnighan (1981) has identified five distinct decision making procedures. They are: ordinary group procedures, brainstorming, statistical aggregation, the Delphi technique, and the nominal group technique. The 'pure form' of each procedure will be outlined briefly and the strengths and weaknesses of all five approaches compared, before consideration is given to the ways in which they can be modified or combined to meet the needs of different situations.

Ordinary group procedures normally involve somebody presenting a problem and inviting comment and discussion. Sometimes the presenter of the problem offers a previously prepared proposal of how to deal with it. Ordinary group procedures are much less structured than some of the other procedures that will be considered. They are open-ended and free-flowing. However, they are also vulnerable to social pressure and conflict. Sometimes attention is focused only on a narrow range of solutions, creativity is stifled, and non-assertive members go unheard. Discussions can seem endless, and people can become fatigued and lose interest. Some members may take up fixed positions and ignore the advantages of other proposals. However, when things go well the process can be rewarding, and the group can become more cohesive and committed to the decisions it makes.

Brainstorming is based on two principles. The first is that most problems have more than one solution and, therefore, every effort should be made to generate as many alternative solutions as possible. The second is that the process of generating solutions can and should be separated from the processes of evaluating and deciding, in order to free people, during the solution generation phase, to be as creative as possible. If this distinction is not made there may be a tendency for members to censor their ideas and only think of 'sensible' or 'workable' solutions. The wild and unconventional ideas that may be suppressed could, on closer analysis, offer the best way forward or may trigger trains of thought that could lead to other effective solutions.

Brainstorming focuses on the process of generating ideas and involves people following a few simple rules:

(a) generating as many ideas as possible
(b) avoiding self censorship,
(c) not evaluating anybody else's ideas during the brainstorming session,
(d) piggybacking or building on other people's ideas.

Normally, one member of the group assumes the role of recorder and writes down on a large sheet of paper all the ideas as they are generated. Sometimes, this idea-generation session is conducted against the clock, thus increasing the pressure and pace. The final step involves looking for ways of combining or modifying ideas. Typically, most people enjoy brainstorming and leave the session feeling that the group has accomplished something. It tends to induce a sense of camaraderie and positive feelings towards the group. However, research results show that individuals working on their own can generate as many ideas as a brainstorming group. Nonetheless, brainstorming is an effective process, because often, when the group is following ordinary group procedures, individual members do not bring to the group a wide range of ideas, even though they may be capable of doing so.

Statistical aggregation is a procedure that uses the ideas of a group of individuals, but does not require that the individuals meet as a group. This procedure, like the Delphi technique, can be very useful when contributions are required from a set of people who have irreconcilable timetables. Its application is limited to problems that can be quantified (for example, estimating the cost of a new project), and it involves several people thinking through a problem and making their own estimate of the best answer. These estimates are passed to one person, who aggregates them to determine the final solution. The mean or median can be used to determine the solution. If the group is estimating the cost of a project, and if one member of the group has offered an extremely high or extremely low estimate, the median might provide a better measure of central tendency than the mean, but normally the mean is a good measure because over and under estimates tend to cancel each other out.

The main advantage of this procedure is that individuals are not subjected to social pressures that could influence their choice, especially if all estimates remain anonymous. The major limitation of this approach is that it can only be applied to certain types of problem.

The Delphi technique extends the procedure used with statistical aggregation to include feedback and re-estimates, and it can be applied to non-quantifiable problems. The focal person or chair of the Delphi panel constructs a questionnaire, which contains a clear statement of the problem and asks others for their solutions. These are summarized by the chairperson, who then feeds them back to the panel via a second questionnaire. The second questionnaire asks panel members for their reactions to the initial summary of responses, which are again summarized before a third questionnaire is prepared and circulated. This procedure continues until a clear solution emerges. If a clear consensus does not emerge, the chairperson may introduce a voting procedure to arrive at a solution.

Because of the iterative nature of this procedure, it is more time-consuming than statistical aggregation. Also, because people respond at different rates, time can be wasted waiting for replies from slow respondents.

The nominal group technique combines many of the good points of the other procedures and mixes the face-to-face interpersonal interaction of ordinary group procedures with a formal and restrictive process for arriving at a solution. It draws from brainstorming by encouraging group members to generate potential solutions individually, and it draws from the Delphi technique by providing feedback on all the suggestions offered.

The procedure begins with a clear statement of the problem being offered to the group. Members sit together, but work alone to generate a list of solutions that they then share with each other. During the sharing process, each member offers one solution in turn, which is recorded for all to see. This procedure continues around the group for as many times as necessary, until all the solutions have been shared. During this process members are encouraged to add to their lists by piggy-backing on the ideas of others. The next step is a brief discussion of the ideas for clarification, and, sometimes, elaboration. The final step involves voting for a group decision via private ballot. One of several voting procedures can be used at this stage. For example, members might vote for the five solutions they favour, rank-ordering them one to five. Sometimes, when the votes have been tabulated, a clear solution emerges. More often, the first vote identifies a small set of possible solutions, which become the focus of further discussion before another vote is taken.

This approach is quicker than the Delphi technique and also offers all the advantages of ordinary group procedures, such as the possibility of building a cohesive work group and greater commitment to the group decision. At the same, time the restricted opportunities for discussion and the formal, secret voting procedures reduce the opportunities for conflict and pressures to conform.

A comparison of the five procedures Some of the criteria against which each of the decision-making procedures can be assessed are listed in Figure 9.6. They include: the number and quality of ideas or potential solutions generated; the task orientation of the procedure; social pressures and the potential for conflict, which can affect the quality of the final solution; non-task outcomes, such as feelings of accomplishment, commitment to the solution and group cohesiveness; and, finally, timescale.

Ordinary group procedures have a number of weaknesses, the number and quality of ideas generated tends to be low, and social pressures and the potential for conflict can affect the final outcome. Nonetheless, Murnighan (1981) reports that research findings suggest that ordinary group procedures are best for emotive decision problems. These are problems that involve value-laden issues that lead to emotional responses by group members: for example, the allocation of budgets in periods of financial stringency. The quality of the final solution and the extent to which the group will be committed to it will be highly

Criteria	Ordinary group procedures	Brain-storming	Statistical aggregation	Delphi	Nominal Group technique
Number of ideas	low	moderate	N/A	high	high
Quality of ideas	low	moderate	N/A	high	high
Task orientation	low	high	high	high	high
Social pressure	high	low	none	low	moderate
Potential for conflict	high	low	low	low	moderate
Feelings of accomplishment	high to low	high	low	moderate	high
Commitment to solution	high	N/A	low	low	moderate
Builds group cohesiveness	high	high	low	low	moderate
Timescale	moderate	short	short	long	short

Figure 9.6 Strengths and weaknesses of decision procedures (based on Murnighan 1981)

dependent upon the way the group process is managed and the interpersonal skill of individual members. Where the required decisions are less value laden and of a more technical or factual nature, the evidence suggests that ordinary group procedures may not be most effective. Which of the other procedures might be most appropriate depends on a variety of factors, such as the potential for conflict, time-scale and the required commitment to the decision.

When deciding what kind of decision procedure to adopt to deal with a particular problem it is not necessary only to think in terms of the procedures outlined above. Brainstorming might be used to generate energy and 'get things moving' before the group adopts ordinary procedures to consider the merits of alternative solutions. The range and quality of ideas can be improved by asking individuals to generate a list of their own ideas privately, before the group embarks on a collective brainstorming exercise. One of the weaknesses associated with brainstorming is the lack of attention it gives to evaluating and choosing solutions. Merry and Allerhand (1977) suggest a number of procedures that can be used to help process the wide range of ideas that might result from a brainstorming exercise. Some are aimed at shortening the list to a number that can be more easily managed by the group. This can be achieved by identifying all the proposals that everybody accepts, thus focusing discussion on those where there is disagreement, or by identifying all those that have no support and eliminating them from the list, or by combining the two. An alternative approach is to divide the group into subgroups, which meet separately and simultaneously, and to share the range of proposals between them, charging each with the task of preparing recommendations for the total group. A variation of this approach is to delegate one subgroup to go away and process all the proposals and bring its recommendations to the next meeting of the total group. Dividing or delegating the task only works well when members have confidence in each other's ability and are prepared to trust others' judgement.

Merry and Allerhand also suggest two procedures for deciding which solution to adopt. Where the group is faced with several proposals, they suggest that they discuss the criteria they should adopt for deciding which to accept or reject, and list these down one side of a matrix, with the proposed solutions listed across the top (see Figure 9.7). The matrix provides a structure for considering and evaluating each proposal. A brief discussion can often produce a quick consensus on each point (ratings being recorded ++, +, 0, –, ––) but, where this is difficult, a compromise might have to be sought.

Where the group has to decide between two solutions, and where there is a history of people taking sides, Merry and Allerhand suggest a procedure that encourages members to evaluate their opponent's proposal positively, promoting a synergistic win–win approach. The procedure involves asking members for their reasons (criteria) for deciding which of the

solution: / criterion:	1	2	3	4	n
contribution					
cost					
people					
commitment					
etc.					

Figure 9.7 Matrix for evaluating proposals

two solutions to adopt. Only positive criteria are recorded, but all the reasons given can be converted into positive criteria. For example, if a disadvantage of solution A is that it will require a large investment, this can be recorded as a positive factor (small investment) favouring solution B. Once the criteria have been identified and recorded, in the form shown in Figure 9.8, each member can be asked to allocate a total of 10 points between the criteria supporting *each solution*, according to the amount of support given to that solution. Making people allocate a given number of points between the criteria supporting each solution encourages them to search out the positive aspects of both rather than only thinking about the positive aspect of their favoured solution.

After everybody has allocated their points, these are summed to identify those criteria supporting each solution with the greatest number of points. These important criteria are then transferred to a new sheet, and each member of the group is given a further ten points, which they are asked to allocate between these remaining criteria in any way they wish. They can allocate their points to criteria supporting one solution or both solutions. When the points are totalled, the most favoured solution usually becomes clear (see Figure 9.9). Attention can then be focused on improving the favoured solution rather than continuing the debate about which alternative to adopt.

Other ways in which decision-making procedures can be combined or modified to make them more appropriate for a particular set of circumstances might be to combine the Delphi technique, which tends to produce a great number of good-quality ideas, with ordinary group procedures that can help maintain the group in good working order and develop cohesion. Another very effective combination is to link an open group discussion with a more structured procedure for deciding between alternatives.

Taking action to improve group decision-making

Diagnosing the appropriateness of current decision-making procedures involves observing how the group defines problems, generates ideas and evaluates alternatives, and the effect these activities have on the quality of the decision and on the feelings and behaviours of those involved in making and implementing

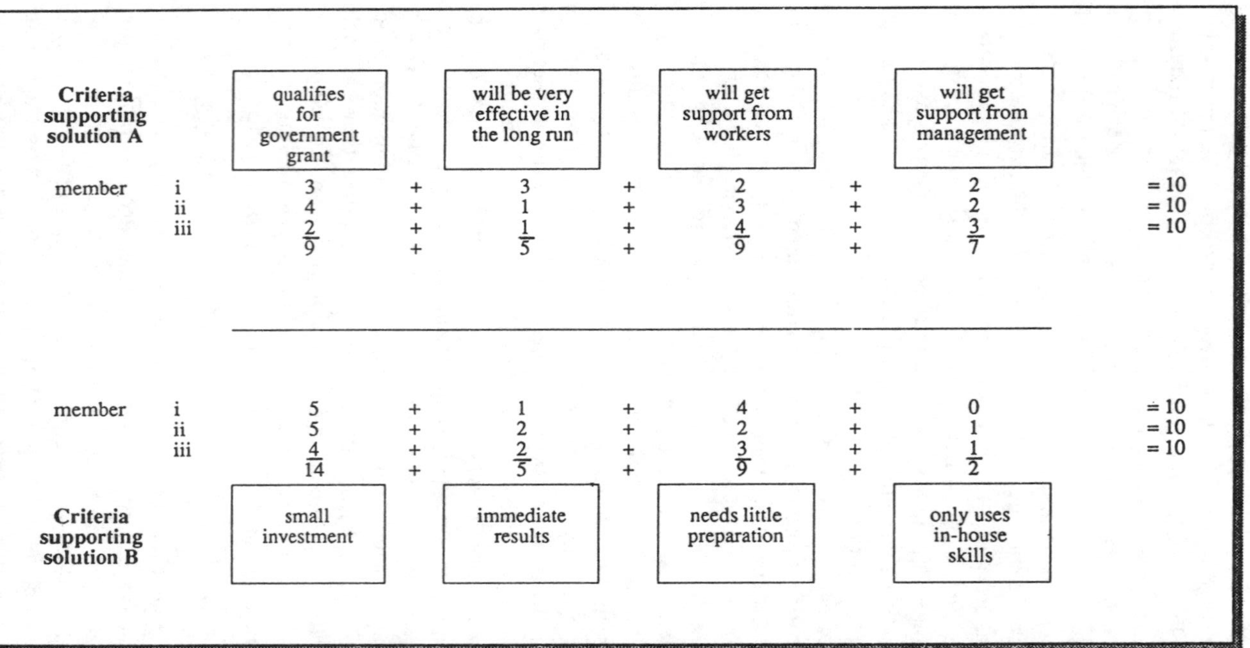

Figure 9.8 Reasons supporting alternativee solutions

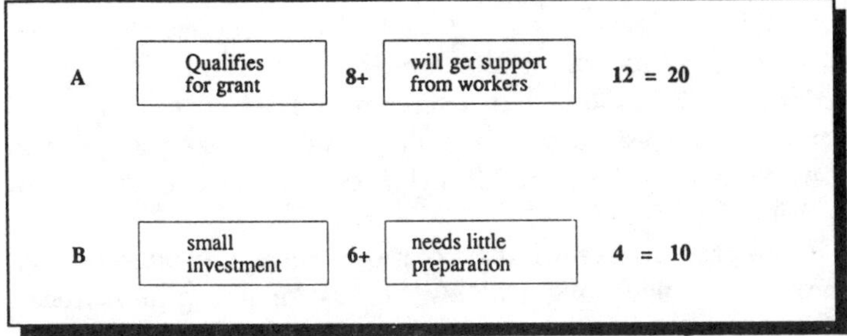

Figure 9.9 Identifying the best decision

it. Figure 9.10 offers a diagnostic checklist that can help highlight some aspects of the decision-making process that might require attention.

In some groups there is a reluctance to challenge the way problems are defined, whereas in others definitions are always discussed, clarified and elaborated. Sometimes, it depends on who it is in the group who presents the problem. Note whether members are reluctant to challenge the way problems are defined when they are presented by some members rather than by others, and consider how the decision-making procedure could be modified to reduce this tendency.

Note the quantity and quality of ideas and alternative solutions that are generated. Some groups latch on to, develop and go on to implement the first solution they come up with,

Definition of problem understood by all	no	☐ ☐ ☐	yes
Number of ideas generated	few	☐ ☐ ☐	many
Quality of ideas/creativity	low	☐ ☐ ☐	high
Pressures for conformity	high	☐ ☐ ☐	low
Willingness to listen to others	low	☐ ☐ ☐	high
Openness to disconfirming data	closed	☐ ☐ ☐	open
Level of risk inherent in decision	low	☐ ☐ ☐	high
Commitment of members to decision	low	☐ ☐ ☐	high
Feeling of accomplishment	low	☐ ☐ ☐	high
Group cohesion	low	☐ ☐ ☐	high

Figure 9.10 Group decision-making checklist

without ever considering whether alternative solutions might be better. If too few ideas are generated or if the group appears to lack creativity, think about how the decision-making procedure can be modified to overcome this. Also look for evidence of risky-shift factors influencing decision-making and consider whether the result helps or hinders the quality of decisions.

Attempt to assess the impact of group norms and interpersonal conflict. Creativity might be low because of strong pressures to conform. Similar pressures might make it difficult for some members to confront the way solutions are defined, especially so for those who are non-assertive. Power plays between individuals and subgroups and attempts to dominate might also induce win–lose rather than win–win approaches to decision-making. People may be closed to ideas other than their own and might reject data that 'disconfirms' their own view. Modifying the decision-making process, possibly by introducing more formality and restricting the opportunities for open discussion, might offer a way of minimizing these problems.

Paying attention to such outcomes as feelings of accomplishment, group cohesiveness and members' commitment to decisions might also point to the need to modify the decision-making procedure.

Summary

This chapter provides a set of guidelines designed to help you to work more effectively in groups. The underlying theme has been that, to achieve this end, you need to develop diagnostic skills that will help you to identify the group's strengths and weaknesses and action skills that will enable you to intervene to correct weaknesses and, where appropriate, build on strengths.

The first part of the chapter identified effort, knowledge and skill, and performance strategies as the key variables affecting group performance. The way in which group interaction processes affect each of these was explored in order to generate a range of indicators that could be used when interpreting data about behaviour in groups and when planning appropriate interventions to improve group performance.

The second part of the chapter introduced a number of ways of observing and recording behaviour in groups. Particular attention was paid to the frequency and duration of communication, communication patterns, role functions, interpersonal style and group climate, performance strategies and decision-making procedures. Suggestions about how these observations can be used to diagnose problems, and indications of how the diagnosis can be used to plan alternative ways of behaving, were also offered.

References: Chapter 9

Belbin, R. M. 1981. *Management Teams: Why They Succeed or Fail.* London: Heinemann.

Benne, K. D. and Sheates, P. 1948. Functional roles of group members. *Journal of Social Issues* 2: 42–7.

Chapple, E. D. 1940. Measuring human relations: an introduction to the study of interaction of individuals. *Genetic Psychology Monographs* 22: 3–147.

Deutsch, M. 1949. A theory of cooperation and competition, *Human Relations*, 2, 2, 129–52.

Hackman, J. R. 1987. The design of work teams. In J. W. Lorsch (ed.) *Handbook of Organizational Behavior*. Englewood Cliffs, NJ: Prentice-Hall.

Hackman, J. R. and Oldham, G. R. 1980. *Work Redesign*. Reading, Mass.: Addison-Wesley.

Handy, C. B. 1985. *Understanding Organizations*. Harmondsworth: Penguin.

Hare, A. P. 1982. *Creativity in Small Groups*. Beverly Hills, Calif.: Sage.

Harvey, J. B. 1974. The Abilene paradox: the management of agreement. *Organizational Dynamics*. Summer: 63–80.

Janis, I. L. 1982. *Groupthink*, 2nd edn. Boston: Houghton Mifflin

Latane, B., Williams, K. and Hoskins, S. 1979. Many hands make light work: the causes and consequences of social loafing. *Journal of Personality and Social Psychology* 37: 822–32.

Merry, U. and Allerhand, M. E. 1977. *Developing Teams and Organizations*. Reading, Mass.: Addison-Wesley.

Murnighan, J. K. 1981. Group decision making: what strategies should you use? *Management Review*. February: 55–62.

Steiner, I. D. 1972. *Group Process and Productivity*. New York: Academic Press.

Stoner, J. 1968. Risky and cautious shifts in group decisions: the influence of widely held values. *Journal of Experimental Social Psychology* 4: 442–59.

CHAPTER TEN

Managing relationships more effectively

This book offers a series of conceptual frameworks, which can be used for reading the behaviour of others and for constructing conduct that will increase the probability that desired outcomes will be achieved. Interpersonal skill refers to the nature of such conduct, and is defined as goal-directed behaviours used in face-to-face interactions that are effective in bringing about a desired state of affairs.

While broad areas of interpersonal skill have been considered under a series of chapter headings, such as listening, information getting, helping, influencing and negotiating, attention within the chapters has also been focused on smaller units of behaviour such as attending, probing and giving feedback. These smaller units of behaviour are often referred to as micro-skills. This apparently reductionist approach to the study of interpersonal skills has a number of advantages, but Hargie (1986) highlights two potential disadvantages, which merit consideration.

A central tenet of Gestalt psychology is that the whole is greater than the sum of the parts; thus, once an overall structure is broken down into smaller units, the original meaning or form can be changed. Studying a number of small units of behaviour in isolation may not be equivalent to studying the whole. This argument has some validity, but it does not apply to the treatment of interpersonal skills offered in this book. The approach adopted here analyses social interaction in terms of clearly identifiable behaviours, while at the same time highlighting the way these behaviours relate to one another. The advantage offered by this approach is that information is presented and discussed in a way that can help people develop their skills by focusing their attention on selected aspects of social interaction. Hargie (1986) describes this approach as one of:

> *homing in and honing up*, where one aspect of social interaction is focused upon at a time and trainees are encouraged to refine their use of this particular aspect. Once the trainee has acquired a working knowledge of a number of skills of social interaction, the ultimate goal is to encourage the appropriate use of these skills in an integrated fashion.

A second danger identified by Hargie is that, by adopting a micro-training approach to skill development, social interaction will lose its natural beauty and become artificial and stilted. Although it is true that, in the short term, focusing attention on particular skills can make people more conscious of their behaviour and it can make behaviour more stilted, this is a transitory stage. A similar pattern can be observed in the process of learning other skills. For example, learning to drive a car requires the driver to become proficient at a number of perceptual–motor skills involved in such tasks as steering, changing gear and slipping the clutch on hill starts. Before allowing a learner to negotiate rush-hour traffic, the driving instructor might focus attention on each of these skills in turn. The first lesson might only involve stopping, starting and steering the car on quiet, level roads. Later, the learner might be introduced to moving up and down the gear box. Later still, these skills might be practised on different roads and in different traffic conditions. When the learner driver is concentrating on perfecting each of these skills, the overall effect might well be a jerky, uncoordinated drive. However, with practice, the skills become second nature and the driver develops an integrated and smooth approach to driving. Much the same happens when people are developing their interpersonal skills. At times the process can seem artificial and stilted, but this is only a transitory stage in the learning process. Eventually, the learner reaches a point where she unconsciously exercises these skills when relating with others.

From micro skills to a more macro perspective

A recurring theme in earlier chapters has been the need to pay attention to the ways in which the nature of relationships can affect outcomes. In Chapter 4, for example, it was argued that it would be naïve to view the interview simply in terms of one person asking questions and getting information from another. The interview is a social encounter in which the willingness of one party to provide full, honest and accurate answers to the questions asked by another is influenced by a number of factors.

One of these factors is the way the respondent views the interviewer's role. In the selection interview, the job applicant is likely to accept the interviewer's right to ask questions and to feel obliged to give appropriate answers. This might not be the case if the same questions were asked by a ticket collector on a railway train. However, the role of the person asking the questions is not the only factor that will determine the kind of answer the respondent will give. The respondent's perception of the interviewer's attitudes, feelings and behaviour will also be important. If the respondent feels that the interviewer is behaving like a critical parent and evaluating all he says, he might distort his answers and provide her with selected information so that she will view him in the best possible light. The needs of both the interviewer and respondent might also have some influence on the nature of the interaction. For example, if the respondent is a subordinate who feels a need for more direction and guidance, he might offer his boss more information than a subordinate who feels that he is being subjected to too much detailed supervision and who feels a need to maintain as much autonomy as possible.

The aim of this concluding chapter is to develop this theme and to point to further areas of study that will help the reader to develop a more holistic view of social interaction. There is a range of factors that can influence whether or not a particular behaviour will produce an anticipated outcome. Some of these have already been considered, but the remaining part of this chapter will briefly introduce some further conceptual models and theories, which can assist in the reading of behaviour and in the constructing of conduct.

Role theory

A person's response to a social situation depends upon how she interprets what she sees. Her perception of others will influence how she behaves towards them. It will also influence her expectations about how they will behave towards her. The way a new employee behaves towards somebody she meets for the first time will depend upon whether this other person is perceived to be her boss, colleague or subordinate. The other's role will also influence how she expects them to behave towards her. Maybe she expects a subordinate to pay more attention to what she says than either her boss or her colleagues.

Handy (1985) illustrates the importance of roles in social interaction with reference to the way Charles Marlow behaves towards Mr Hardcastle in *She Stoops to Conquer*. Marlow is under the impression that Hardcastle is the innkeeper and, therefore, behaves towards him in conformity with his stereotype of the role of innkeeper. However, Hardcastle is not the innkeeper. He is Marlow's prospective father-in-law and he behaves towards Marlow in a manner appropriate to a future son-in-law. As Handy reports, the ensuing bewilderment and frustration on the part of the two characters, who both receive information that so vehemently conflicts with their stereotypes of the other's role, provide great entertainment for the audience, who are party to the role confusion. Marlow and Hardcastle were bewildered because their behaviour towards the other did not produce the anticipated response. Their role expectations were not confirmed.

The example of Marlow and Hardcastle illustrates the point that people play many roles. Sometimes, it is relatively easy for one person to identify the role being played by another. A man in a blue uniform in a car fitted with blue flashing lights is likely to be a police officer. Costume, terms of address, the words used, body language and other cues provide the signs that designate roles. However, there are some occasions when it is difficult to determine another's role, particularly if that person is known to occupy a range of different roles and when the available role signs are ambiguous. Even within the course of a relatively short period of time the same person can play many roles. Before arriving at work in the morning, a worker might have played the roles of wife, mother, passenger, friend and customer. These roles are not necessarily tied to situations or relationships. Within the context of the same conversation, role relationships may change. In the early stages of a conversation two negotiators might relate as friends before they eventually 'get down to business'. Sometimes, two people may have the opportunity of conducting their interactions in terms of several different role relationships. The same two people might be husband and wife, subordinate and boss, or political rivals. This kind of situation heightens the chance of the people involved experiencing role ambiguity and role conflict.

Role ambiguity arises whenever a person is not clear what role she should play in a situation or what role somebody else is playing. Role conflict arises when a person has a possibility of playing two incompatible roles at the same time. For example, a policewoman might observe her brother committing a crime and have to decide whether to play the role of police officer and apprehend the criminal or the role of sister and protect her brother from the force of the law. The offending brother might also be faced with a dilemma, especially if he is not clear what role his sister is likely to perform. Does he attack the police officer in an attempt to escape or appeal to his sister for help?

People use role signs (for example, speech and body language) to signal the role they have in mind for themselves. Sometimes, others are happy to accept a person's definition of their own role, but this need not always be the case. For example, when a marketing executive and a product development engineer meet to consider their approach to an important customer they plan to visit later in the day, the marketing executive might see the customer visit as *his* meeting and signal to the product development engineer that she should follow his lead. The engineer, on the other hand, might be convinced that it should be *her* meeting, because the profitability of the deal depends upon agreeing the right product specification. She might therefore reject the role the marketing executive proffers for himself and respond in an uncooperative manner to his assertive behaviours. Her lack of cooperation might force the marketing executive to redefine his role and persuade him to adopt a more conciliatory and egalitarian response to his colleague.

Developing a better awareness of role relationships and of the ways in which others interpret roles can help a person construct conduct that has a greater probability of leading to desired outcomes.

Transactional analysis

Transactional analysis provides a useful model for understanding the nature of interpersonal relationships. It was pioneered by Eric Berne (1964, 1972) and offers a theory of personality and personal interaction. Personality is presented in terms of three ego states: Parent, Adult and Child.

The *Parent* ego state comprises a set of feelings, attitudes and behaviours that have been copied from parental figures. Most of a person's interactions in early childhood are with parents or surrogate parents, and this experience, according to Berne, is never forgotten. Whenever a person behaves in ways similar to the ways she remembers her parents behaving (nurturing, standard setting, criticizing and judging), the source of her behaviour is the Parent ego state.

The *Child* ego state comprises a collection of feelings, attitudes and behaviours that are the remembered reactions to parental behaviour. They include guilt, anger, rebellion, excitement, joy, sadness and fear.

The *Adult* ego state comprises a set of feelings, attitudes and behaviours associated with information processing and the objective testing of reality. In Transactional Analysis the structure of personality is presented diagramatically as three circles, see Figure 10.1.

The balance of these ego states may vary from person to person, and within the same person from time to time. According to Berne, it is the ego state that predominates that determines behaviour. On one occasion a person may behave as an Adult and on another occasion the same person may behave as a Critical Parent.

This model can be usefully employed to improve a person's awareness of her own personal style. The basic unit of behaviour is referred to as a transaction. It involves one person doing or saying something to another and the other responding. By paying attention to the nature of a transaction it is possible to diagnose the ego state from which it has originated. For

Figure 10.1 Ego states

example, transactions originating from the Critical Parent ego state are often spoken in a critical condescending way, include the frequent use of words such as never, should, ought and don't, and are accompanied by non-verbal behaviours such as frowning and pointing. The attitudes being expressed by such transactions tend to be judgemental and authoritarian. Transactions originating from the Adult ego state tend to be associated with a confident voice, thoughtful or interested expression and include words such as where? why? what? The attitude of the person behaving in an Adult manner tends to be open and/or evaluative. In contrast, the Free Child ego state tends to be the source of transactions that are spontaneous, uninhibited and expressed in an excited voice.

This structural analysis of personality provides a basis for analysing and understanding the nature of interactions. According to Berne, every interaction between people involves a transaction between their ego states. The originator of a transaction targets her behaviour at a particular ego state in the other person and assumes that the recipient will respond from his targeted ego state. When this happens, the transaction is described as a parallel transaction. For example, when a manager asks her secretary where the telephone directory is, she might originate the transaction from her Adult ego state and target it at her secretary's Adult ego state (see Figure 10.2).

The transaction will be a parallel transaction when the secretary replies from her Adult ego state (see Figure 10.3).

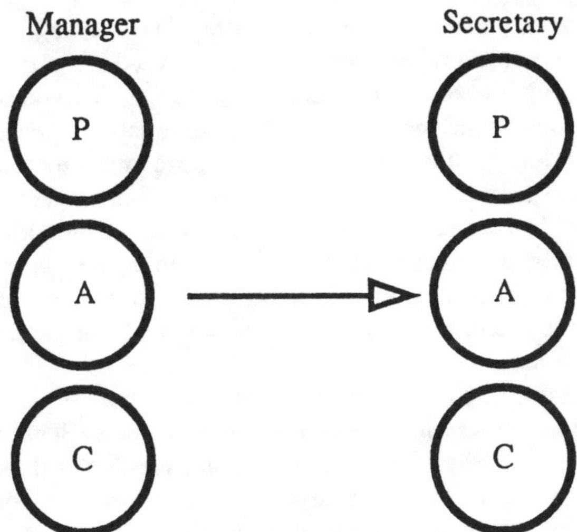

Figure 10.2 'Where is the telephone directory?'

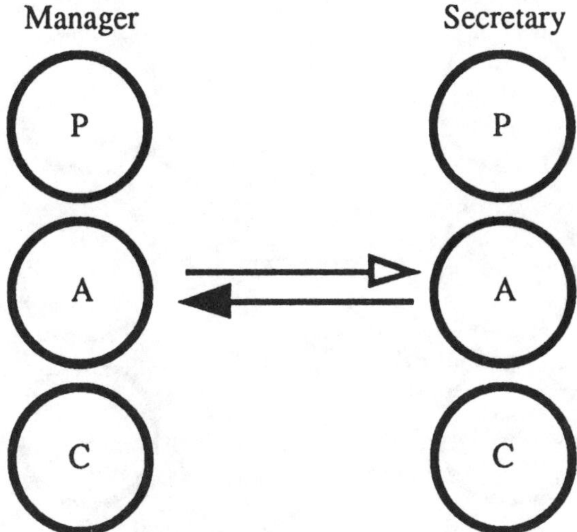

Figure 10.3 'You lent it to Bob'

However, if the manager fails to hook the targeted ego state in the secretary, the transaction will be crossed. An example of a crossed transaction would be if the secretary replied from her Parent ego state and targeted the Child ego state of her manager (see Figure 10.4).

In crossed transactions the originator of the messages receives a response from an unexpected ego state, whereas in parallel transactions the originator receives an expected response from the ego state that she targeted. Transactional analysis offers a useful model for understanding and improving interactions by helping a person to identify the ego state that tends to be the source of her transactions in particular situations or with certain individuals. If a person decides, on reflection, that the source of some of her transactions adversely affects outcomes, she may attempt to modify the ego state from which she originates these transactions.

For example, a person who has taken a day off work to await the arrival of a telephone engineer to install a new telephone may feel let down when he fails to turn up. Her normal response in such a situation might have been to phone the telephone company and issue a stern rebuke: that is, to engage in a

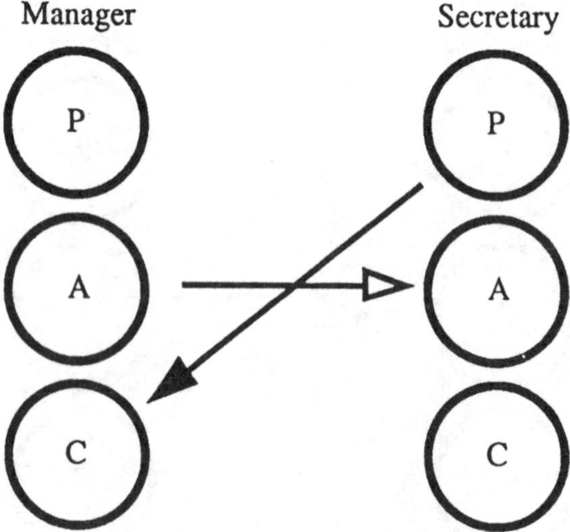

Figure 10.4 'How come you can never find things when you want them?'

transaction originated from her Critical Parent ego state and targeted at the Compliant Child ego state of the company's customer service manager. She might, however, remember that in the past such complaints have resulted in acrimonious arguments and little action. On this occasion, therefore, she might deliberately decide to originate the transaction from the child ego state and target it at the nurturing parent ego state of the customer service manager. She might explain that she lives alone in a large, isolated house and that she is afraid of intruders at night. This might motivate the customer service manager to do everything possible to help her feel more secure.

Thinking about interactions in terms of ego states can yield useful diagnostic information that can be used to manage relationships more effectively. Only a very brief review of some of the most basic ideas of transactional analysis are presented here, but they at least illustrate how important it can be to pay attention to the personalities of those involved in social interactions.

Interpersonal needs

Schutz (1958) advanced the notion of three basic interpersonal needs: inclusion, control and affection. Inclusion refers to the need to be with people and to be alone, to have enough contact to avoid loneliness and enough aloneness to avoid enmeshment and enjoy solitude. Control refers to decision-making processes between people and areas of power, influence and authority. It involves the need to achieve enough influence to be able to control important outcomes and to be able to relinquish enough control to be able to lean on others and allow them to take responsibility for outcomes. Affection refers to close personal emotional feelings such as love and hate. It involves the need to avoid being engulfed in emotional entanglements and the need to avoid having too little affection and a life without love and warmth.

Schutz makes an interesting distinction between *expressed behaviour*, the behaviour we feel comfortable expressing towards other people, and *wanted behaviour*, the behaviour we want from others, that is, the behaviour we want them to express towards us. He developed FIRO-B, an instrument that explores the levels of behaviour that people are comfortable with in relation to these three needs. He argues that people have different levels of need. In terms of wanted behaviour, if they experience more than their preferred need for inclusion they will feel crowded, whereas if they experience less than their preferred need they will feel left out. If they experience more than their preferred need for control they will feel pushed, whereas if they experience less they will feel that they are not being offered sufficient direction. Similarly, if they experience more than their preferred need for affection they will feel smothered, whereas if they experience less they will feel unloved and rejected.

The success of a relationship is affected by the degree to which the parties to the relationship see the potential for satisfying their needs. For example, a person who has a high need for expressed control is likely to attempt to exert control and influence others. If she relates with others who have a high need for wanted control the relationship is more likely to be mutually satisfying than if she relates with others who also have a high need for expressed control. People with a high need for wanted control are comfortable when somebody else tells them what to do and, therefore, are likely to respond positively to those people who want to take charge. If, on the other hand, both parties to the relationship have a high need to control others and a low need to be controlled, then the relationship is less likely to be satisfying for either party. They will both want to take control and tell the other what to do and they will both resist accepting directions from the other. In such circumstances there will be a high probability that their goal-directed behaviour will fail to produce desired outcomes. However, being aware of why the relationship is not as satisfying as it might be offers the possibility of managing the relationship more effectively. If the stakes are judged to be high enough, one of the parties involved may decide to modify their behaviour, adapt to the situation and, for example, allow the other person to take control. On the other hand, they may both agree to modify their behaviour, and they may seek to identify areas where they are compatible and to build on these.

Managing relationships more effectively

The conceptual models presented in this final chapter provide a basis for understanding why some goal-directed behaviours might be less successful than others, or why relationships with certain individuals might be more satisfactory than relationships with others. These models suggest a range of diagnostic questions and action strategies, which offer a basis for managing relationships more effectively.

Role theory focuses attention on the roles people play and the ways they perceive the roles played by others. Sometimes, it might be possible to improve a relationship if people signal more clearly the roles that they think are appropriate for themselves and others, and if they challenge what they believe to be inappropriate role expectations and behaviours.

Transactional analysis may also offer an alternative perspective and suggests ways in which desired goals might be achieved more effectively. For example, a person's lack of success in negotiations might be attributed to her tendency (when negotiating with people who originate transactions from their Parent ego state) to allow others to hook her into responding from her Compliant Child ego state. The way forward might be to modify this response pattern and for her to respond from her Adult ego state. Deliberately crossing transactions in this way could have the effect of forcing the other negotiator to follow her lead and to engage in a parallel transaction by also originating transactions from his and targeting them at her Adult ego state.

An awareness of her own and others' needs can enable a person to assess what she needs to do to make her behaviour more effective. For example, if she is aware that she has a high need to exert control she might be alert to the possibility that her helping style might be too prescriptive. On the other hand, if she is aware that her clients differ in *their* need for control, she might be able to tailor her helping behaviour so that the help she offers produces the maximum benefit for each of them.

Interpersonal competence involves the ability to understand the nature of social interactions, to be able to read behaviour, and to act in ways that will bring about desired outcomes. This book provides an introduction to some of the key diagnostic and action skills that can help a person to achieve this end.

References: Chapter 10

Berne, E. 1964. *Games People Play*. New York: Grove Press.

Berne, E. 1972. *What Do You Say After You Say Hello?* London: Corgi.

Handy, C. 1985. *Understanding Organisations*. Harmondsworth: Penguin Business Books.

Hargie, O. 1986. *A Handbook of Communication Skills*. London: Croom Helm.

Schutz, W. C. 1958. *FIRO: A Three Dimensional Theory of Interpersonal Behaviour*. New York: Holt, Rinehart. (Reprinted 1966 as *The Interpersonal Underworld*. Palo Alto, Calif.: Science and Behaviour Books.)

Author Index

Subject Index